Y0-BSN-825

THIS PILGRIM'S PROGRESS

A Correspondence with Joel Goldsmith

by

Barbara Mary Muhl

Published with the gracious permission of Mrs. Geri McDonald, daughter of Emma Goldsmith, and legatee of the Infinite Way, its writings, and administration.

Published by
Christus Publishing
30035 Bouquet Cyn. Rd.
Saugus, California 91350
Fax: (805) 296-2182

ISBN 1 - 880863 - 25 - 1

Printed in the United States of America.
First paperbound printed 1991.
Second paperbound printed 1994.

A NOTE ABOUT JOEL

Joel was born into a Jewish family which, he said, was "...not religious; my mother taught me the *Ten Commandments* and that was it."

His father was a successful lace importer who took Joel with him into the business at an early age. Joel recounts that, "Upon seeing the flesh-pots of Europe and man's inhumanity to man, I began to wonder, where is the God in all this?" And he felt driven to find out.

He told me that when he was pondering this, one night in New York, something inside of him said, "If you would find the Truth, study the life of the man, Jesus. The Truth is contained therein." As Joel said, "That was a funny instruction to give a Jewish boy, but I did as I was told."

His study led him to Christian Science, where he had many years of great success as a healer, a Board member, and as First Reader in the Mother Church in Boston.

Joel said he was "happy there" until the time arrived when his healing ability became so widely known that he was getting letters asking for help from all over the United States and even from Europe. At a crisis point the Board called him in and told him that he would have to restrict his healing work to his "own area." His answer was, "Don't try to take the freedom away from a Jew; we have worked too hard for it." So he decided it was necessary to resign from the Church.

However, the parting was amicable, and Joel has always acknowledged his debt to Mrs. Eddy.[1] In fact, shortly before he made his transition he said to me,

---

[1]   Mary Baker Eddy, founder of the Christian Science Church; author of *Science and Health with Key to the Scriptures* and related writings.

"Barbara, if I live I'm going to make the world acknowledge its debt to Mrs. Eddy." Indeed, she was the 'mother' of psychosomatic medicine, and mental healing. Subsequently, some of the principles of spiritual healing could be found in her later writings. However, they still contain elements of mental healing and this is where they differ from Joel's unfoldment in the Infinite Way, which contains no element of mental healing.

After about sixteen years of doing healing work, in response to students' requests, Joel began to teach. He was an effective, valid, spiritual teacher and, today, there are Infinite Way tape meetings being held all over the world. His books are available in most bookstores and public libraries.[1]

Personally, Joel was interested in everything – read everything. He had a wonderful sense of humor, and loved the theater. In fact, he once said to me, "The only reason I would come back would be to do a turn in Vaudeville." With his little string tie, his twinkly eyes, and his quick wit, he would be a great success.

I am waiting, Joel...

Joel S. Goldsmith

1   If anyone wishes further information about Joel's tapes or his writings, please write to Mrs. Geri McDonald, The Infinite Way, P.O. Box 2089, Peoria, Arizona, 85380.

TABLE OF CONTENTS

INTRODUCTION

I had been taught in Sunday School that Jesus "...died for me and saved me from my sins." Many years later I learned that this was error. The truth is that Jesus *lived* his life for me and in the process taught me how to save myself. He taught the rest of us what Truth was; how to be *real*; and how to reconcile ourselves to God (as we understand that term in the Infinite Way). He taught that the secret of life is Love. But no one can love until someone has first shown him how, by loving him. Jesus did that, demonstrated that; and in so doing gave us all the Keys to the Kingdom.

Ever since I was fifteen years old I had been chasing messiahs and looking for a spiritual teacher. Actually, my "rite of passage" had begun at age nine when I was baptized (with full immersion) in a giant font resting on the backs of twelve bronze oxen (built to the exact dimensions of the account in the Old Testament). I was really looking forward to this baptism because my father told me every day how filled with sin I was, and emphasized it with a slap to the face, or the bottom, or wherever he could reach. I thought if I could be saved from my sins that would mean the end of the beatings. I fantasized every day for a month how glorious it would be to feel sinless and pure – and *spiritual*. I walked up the stairs of the font with a nine-year old fluttering heart, was pushed down under the water, then guided to the opposite stairs for my descent. And *descent* it was. I was shocked and horrified that I still felt as sinful as I had before.

After the baptism I told my uncle, who was a dignitary in the church, that I was very disappointed in God who had not "fixed" me, that His promises were worthless, and that I wasn't even sure that He existed. He answered, "You must just take that on faith." I said, "Faith isn't good enough for me. I have to *know* if God exists or not. I haven't found Him here in the church, and you don't really know, either. I will be perfectly willing to live with the fact that God does *not* exist, if that is the *Truth*. But I have to go and find out." And so my journey began.

I considered leaving out any mention of my father, but this book would be of no value unless it were honest, so I left it in. My father was 'heavy-handed' and that was a large part of what motivated me to try to "find a better way." For a long time I felt sorry for myself about my father's behavior, in fact, until I became a student of Joel's and *accepted* the primary axiom of *The Infinite Way*: "Nothing can happen to me that is not an outpicturing of my *own* state of consciousness." When I was working with that principle one day I was thinking of my father and my "inner voice" said to me, "Who loved him?" I realized, "No one!" His parents had treated him the same way, and their parents the same – and so on back in time, and so on back...

It was then I understood the real meaning of the scriptural statement, "The sins of the fathers are visited on the children until the third and fourth generations." It meant the *ignorances* of the parents and the *conditionings* of the parents are perpetuated onto the children down through the generations. I then also knew why I had said to myself when I was seven, "When I grow up I am not going to do this to my children. This insanity is going to stop with me." (I was almost successful with that – not totally – but almost).

After I could see that my parents' errors were due to ignorance – the same as mine were – it became very easy to forgive them. It took me longer to forgive myself.

In my search I talked to a lot of people about God but no one could prove to me that He existed. Finally, at age fifteen, I began to search for myself, and spent the next twenty-five years looking for a teacher. The search took me through Lao Tzu, whom, at that time, I didn't understand; through Confucius, whom I did understand but who left me cold because I wasn't searching for an ethic (which was his message) I was searching for Truth – whatever *that* was. I read all of Kahlil Gibran, who made me feel wise and good. I gleaned bits and pieces from the *Rig Veda*, the *Bhagavad-gita*, Buddhist texts, Dr. Suzuki, Alan Watts, the Sufists, and others who claimed to know. But they all kept describing the *what*, and they never seemed to agree as to *just what*.

Then back to Christianity with Origen, St. Augustine, St. Thomas Acquinas, St. Catherine, St. Theresa, Molinos, St. John of the Cross, Jacob Boehme, Eckhart, *The Cloud of Unknowing*, New Thought, New Age, Divine Science, and Religious Science. Those who were really mystics (and not all were) *described* an experience. But none of them told me how to get it.

Finally to Christian Science. My Practitioner was the first person to tell me I needed more than reading, that I needed to *study* and do the daily lesson. This began to work fine for me. Healings were showing forth and a friend of mine urged me to join the church, in gratitude for the healings.

I succumbed to this. But being a congenital *non-joiner*, I decided to join the Mother Church in Boston rather than a local one. When they sent me a paper to sign stating that I would agree never to read anything but the Bible and Mrs. Eddy's writings, I wrote back, "I can't promise to restrict my learning. If my reading had not been eclectic I would never have found Christian Science." They said that I "...was not ready for Christian Science." So I became a non-joiner again. God knew what He was doing. Two months later, when I found Joel, I would, in any case, have considered it necessary to resign from the Church.

I almost missed Joel. I was talking about Christian Science to one of my husband's secretaries when she said to me, "Did you ever hear of a man named Joel Goldsmith?" I answered, "No, I haven't." Inside myself I added, "And I don't want to; Christian Science is working for me and I am through chasing messiahs."[1]

When I got home something inside of me said, "Barbara, you have never in your life had a closed mind. Why are you beginning now?"[2] I called the secretary back and said, "Well, send me the book." When *The Infinite Way* arrived, I read on page 40: "Illumination dissolves all material ties and binds men together with the golden chains of spiritual understanding..." I knew then that I was 'home', and I have never left home since.

This Pilgrim's Progress is my correspondence with Joel, which took place during the seven years I had him as my teacher in the flesh. Through his books, and tapes and, often, his Presence when I am teaching a class, his guidance and *correction* still go on – and will go on eternally. I have learned over the years that the "golden chains" that Joel speaks of are the link between the *real* spiritual teacher and his student and, as Joel says, "The relationship between a spiritual teacher and his student is established by God itself, and it is far more sacred and binding than any other tie, including the marriage tie." This is so, because the binding is not human, not personal, but from God Consciousness to God Consciousness.

---

[1] I haven't done too well making my own decisions about what I would do with my life. For instance, I met my husband two months after I had "given up men, *forever*."

[2] At the time I thought this was my "intelligent self" talking to me. Now I know it was, but one of its names is "God."

iv

In re-reading these letters in preparation for the book, I am actually embarrassed at what a beginner I was. But to paraphrase Gertrude Stein, "a beginner is a beginner is a beginner" and, like everyone else, I had to start where I was; and where I *was* was a very human place. I have told my students that I have never met anyone who was more attached to his humanhood than I was. It just happened that I was more attached to God.

I remember when I was a child of seven saying to myself, "You know, if someone were to write a book about his life and really tell the *truth*, it might help other people." Actually, I didn't fully understand that rumination myself, and I certainly was not thinking that it could, or should, be *my* life. But, as it unfolded, my students have often told me that when I tell them that I started "farther behind the 8-ball" than they did, and that I have made more mistakes than they have, it has been a source of encouragement and comfort to them. I was always telling them, "If *I* can make it, *anyone* can make it," and the last twenty-nine years have proved that again and again. All it takes to make it is the right message, the *right methods*, great courage, and great perseverance. All of that is *possible* for *anyone* who truly wants a way out of the human mess. My students and I have done it, and none of us is a 'special case'. Our progress has been due to our serious practice of right methods.

It is *possible* to learn how to surrender one's life to the government of Divine Love, to *learn* to "die daily" to the *false* sense of self,[1] and to *achieve* gratitude, peace, and Love.

Since Joel "had it all" when I met him, I found that when he shared with me his own struggles on the Path, it was of great comfort and help to me. I recognized the

---

[1] St. Paul, I Corinthians, 15:31.

v

greatness of his Consciousness and, without those glimpses into his sometimes 'humanity', it would all have seemed too much for me, and impossible of achievement. My students have told me the same. Even though sometimes, when I tell them about some of my former shortcomings, they will say, "You *say* that, but who can *believe* it?" Believe it!

It is all exposed in these letters. My struggles did not cease when I began teaching. I have always referred to myself as "only student number one." What comes through me in class is of the *Father*. It is pure, and I am student to that, just as they are. I *hear* it first, but then I must begin to do the hard work to *demonstrate* the lesson. Just like everyone else, I must walk the road, meet every stumbling block, pass every milestone. The milestones are the same for all.

One of the first things I learned was that I had to correct my understanding of many of the words used in the Infinite Way; words which are in common usage in the Christian religions but which have a totally different meaning when used by Joel. For instance, the words *God*, *Consciousness*, *Christ*, *devil*, etc. Until I understood and accepted the new meanings, progress was difficult.

Consequently, as an aid to better understanding, at the back of this book there is a Glossary of some of the major terms. It might be helpful to peruse it before beginning the Correspondence.

In spite of the struggle, God has graced me over the years with continuing unfoldment of consciousness and I have continued to be able to help those who come to me.

One thing I know: we are all in this together, we are brothers. And loving our neighbor as *our* Self is what life is all about. One of the stumbling blocks is that we first

have to learn what "our Self" *is*, before we can love it —
or anyone else.

It is not an easy task to achieve understanding and,
one by one, remove all the onionskins of our
"humanhood" (which is nothing but our "mistake
making faculty"). But it is achievable – and well worth
the effort, because it puts us in control of our lives and we
no longer have to live, like flotsam and jetsam, just being
buffeted by circumstances, with no power to direct our life
in the way of our spiritual destiny.

My hope is that this book, which is just one pilgrim's
progress, will be of some service – and also afford a
glimpse into how Joel dealt with a private student.

Aloha love,

Barbara

Renaissance World
30035 Bouquet Canyon Road
Saugus, California, 91350
June, 1991

CHAPTER 1

CORRESPONDENCE 1958

Note: Early in 1958 I had gone to New York to take a class with Joel. It was then he gave me permission to hold a tape group in my home. (Little did I know what that seemingly simple service would lead to). My letters are not in this chapter, because it was not until 1959 that my "inner voice" said to me, "Keep copies of your letters." These are the first of Joel's letters to me.

Dear Friend: October 6, 1958

We are at home now, and I have just received your letter of September 30th, and your very thoughtful check enclosed. This, of course, will immediately go into the activities of the Infinite Way.

I am happy, indeed, that you have written me, as both Emma and I have spoken of you so often in our travels, and often in my meditations I would be consciously with you in your spiritual unfoldment.

As you know, we will be at home the balance of the year, and so will look forward with great joy to hearing further from you.

Emma joins me in Aloha greetings,

Joel

Dear Friend: October 16, 1958

My very sincere thanks to you for your message and for your thoughtful sharing with our work.

Indeed you know that I will be most interested to hear of the experiences that you are having with the message of the Infinite Way, or the experiences that those who come to you are having, and of course you know that any help I can give, at any point in your work, you need only ask.

I am sure you already know how wonderful it will be if you can arrange to be in Honolulu in December.

Aloha greetings from Emma and from me,

Joel

Dear Friend: October 31, 1958

Thank you sincerely for your letter of Sunday. Indeed I do understand how impossible it is to talk about our spiritual unfoldments. In fact, the very fact that we cannot talk about these things is proof of their reality.

I am grateful that your husband has become interested in the message of the Infinite Way, and that it has found a response within him. You cannot know how wonderful, how really wonderful, it is when husband and wife are together on this Spiritual Path.[1]

---

[1] My "husband" is, of course, Edward Muhl. Perhaps we need a word about him.

Edward began working for Universal Pictures when he was nineteen. He learned the business from the ground up, beginning in the Accounting Department. Some years later he was made head of the Legal Department. After that he became General Manager of the studio proper and, finally, for the last twenty years of his tenure he was Vice-President in Charge of Production, responsible for making about thirty-five pictures a year.

Universal made some of its most successful pictures under his aegis and never lost money while he was there.

In 1973 Edward retired from Universal and , just to keep his hand in, became a consultant to budding film ventures.

Joel had an abiding interest in film and theater and one of the things he enjoyed about Edward was being able to "...talk about the movies."

Note: While I was in New York I had asked Joel to work on the decaying teeth of my four-year old daughter, April. While I had been away, the nanny had allowed her to have apple juice instead of milk. It is true that the child was very persuasive, but the adult should have known better. The apple juice literally dissolved her front baby teeth. We were not successful in meeting this.

Regarding this matter of April's teeth, I would like you to know that there is nothing personal about this, because *such things are the products of universal belief.*[1] Now, the remedy for all such things, and the overcoming of them, is embodied in the healing principles of the message of the Infinite Way. I would like to suggest, for your daily study for several months to come, the March and the October 1958 *Letters* and the chapter "Love Thy Neighbor" in *Practicing The Presence.* The study of these writings, and the daily practice, will bring you to a place in consciousness where you will, in every case, instantly recognize that you are not dealing with certain persons or certain conditions, but with *universal hypnotism,* and you will be able to instantly dismiss it, and thereby prevent many things happening, and heal others that have already come to pass. The entire secret lies in *impersonalizing good and evil.*

It is true, that in certain forms of discord, there is more difficulty in meeting the situation than in others. Dentistry, broken bones, and a couple of other items still seem to present difficulties, and of course, the greatest difficulty of all, are the cases of children who come into this world at birth with physical or mental handicaps, and sometimes with both physical and mental handicaps, and while we are devoting a great deal of time

---

[1] Italics that appear in a letter of Joel's are mine. They represent phrases that I underlined at the time so as to study them more deeply.

and attention to this form of work, it is not proving to be an easy matter.

Please know how much we would enjoy seeing you over here, but probably if December does not prove practical, there will be a later date.

Emma joins me in love to all of your family,

Joel

Note: A few days later he said to me, on the telephone, "We don't have much luck with teeth and broken bones." Nonetheless, in spite of this acknowledgement that some things were "very difficult," in 1963 he grew hands and arms on a Thalidomide baby – in three months! As to his statement, "The entire secret lies in impersonalizing good and evil," that is absolutely true. My students and I have really worked with this one over the years, growing in understanding all the time, but it took us twenty years to be able to fully demonstrate that on a regular basis.[1]

Dear Friend: November 10, 1958

Happy, indeed, for that flash of light which came to you, and of course there will be signs following.[2]

The secret of the Infinite Way is this: that what you read and what you hear of the message is, at first, only intellectual perception, and of course, *this has no spiritual significance whatsoever, nor does it bring forth spiritual harmonies.* However, the continued practice of these specific truths, and the daily meditations, all are seeds taken into consciousness which gradually open, take root,

---

[1] "Us" or "we" always means my students and me.
[2] "flash of light" means a flash of understanding. See "Revelation" in the Glossary.

and then grow into a whole new consciousness, at the same time dispelling the old man and his ways, and his garments, and revealing the new birth, the new body, the new business, the new consciousness infinitely expressing itself tangibly.

Aloha greetings from both of us to all of you,

Joel

CHAPTER 2

CORRESPONDENCE 1959

Note: In December, 1958, Edward and I went to Honolulu to see Joel. Later, I hadn't written to Joel for a month, for reasons explained in my letter below. But in late January I received a letter from a student in Honolulu saying, "Joel is wondering what is going on with you. How about a letter for Sensei."[1] So I wrote:

Dear Maestro,   February 3, 1959

Well, well, don't start this one till you have some free time. One reason I have delayed writing (besides the five bustling human ones I have) is that I have so much to say I am appalled at having to write it, and at your having to read it. I really do have the feeling that with the mountain of mail you have (and since I have discovered that you kindly answer each and every one) one shouldn't write you unless he has something important to say. And the only important thing I have to say is "thank you."

The reason why I wrote you before that there was really nothing to write about our development was that I realized that our little steps of growth, and pieces of understanding, must be almost exactly like those of everyone else on the Path, and you must have heard about *their* experiences ad infinitum. Not feeling that we could add anything really new or startling, there was no point in taking up your time just recounting our daily climb up "dem golden stairs."

---

[1] *Sensei* is Japanese for "teacher."

I won't pretend to any organization about this – just must go along with free association – because if I take time to edit it, it won't get written.

To begin with – my main reason for having wanted to come to Honolulu was so that Edward would be able to make his own direct contact with you. This is also the reason I sent him alone to the first private session. He had not at that time really seen the value in meditation and I thought perhaps by seeing how easy a thing you make it, and how simple, he would be encouraged to try it.

You see, as I am sure you realized while you were with him, he has so much *human* power and *human* intelligence that he has been able to make his long, successful career on "Edward's ability" alone and consequently has never (until now) been forced by the exigencies of his business to find some answer greater than himself. The goings on in his business, this last year, have been too much for him alone, and this ability to make *conscious* contact has not come a day too soon. I emphasize *conscious* because, as I told you in New York, I think he has always operated at a higher or lower degree of *unconscious* contact.

For whatever reasons, such as time, a sheltered life, greater interest, etc., I have always been the searcher in our lives in these spiritual matters. For about the last two years I have been very anxious to turn Edward loose to stand on his own feet with God; but until you came along, I have never found anyone whom I felt would or could inspire sufficient respect in Edward to make him take the principles seriously. Also, he has a very sharp radar for anything the least bit phony, which would have turned him away quickly. Until now I've just never found a sense of security in anyone's spiritual integrity, and I am at least sure of my own *sincerity* – if not ability – so felt it better to continue trying to explain this to him myself.

I have now turned him over to you 100%. This is a great relief to me. It is perhaps a chore I need never have carried – since it can also look like "bearing false witness" to consider that he *needed* any growth, I suppose – nonetheless I operated at the best level I knew how at the time. I really need the attention units to work on my own character, so I am very glad to have him row his own boat.

Last Thursday we ran Reel 10 of the Kailua Study Group and I got a great deal of merriment out of your explaining how you sometimes "strive with God."[1] This shot very close to home with me because (sometimes feeling sacrilegious) I have always felt very, very personally about God and was reminded of a time in my own experience which was similar. This, by the way, was the second time God has spoken to me with a real voice.[2] I had forgotten it until I heard your tape – and remember telling you that the only time He had so spoken was about my father one day.[3]

This second experience was about five years ago and Edward and I had been having particularly stormy experiences together and communication had seemed to be almost completely shut off between us. I was alone in my bedroom and quite upset – and I can remember storming up and down the room addressing the Father in terms something like this, "Now look here, you know me better than anyone – you know my real motivation – you know what I am really after – why are you making it so damned tough?! I try this, and I try that, and nothing seems to make any difference. Why don't you *tell* me what it is you want me to do – I'll do it! I want to do it! But why do you leave me floundering around without any instructions – why don't you tell me what it is you want of me?!" And then the Voice spoke - so soft

---

1   Regarding this mention of Tape 10 of the Kailua Study Group – we continued to study it from time to time. In 1989, when we, ourselves, had reached the ability to "strive" with the Fourth Dimension, that tape saved our lives.

2   See Glossary, "Voice."

3   For many, many years I had always felt God as "Father." Thirty years later I learned that even that concept of God must go. There simply is a higher state of consciousness to be attained than the awareness of God as "Father." However, one only reaches that one day at a time. In the meantime, it is all right to cling to God as "Father," because that *is* one of His *functions.*

- so kind - so fatherly – and He said, "*Then be still, child.*"
Well, I was stunned – and I remember sitting down on
the bed and saying, "Is that what it takes?" He didn't say
any more – but I knew He meant that with me storming
up and down and shouting and being so busy all over the
place He just couldn't get through. That was the first time
I realized what a gentleman God is – He won't ever
interrupt you! And when I am enthusiastic, it's always
been pretty hard to get a word in edgewise with me.
Which is also the reason I wanted Edward to come to you
alone – it sometimes seems that with me around he's
kind of inhibited, or something.

> *Note: I am fully aware that to a beginning
> student, or to anyone who has not had the
> experience, the statement, "God said to me..."
> can sound, at best, "touched." Nonetheless,
> after sincere effort, contact can be made with
> the indwelling God Consciousness, and we can
> "hear" or "feel" an inner communication
> which we know that we did not "think up." In
> fact, what it says is usually startling (never
> fearful), and it is the last thing we would be
> likely to tell ourselves. When this contact
> becomes habitual we find we are being guided,
> or "fathered."*

By the way, this seems as good a time as any to tell
you how wonderful, absolutely wonderful the Father has
always been to me. It took a long time for me to realize it
– but at about 35 I could look back over the years and see
how gently but firmly I had been guided, step by step,
without my knowing it. The other day I was trying to
figure out *why*. Because I have really made a lot of
mistakes in my life – and yet, slowly but surely, He has
always been bringing my ship into harbor. I couldn't see
any reason *why* – until I thought over how I had behaved
with Him. And, you know, it surprised me! *Never*, not
ever that I can remember, have I asked God for *things*. I
have actually never sought them, either – due to no credit
of mine; it wasn't on purpose – and I have appreciated the
beauty of nice things as they have come along. But I

really have never sought them. I didn't even ask God for Edward, which was the one thing that I wanted the most in the whole world. Of course I stormed around on a surface level – but down deep I always felt, "If it is to be, it will work out. " The only thing I have ever asked Him for is understanding – of course I really meant a kind of human understanding – I wanted to be loved, I guess. And it's only recently that I have realized that He has been loving me all along.

I have a sharp "Radar for Truth." No credit to me. I guess God felt I couldn't be expected to dig my ditch without some sort of shovel – and He gave me the ability to recognize Truth when I saw it, or read it, or felt it. I didn't know this consciously for a long time, either. At first it was an intellectual recognition, but in recent years it has become a recognition of "feeling." A bell goes off inside of me when a truth is presented to me – that is my simple rule of thumb now for knowing whether or not a thing is true. I have learned by experience that I can trust that bell, and it always, or most always, also brings up tears of joy. For instance, I nearly always cry all the way through your tapes, or your classes – or at least get one or two good lumps. And I have such a good time at it!

Oh dear, I haven't even got a good start and here it is 12 o'clock already. I have 400 things left to say – but must go about my human responsibilities.

But I did want to tell you that very quietly the other night Edward said, "That is without any question the most brilliant man I have ever met in my life." And I said, "Yes, and his brilliance is really the least about him." I saw the size of the man who sits behind Joel – and he is nine feet tall and three feet wide and just smiles and smiles.

And we all just love you all.

More in the next.

P.S. Oh, yes, I forgot – am enclosing a "thank you" for your private talks. Half is from Edward.

Think about me being peaceful, would you? And if you ever have time around 7 p.m., our time, on Thursday, be with us for a minute.

Dear Friend,   February 10, 1959

My heartfelt thanks to you for your beautiful letter of February 3rd and for your very thoughtful enclosure.

Yes, indeed, it is my joy to be in touch with our students all around the globe, and it is for this reason that my mail is so heavy. I am not only interested in their welfare, but in helping them with their specific problems until such time as they, themselves, are helping other students.

I can assure you it was a great joy for me meeting and getting to know Edward. His consciousness should certainly open wide a new era in the moving picture industry, because you know it only takes one to really start the ball rolling, and to create a whole new pattern.[1]

I am happy that both of you experienced the joys of meditation and you now know that there is no other way to contact the Spiritual Kingdom which is within. People have often wondered why it is that with years and years of study they have not made a single gain in spiritual development, and the answer is that *there is so much more to spiritual consciousness than brain development or acquisition of knowledge,* and that something more is only to be found and experienced

---

[1] This actually did happen. When Edward was head of Universal Pictures, he created a whole new relationship with agents and managers. Those who previously had fudged or lied to him stopped it, and an era of trust was initiated there. I was present in the studio commissary one day with Edward and a number of studio executives when an agent walked in who had unilaterally changed the language in a contract without telling Edward. He saw Edward, smiled at everybody and said, "He doesn't like me." Edward answered, "You're damned right I don't like you, and I'm not going to like you until you change." An example of "one-trial learning," the agent changed.

through meditation. The deeper we go into meditation, the greater our spiritual unfoldment and attainment.

I suppose the part of your letter that made me happiest was that you perceived the He that is within me. This is indeed the mystery and the miracle.

And so, for now, Aloha greetings from all of us over here to both of you and to your family,

Joel

P.S.

Dear Edward – Please think about that subject of drug problem. Our YMCA writes it is a major problem.

Aloha Joel.

Dear Maestro,   February 10, 1959

Well, you keep pulling the rug out from under me. I no sooner ask you to see me peaceful than I run a tape which tells me I mustn't ask for this. Last Sunday night I was just about one step ahead of a fit, the children had been so noisy (and thoroughly human) all day and I was tired because I still have to get up two or three times every night with the baby to give him a bottle, and still have to get up at 6:00 every morning with the school children – and all in all it doesn't add up exactly to a vacation. Anyway – I felt I had to hear a tape or bust – so I ran Side 2, Reel 1, of the Kailua Study Group over again.

I haven't heard this tape now for about 6 months and first of all, I heard it with brand new ears. I really didn't hear before that we aren't even supposed to ask for "peace." Yet on this tape you say exactly that. That we are supposed to ask only for (or seek for) the presence of God. So, I withdraw my previous request. See me in the presence of God instead, please, and I'll try, just try, and stop jerking until it's set good!

"Letter to Sammy" was a great, great success. We are just overwhelmed by it. It is really the finest credo for living. Also, it was *the* thing that kicked over a limitation for one of our group who had been struggling with the question of just where God *was*. "Letter to Sammy" showed her, and now the message of the Infinite Way has opened up a new dimension for her.

Well, tonight I'm not very cheerful – in fact for a nickel I'd run to Australia and change my name and start over. So guess I'll close.

Bye for now,

Dear Joel,   February 13, 1959

Just a couple of quick thoughts:

First, I hope you didn't misunderstand me when I said I had turned Edward over to you 100% – words are such meagre things for accurate communication – naturally I can't turn him over to you or to anyone. He is his own man, and has always been, and however much of your teaching he uses will always be entirely up to him – I merely meant the blind had decided to stop leading the blind.

Secondly, I withdraw the request about the meditating with us on schedule. I realize that you are really with us all the time.

Third, what is your viewpoint on the loss of material things? I have gone for years without sustaining any material losses. I have no insurance against this. I have felt God had us in his hands all the time. However, beginning with the day before we left Honolulu, with the loss of my camera, I have been beset the last few weeks with losses of jewelry, most of it pieces I had recently purchased. It doesn't involve a large investment, but, for instance, a topaz piece I lost last week was one I had just bought after looking for such a pendant for years. It seems very mysterious to me. I can't figure out the *reason* for it. Do you think it is paraphrasing a "loss of materiality?" Or is that too silly? Or does it mean that I'm not supposed to buy any? I don't mean to indicate that I am particularly fastened to them – I never have been very fastened to material things – rather just enjoyed them as they came along – but some things, this pendant particularly, had a distinct aesthetic value for me. What do you do about this? Do you carry insurance? Should I take out insurance – or just forget about the whole thing? And should I continue to buy things that interest me – or forget about that, too?

I realize this is not a very important problem, but what makes it important to me is that I don't *understand* it. I find over the years that I can easily forget about things like this once I *understand* them, but until I have the understanding, I have a tendency to worry them like a dog with a bone.[1]

Next morning – (had to stop and take the kids to South Seas Holiday).

Edward bought *Zen Flesh, Zen Bones*[2] while we were in Honolulu, and I have been really enjoying reading those stories. I'm going to read them to my children. They can sort of get it "through their Bones." Zen interests me, anyway. It interests me as a doorway to a better understanding of the Japanese people. It's really funny how very many doors towards the West (or really towards the "East") have opened up to me since beginning the study of "Mme. Butterfly" a few months ago. If you really get to the point of planning a lecture trip to Japan, I

---

1 Two years later my mother handed me this very pendant saying, "Is this yours? I found it in my jewelry box and it isn't mine." I guess God decided it was mine, after all. I still have it.
2 Reps, Paul, ed., *Zen Flesh, Zen Bones; a collection of Zen and Pre-Zen writings.* Tokyo: Charles E. Tuttle Co., 1957.

wish you would keep me advised of its approximate date.
It would be just wonderful to do it with you and Emma.[1]

I will tell you how I know that you are my true
teacher. About 6 years ago I had a healing in Christian
Science and at that time began a serious study of Mrs.
Eddy's works and the *Bible*. I think I told you in your
home that I had decided just for ducks to read the *Bible*
from beginning to end, just to get an overall picture.
Anyway, at some point in the *Bible* reading, I came upon
a statement, the beginning of which I can't exactly
remember (I will have to paraphrase since my little
heathens are knocking at my gate and I haven't time to
get a concordance and look it up accurately). I think it
was "after the something and something he will be given
a *white stone* with his secret name engraved on it, which
he will thereafter tell no one." Now this flashed out at me
with neon lights, and I knew that "name" meant
"nature" and I thought, "Oh, I wonder when, *when* I will
be given the stone with my secret name on it. What,
what is my secret name?" etc. Well, for years, from time
to time, I kept asking the Father, "When are you going to
tell me my secret name?" But whereas He usually
answered me rather quickly on serious things, He
remained silent as the sphinx (or rather silent as Himself)
on this, and I just kept wondering and wondering. Of
course, I knew He would tell me some day – but I was
impatient for it. (Of course, I don't have to tell you that
impatience is *the big defect in my character*). But my being
impatient didn't seem to impress Him in the least. He just
stayed silent, for 5 years. Last year when I was reading
The Infinite Way, and I wish I could remember on what
page, you gave me my secret name; and I knew it was,
just as surely as I knew that day on reading it in the *Bible*

---

[1] In 1986 I fulfilled this desire. I went to Kansai University to study Japanese and to find
out if there were any Zen masters left. Joel had told me there were not. He was right.

In studying the Japanese language, and their religions (I really mean plural; they have
religions for coming and for going), and culture, I also found out that Kipling was right. We
do not *see* alike, nor *think* alike, and it will take many decades for "the twain to meet,"
although there is much we can learn from them, and vice versa. The real problem is, they
are learning from us much more quickly than we are learning from them. I predict some
stormy days ahead.

that it would be forthcoming some day – and just as surely as I knew that I had never had it until then.

Now, the really funny thing is that many years ago I had told Edward this thing I read in the *Bible*, and had also mentioned to him from time to time that I wished it would come to me. Well, I was so impressed with the whole *Infinite Way* that I was terribly anxious to have Edward read it and I thought I would tell him this experience to awaken his interest in the book, so I started to tell him about it – and about one-third of the way through – long before I ever got to the point about the name – my mouth was stopped. I just hung up on myself and I could go no further. I absolutely couldn't tell him. And then I remembered that it had also said, "...after which he will tell no one." And I couldn't. And I can't even tell you – but then I don't have to, do I?

Do you wonder why I keep saying that all this is so *exciting*!

I was interested to note in reading the Zen stories that some of them left me unmoved, but some brought up my "testing tears" that I told you about. These were always the stories about the "big unchangeable." Whereas the ones about the human vagaries didn't have this effect. The ones about "silence" strike me the most.

That's all for today. Love from,

Dear Barbara,   February 16, 1959

Your letter of February 10th makes me very happy indeed. Now, when you go back to the December 1958 *Letter*, it will be as clear to you as a blueprint. Now you have really caught the essence of the message of the Infinite Way. You see, it was a strange thing to me when I first learned that people prayed to God for things like health, and supply, and happiness, and automobiles, and employment, and all of these things of the world. People prayed actually for homes, and for the sale of properties, and all of this mystified me. *This makes God a servant of man, doesn't it?* This has God doing the will of man. *This makes the wisdom of man superior to God's, since man is able to tell God what man needs, desires, wants or should have.*

The whole message of the Infinite Way is based on the premise that you *cannot enlighten God,* you cannot tell God or advise God, but that you can be receptive and responsive to God and let the will of God be done in you and through you. Now we learn, "Where the Spirit of the Lord is, there is liberty." And so it is that whenever we open ourselves and become receptive to the Spirit of God and permit it to fill us, then are we free of the discords, the inharmonies, and the lacks, and of course we are fulfilled with spiritual harmony appearing outwardly as human good in all forms.

I am truly grateful for this uncovering in your experience and for your receptivity to it.

Happy also that the "Lesson to Sammy" has met such a great need. We have sent it to press as a pamphlet similar to "Deep Silence" and it will be available some time this summer.[1]

Our united love to all of you.

Joel

P.S. Please remember the art book on Oriental art. Would love it.

Dear Joel,   February 19, 1959

Thank you for your letter of the 16th which in a large

---

[1] "Letter to Sammy" was published first as a small pamphlet. In 1986 it was included in a new book, *The Collected Essays of Joel Goldsmith* (pub. Devorss), which is an anthology of most of Joel's pamphlets. I highly recommend this book to all students, because each of the pamphlets was a little gem.

way answers my letter of the 13th which, of course, was already on its way before yours came. Believe me, I do see how unimportant these material things are, and it is not the *things* or the loss of them that really concerns me, since heaven knows the Father continues to supply me very well. The thing about it, rather, that troubles me, is the *experience* of loss which seems to me to be an expression of discord, or confusion, the same as April's teeth seemed an expression of lack, or Tony's broken arm.[1] I perhaps am terribly naive, but it always really shocks me – and I do mean exactly that – shock – when these experiences or so-called problems come into my environment.

> *Note: How many times in my twenty-nine years of teaching have I had the same woebegone question from a student. It takes a long, long time to come to the realization that, as Joel says, "...as long as there is one drop of humanhood left in us it will externalize itself." I had quite a few drops left! (See Joel's letter of February 26, 1959, p. 24).*

Now I remember the tape very well in which you state that we are never without problems to solve and can actually look on them as a blessing. I certainly do see that – and I can look back on some really serious problems that have beset me in the past, such as drinking, smoking, lack of health, not knowing who I was or where I was going – but all of that kind of major problem seems to be behind me. It is only these dinky, little, annoying, unimportant pieces of discord that keep cropping up – and I suppose the feeling at the bottom of it all is one of not being able to understand why I have not progressed to the point where

---

[1] April is my middle daughter. Tony is my second son.

this kind of petty annoyance simply does not occur in my life.[1]

It's a little like the two cavities I got in my teeth after Suzi[2] (which are the only ones I have had with any of my children). I was surprised, shocked and even (although I am ashamed to admit it) hurt, that such a thing had happened to me because I felt the health problem had been solved long before. Now whether or not this is "pride going before a fall" or whether God just doesn't want one ever to take anything for granted, I don't know.[3] Anyhow, it isn't the *things,* or the *circumstances* – it's the experience of lack of harmony that troubles me.

If all this nonsense does ring any kind of bell as human experience, and if you can give me any light on *what* is wrong when these things happen, so I can correct it, I will appreciate it.

Now, my dear, I must be straightforward and tell you that while your reference to the book on oriental art rings some kind of bell, things were changing so fast in Hawaii and have continued to change so fast since I got home, that I have remained in a slight state of diffusion and I can't remember exactly what we talked about in reference to this book. Was it that I told you I had a lovely book on the art of Japan? Or just what was it, please? I feel guilty to have to ask you to elucidate because I have learned that you never forget the tiniest reference in a conversation. But then I'm not supposed to be able to operate at your level, am I?[4]

I do see that ultimately, as you state in your letter to me, "When we open ourselves to the spirit of God and permit it to *fill us,* then are we free of the discords, the

---

[1] I was demonstrating the ignorance that I have often had to chide in *my* students, "You mean you are so *good* that you ought to be better." It seems to take a long time to let go of that one.

[2] Suzanne is my eldest daughter.

[3] The Truth is, God knows nothing about it.

[4] And so began a Comedy of Errors!

inharmonies, and the lacks," – so the answer to all my wondering about these little things must just be that I am not sufficiently opening myself. I am trying very hard to do this, and shall continue to do so. In the meantime, should I take out some insurance!?[1]

Love,

Dear Friend Barbara,   February 18, 1959

First of all, I wrote a post-script on your letter this morning that wasn't intended for you at all. My mind was somewhere off in space when I wrote this on the bottom of the wrong letter. I am sure you will understand and overlook it.

Now, as to your letter – on two points. Number one, insurance. If one has attained the *fullness* of spiritual consciousness to such an extent that one's possessions are of no moment, and the loss of them or gain of them is *entirely* of no consequence, then I would say that it is not necessary to have insurance or to lock one's doors. This would not necessarily prevent goods being stolen, but since their loss would mean nothing to one in that consciousness, there would be no loss. Before anyone can assure that there will be no losses, *one must be certain that the entire world has attained Christ-consciousness.*[2] As long as there is *a trace* of human consciousness, there will be human skulduggery in one form or another, but it will not come nigh the household of those who have *attained the fullness* of the measure of manhood in Christ Jesus.[3] Now, if one is not living alone unto themselves, but has a family, then something else enters the picture, and the rights of others must be considered, otherwise we are not

---

[1]   This is an example of Joel's "hidden absolutes" which, as beginners, we do not see, because we rush to the "good part." Joel forgot to say, "When we open ourselves to the spirit of God, *totally,* and permit it to fill us, *totally...*" He also didn't mention that that "totally" comes after the "death" of the human sense of self. (See my note following my letter of 2/19/59).

[2]   Year 5001?

[3]   It is so easy to overlook Joel's "absolutes."

loving our neighbor as ourselves. The same is true with automobile insurance. Regardless of where one might be in consciousness, it is a gesture of love to one's neighbor to carry adequate insurance so that the neighbor may be protected. I can assure you that in my own experience, when I was single I carried no insurance except such as was necessary on automobile insurance. But as a married man, I carry adequate insurance on the automobile, on personal property, on the home, and on everything that is insurable. This is my recognition of the rights of others.

And now for number two. You ask for my viewpoint on the loss of material things. Actually, there is *never any reason for loss*,[1] and so there is no use delving around trying to find out the why's and wherefore's of losses – there just is no reason – I mean from the standpoint of some invisible reason. *The outer reason, of course, is just carelessness* as a rule, and this calls for a little more conscious thinking when one is handling anything of value. My own experience there, also, is that I have suffered quite some losses through human relationships, because I am inclined to be careless in that direction, and assume the integrity of those with whom I come in contact. But I have not known any of this other type of loss.

As long as we have possessions, we are putting a value on them, or we wouldn't have them, and so I would say that care and discretion should be used with one's possessions, or can I put it this way – that *we should be good stewards* of that which is given to us. This may, of course, be a throw-back to my childhood, when my mother was an active worker in charitable organizations and impressed upon us the fact that while we could be as generous as we wanted to be in giving of our possessions, we must never be wasteful of them, or careless in the handling of them, and probably that has something to do with the fact that I sort of respect money and the things

---

[1]   Over the years I have learned there is always a *reason* for everything. That does not constitute an *excuse*.

that money will buy to the extent that I cannot be either careless or wasteful.

Paul Reps, who did that *Zen Flesh, Zen Bones* is in Japan right now, and just sent me a Japanese magazine in which he has a few new drawings. I am giving those to D., and when she's through with them, she can send them on to you. I may also have a copy of his book which followed *Zen Flesh, Zen Bones* and if so, I will mail you a copy.

Thursday night, the Consul of Japan and his wife will be out here at Halekou for dinner, and he is very much an Infinite Way student, in fact both of them are, and he is desirous of having me make a tour of Japan to speak in the Zen temples on *The Art of Meditation* and *Practicing the Presence*, and our approach to God. Do not yet know when that will take place, but will surely let you know when it happens.[1]

Thank you for telling me the experience with the Infinite Way and how you learned that I was your teacher. And I am sure that when you were here you saw what you saw, and thereby know all the rest.

And so, from Emma and from me, Aloha greetings,

Joel

Dear Maestro,   2/24/59 12:30 a.m.!
                                           (it's quieter this way!)

Oh I had such a good laugh over the now infamous "post-script" I really rolled on the floor. Thank you. I think sometimes the kindest thing a teacher can do for a student who is all boggled down in human things is to

---

[1] The Japanese Consul and his wife must have been the *only* I.W. students because the trip was a great disappointment to Joel. When he returned he said to me, "They didn't have the slightest idea what I was talking about." My trip in 1986 made it clear to me why this was so.

get down there with him for a few minutes. Sometimes living can seem to me to be a desperately serious business – and to be desperately serious is not my nature at all! Anyhow, I welcomed the opportunity for a good laugh.

Also, your last letter on the insurance question was so clear, brilliant, and to the point. It is too bad one has to be concerned with such issues, and I regret taking up your time, and my own, with these things in the world of effect. But, unfortunately, I do find that some such things can actually be hampering my growth – it's like a blot on the paper – and I'm not free until it is erased. You see, it is a great relief even to be told, "Now, girl, all that is just nonsense." At least then I know I don't have to worry about that any more, and I don't. When you said there's no use digging around about it, that did it. I accept that.

However, I find from time to time that the issue of how to bridge the gap – in practice! – between the human effects and the divine causes, can be very cloudy for us inexperienced ones. Your last letter sets up the problem and knocks it out with such clarity that I wonder if you would mind if I let the others of our group read that particular letter. It's a little like the relief I got in talking to Emma about how she handles the food aspect in your home. You see, I was concerned about proper diet for our family: vitamin supplements, holding down the free white sugar for the children, etc., because it seemed somehow to conflict with "take no thought." I mean, if one is to take no thought I suppose one is to take *no* thought! Anyway, it was a great relief to me to find that Emma, too, felt about it much as I did, and now, in this other instance, I find that the proper way is to act with intelligence – human intelligence, if you will – or what looks like human intelligence.

As to the actual losses. Nothing was stolen. It was, as you said, just carelessness on my part. I was confusing a careless attitude as being just "sure that God would take care of everything." Well, he spanked me on the bottom, and I see now they are not the same thing.

The line in *The Infinite Way* was, "...those of us who have taken the name of the Christ." And practically in the same instant that I recognized it as my own secret name, I realized that it is really everyone's secret name, isn't it? Isn't this exciting!

Goodnight, and love to all from,

Dear Friend,   February 26, 1959

Now we come to the crux of the entire situation as it relates to these problems that are now coming up in your experience. Let us go back again for a moment to the word "God," and remember that God is *infinite consciousness, divine consciousness, spiritual consciousness, without a single flaw.* Originally, before what is termed the "fall of man," or the "prodigal son's leaving home," this infinite, divine consciousness was also *individual* consciousness – yours and mine – and into this consciousness nothing entered that defileth or maketh a lie – no evil experience, no power of evil, no untoward circumstance. And then comes this experience which is known as Adam and Eve's expulsion from Eden and is also known as the prodigal son's leaving home, all of which really means that *a separate state of selfhood was set up – a personal sense of consciousness – and this based on accepting two powers – that of good and of evil.* Let us not quibble about how it began or why, but just let us acknowledge for the moment that it happened, and that you and I are the result of it having happened.[1]

That is, our entire human experience is due only to the fact that we have accepted a selfhood apart from God, and that *we have accepted a mind consisting of two powers – that of good and that of evil.* This, then, *constitutes our humanhood*[2] – at the moment when God placed our

---

[1] In about 1969, the Voice brought forth in one of my classes the full explanation of "How it all got started." This will be fully explained in one of the Volumes of my series of books: *The Anatomy of Spirituality.*

[2] See Glossary, "Humanhood."

footsteps on the Path back to the Father's house – back to the Garden of Eden. This Spiritual Journey which we are taking now is that trek back to God-consciousness. And now remember this – *as long as there is a trace of humanhood in your consciousness, even that trace must externalize itself in the forms of human good and human evil.* And so – experiences will for a long time continue to take place of the nature of good and of evil and bit by bit, onionskin by onionskin, these will drop away from us, so that instead of "seeing through a glass darkly," we will ultimately see "face to face," and then, of course, our purification will be so complete that we will no longer have human experiences *even of a good nature.* And so you see now that you have arrived at a very important milepost on your Journey. Up to this moment, you are able to accept all of the good experiences of your human experience with good grace, but not the evil ones, and therefore you are now face to face with the situation where you ask yourself, "Am I forever to be satisfied with merely a falling away of evil human experiences, or must the day come when I face the situation squarely and realize that my goal is not merely overcoming evil human experiences and experiencing only good ones, but that I have arrived at that place in consciousness where *both the good and the evil must go*, and I learn the nature of spiritual demonstration."

Paul refers to this when he says, "Neither circumcision nor un-circumcision availeth anything." Now, regarding the matter of the art of Japan; you actually have me thinking again. You see, when you were here and also when E. was here, we talked a good bit about the ivories and the Oriental art which I have, and which either you or she has, and I felt that she had said to me that she had a book on the art of either Japan or the Orient, and that she wanted to send me a copy of it when she got home. By some – what seemed to be accident – I made that notation on your letter, but actually intended it to be on E.'s letter. And now I am beginning to think – was it really you who spoke of a book which would explain these ivory pieces. With this explanation, you will know now whether it was you or was not you, and so I am going to leave it there.

Thank you sincerely for the wonderful pictures you took of us on Maui, and the pictures of your family. Indeed they have arrived, and I have them here. We are both grateful to you for this thoughtfulness, and when you come back to Hawaii, you will find them here on my desk.

Aloha greetings to both of you from both of us.

Joel

Dear Barbara: March 2, 1959

Be assured you may read to your group anything that I write to you. Always, truth is for everyone receptive and responsive to it.

One thing I would like to make clear to you, because it has been a major point with me in all of my teaching throughout the world. A transcendental teaching only has value in proportion to *its practicality in our daily experience. To sit on cloud nine is wonderful, if our feet reach down to the ground.* Our heads must always be in Heaven, and our hearts likewise, but *our feet must be on the earth.* Otherwise, you have nothing but an abstract teaching without real value except as either a mental exercise or an emotional experience.[1] My whole understanding of the Master's mission was that He came to reveal that the Kingdom of God was made practical on earth in *bringing forth harmony of body, of purse, of human relationships,* and that is the function of the message of the Infinite Way.

---

[1] Many, many times, in my teaching ministry I have had students come to me who had been reading Joel and hearing his tapes (some of them for years) but they still were unable to *live* the Infinite Way or deal with their human problems. Almost without exception they were either 'cloud 9'ers', or they had failed to understand the *practical* aspects of Joel's teaching, or they had leaped over his subtle *absolutes*.

And so, for now, Aloha greetings from all of us to all of you.

Joel

Note: The following letter was my first sortie into trying to understand the "absolute." Joel's wonderful patience gave me patience when I have had to deal with it with my students. Sooner or later, every serious student tries to come to grips with the concept of good and evil. It has also beleaguered the philosophers. Joel's answers were cryptic and I continued to struggle with them for some time. Clarification does come, but it requires a change in awareness, and growth in spiritual perception. Perhaps the Buddha's answer is as good as any. When he was questioned by his son, who had asked about life after death, he said, "I do not elucidate life after death. I elucidate the cause of human suffering and its elimination." When the Belief System about good and evil goes, so do the questions. The "mirage on the desert" is seen through and we drive on.

Joel's answer to the "absolutists" was, "The Infinite Way is not an absolute teaching. We acknowledge that we are living in a world of seeming duality."

The letter was too long to be answered in the usual way. Joel just sent my letter back to me with his comments written in the margin. I have reproduced them as they were expressed, and have put them in parentheses, and in bold-face type. I hope it is not confusing.

Dear Joel,   March 5, 1959

Well I don't know whether or not I'm going to be able to communicate what I am thinking. But I can only try. This is in answer to your letter of 2/26. In trying to formulate my thoughts I have gone back and re-read all your letters since we came home, to try to get a unified view.

In your letter of 2/16 you mention that it seemed strange to you when you found that people were actually praying to God for health, supply, happiness, homes, etc. I can easily see that such things would, indeed, be making a servant of God. I can also see that since that would be "praying amiss," in all probability those prayers would not be answered. I have completely accepted your teaching that true prayer is not words from man to God but *from God to man*. I know one cannot "tell" God nor "enlighten" God – and would not dream of trying to do so.

However, you also say that the grace of God is often manifest as the "added things" – as companionship, and love, and you say that it must come *through* Man. On Maui you said that God has no way of entering into form except through human consciousness (I use human consciousness in the sense of *individual* consciousness). So, wouldn't it be true that if one were living totally under Grace, in constant direct communion, his outer life might still, to the outer eye, look as if it were being lived on a human level?   **(Yes indeed).**

Now, if that be the case, I admit that it is rather difficult for me to see the "absence of human good." I can certainly see there is no evil – since it does say in the *Bible* that, "God created all, and he created it good." Now, if God is all in all – doesn't that automatically make Good all in

all? And if Good is all in all, then certainly there can be no power (evil) opposed to it.
(Absence of human *sense* of good).[1]

Also I can certainly see that all human life and *things* are illusion, hypnotism – as far as they are conceived to be *human*. But if, as you say, we can live under Grace and be "in the world but not of it" – then we are still, are we not, *in* the world? Now granting the hypnosis of anything human – this does not negate Reality, does it? Suppose, just for the sake of argument, that I stop – right now – being subject to the illusion or hypnotism that I have *any* kind of human existence at all. That would not necessarily mean that I would disappear to the eyes of my husband or children would it? Or that I would be relieved of the responsibilities I have undertaken toward them in this form? **(Correct).**

In fact, would it necessitate giving up form altogether, or would the 'I' still be maintained as me in this form? **(Not necessarily now, altho' eventually).** Presuming it would, or could, would it not follow that this individualized 'I' would be living in a state of Grace, or in a state of *Reality* – and if so, would that not preclude the entrance into my experience of any of the hypnotism or hypnotic forms of so-called evil? **(In proportion to degree of *realization*).**

To try to be simpler – it would seem to me that if one were really living in total *awareness* there would be nothing but good in his experience – the same as there would be nothing but God in his experience; and that any deviation from that absolute Good would only be the proof that the awareness is not yet complete. **(Yes).** And this is what hurts me about experiences of discord – not the experiences themselves – but rather that they are signposts that I "ain't made it yet." **(No one *ever* has while on this plane).**

---

[1] In 1990 I had the Realization (see Glossary) that whenever Joel speaks of "sense, human sense, fleshly sense," etc., he is referring to our "Belief System." It is this that has to go.

What I think I mean is that in your letter of the 26th you state that when our purification is complete we will no longer have *human* experiences of any kind, good or evil; I can see that as regards *human* experiences – but do you actually mean then that we will, by that time, have ceased to have this kind of body as an instrument? Have ceased to manifest into this kind of *form*? Or, in other words, that we will no longer be evident to this world? Or do you mean that we can still come into this world but in a purified state?   **(Yes).**[1]

If you mean that after   **(Complete)**   purification we will no longer *need* to come back   **(Correct)**   into the world, then I think I can see the source of my troubles. If human living is proof of non-purification then I can see that one must only work to rid oneself of attachment to all things human – and that would, of course, include human good – such things as husband, home, children, friends, etc.   **(Nonsense).**[2]
And I am not quite ready to give up the pleasure I receive in holding a baby. On the other hand – and this certainly is only my own opinion and may be erroneous – it has seemed to me that all *true* pleasure is of God. The pleasure of loving a baby – so it is God loving that baby – but it is pleasurable to me to have the feeling of that love flowing through me. The pleasure of spiritualized sex.[3] So it is God loving and giving – but it is pleasurable to me to feel it flowing through me – just the same as it was pleasurable to me to feel the healing light flowing through me when I have been a channel for healing.   **(Yes).**

Now, in all of the above I do not exclude the 100% concept of "thy will be done," if that means to sit back and not plan, and not decide, and not desire, but wait for instruction. But I do not see that it is in any way irreconcilable with having gratitude for, or enjoying, the

---

[1]   I wish I knew to which of the two questions he answered "Yes," since they are mutual contradictions.
[2]   "Nonsense" is a terribly important answer. It re-arranges one's view of "this world," and one's place in it.
[3]   I wonder what I meant by that?

blessings of experience which (by virtue of our listening attitude) *He* brings into our lives. And isn't it true that if He were bringing in *all* experience that all experience would be Good? **(Yes).**

I don't know whether or not I have made myself at all clear – but to sum up, I find it very easy to give up the belief in evil. I don't think I ever really believed in it anyway. But right now, anyway, I would find it as difficult to give up my belief in Good as I would in God, since to me they are synonymous.

My goal has never been the overcoming of evil experiences. My goal has always been the search for Truth-God. But as a result of that sincere search over the years there has been an increase of good experience which I have construed as meaning I have been getting closer to *reality* – and when an experience of discord comes I have construed it as having slipped away from reality. **(Yes).**

Now if that be true, then certainly I can understand the *reason* for the slip from reality being that I have set up a sense of life separate from God. I now know that such a concept is not only egregiously egotistical, *ridiculous*, and stupid, but damned dangerous. And the desire to totally eliminate that concept is why I am at your feet. **(Yes).**

I remember that it was D. and I who talked briefly about my book on Japanese art – and your talk must have been with E., since my book deals with painting, not sculpture. I am sorry. I wish it had been my book, because I would like to be of service to you.
(Have received the book from E.).

Well, so much for *that* struggle.

I have another one.

It looks like the Muhls are producing again. And I was at first at a loss to understand it, because I had the distinct feeling that after five I was through. I'll admit there were some personal things I wanted to do after the baby got to be a little older – go back to school for one.

Now I would like to have your opinion on this. I actually never gave another child a moment's thought. Also, I have not for years used contraceptives of any kind because I felt the bearing of children was under the control and guidance of God. That He would not send you any He didn't mean for you to have.

Edward the other night, when I told him what I suspected, said that he didn't think God knew anything about it at all, or had anything to do with it. That it was purely human experience and must be dealt with on that level. And he quoted you on this saying that you had told him, "There is no God in human affairs," and so, since there is no death in reality, there must also be no birth in reality, and therefore God has nothing whatsoever to do with it.
                    (Edward is correct – absolutely!).[1]

Now I have always felt He did, and I wish you would please tell me your viewpoint on this. Do I have the right to decide not to have any more children – and if so, how does that reconcile with "Thy will be done?" Or is it like the insurance matter? I am not talking about *this* child, since I would not dream of interfering with or blocking a life process once begun – but what about the future? I know you'll probably say "give up sex" but I ain't ready for that, yet. I've got lots more humany human problems to work on before that, such as impatience and anger.
(I never have said, "give up sex." I do not advocate "giving up." Ascetism is no part of the Infinite Way. As to contraceptives – be guided by your own sense of right. This is an individual demonstration. Seems to me you have done well by society already!!).

---

[1]   I think Joel meant, "In the absolute."

Oh, dear, I hope you're not bored with me. I do feel that all this grinding down will serve some purpose one day. Anyhow it's a little like the story about the couple coming into the court for a divorce where the wife was the complainant and said that she couldn't any longer live with a man who was so bitterly cruel to dumb animals; that her husband had caused her German Shepherd dog to have a nervous breakdown. When the Judge asked her just what he had done to bring about this terrible thing, she answered that every night when her husband came home the first thing he would do would be to fix the dog with a baleful eye and ask him,"If you're a Police Dog, where is your badge?" And that this had finally rendered the poor dog a trembling neurotic.

So, without wishing to bring about the same result, I will continue to impose on you and say that since you are a Teacher, you must teach!

Love to all from

P.S. Oh, dear, in re-reading my letter I am afraid I have just taken up your time with a lot of gibberish and never really said what I meant.

I think what I mean is, is the goal then "no human experience" – and if so does that mean no home, no family, no friends, no nothing? Or is it just to take the *human* out of home, family and friends?   **(Nonsense).**

As they write in the letters in the lovelorn columns:

"Bewildered."

(continuing)
March 6, 1959

Well, I seem not to have done with this subject yet. I labored over it all night and since the other letter is not yet gone will add this to it.

I do think my twistings and turnings have at least clarified a little for me what I *mean*. And I think what I mean is this:

Does *purification* mean no more death and birth, no more going out and coming in, no more change of form, and consequently no need for marrying, having children, going to work, etc.? If so, then obviously all this is nonsense and one should just seek for God Consciousness and ignore all the other until it goes away, at the same time, of course, going through all the play acting of so-called living.   **(Absolutely correct).**

I have heretofore thought not the *absence* of a thing indicated spirituality, but rather the *how* of a thing. To illustrate:

I had my first child in the hospital, with anaesthetic, with pain, with horror. I was full of fright and full of anguish – not at childbearing, but at the pain of it.

Now after that, I decided there had to be a better way, and in the conscious pursuit of the concept that giving birth was a God-controlled, God-governed function, I was lead (I thought) to the understanding that if God could create the child and maintain it for nine months with all the miracles that gestation contains, then He certainly could get the child in here without my help. And by the time the next one came I was able to have it (still in the hospital, since I couldn't talk the doctor into having it at home) without anaesthetic and with a minimum of pain.   **(Improved belief).**

However, I changed doctors for the third and was absolutely determined to have it without human interference of any kind. Now just as the child was about to be born the head was pressing very hard on my pelvis and my mind was flushed through with the thousands of years of junk in the thinking of the world about pain, anguish, tearing, death in childbirth, etc., but I decided in a flash that I would really rather be dead than *afraid* any

more and literally said to myself, "I'm going to go with God or nothing." **(Greater improvement).** At that exact moment out popped the child's head, perfectly free, *without any tearing at all*, and all of my children since then have been born at home, without any anaesthetic, in a very short time, with an absolute minimum of pain, and certainly without any *fear* of pain. Now, I have always construed this as a very definite God experience in my life and have felt that this growth, development, or evolution in the way I was able to bear children was a direct result of God-seeking and God-awareness.
(All this leads up naturally to final revelation).

Now, is this not true, then? Does God really know nothing about these goings out and comings in, and does this merely represent a human good? If so, I want to know it, because I am definitely on the wrong track in that case.

I'll admit that in this case I was definitely after an absence of pain, but I felt that the way to achieve this was through God awareness and thought I so did. Is this a wrong goal, too, in the sense of achieving a bigger house, etc? **(Not wrong – but correct).**

It's very difficult for me to conceive that the bearing and rearing of children is a human activity, or nonsense. Yet according to Edward's theory this is exactly the case. If so, I'm perfectly willing to accept it, but it will certainly call for a reversal in my thinking.
(Edward is correct!).

In other words, I have actually felt that over the years the increase of balance and harmony in my experience has been due to an increasing God-Consciousness and the increase of God governing my life; and that the periods of friction have indicated those places where I am not yet aware, and am not letting Him govern. **(Yes).**

Isn't it just that the "seeking" after this would be wrong?

Oh, lord, this is a weighty subject for such a beautiful morning. Next time I shall be a tree, and "leaf the driving to Greyhound."

I'm exhausted and I know you are.

Love from,

(Dear Barbara – Spiritual living is not a giving up. And it appears outwardly as a human life of health, beauty, wholeness, clean-ness, etc. We do lose our old concepts of love, wealth, government, etc etc. When ripeness is attained we drop this concept of body in order that we may do our work from an invisible plane).

Aloha,

Joel

Saturday night
Dear Joel, March 14, 1959

I got the message. I see now that, yes, I have taken the human good (didn't know it was human) and tried to get rid of the evil. Showing me the non-reality of birth did it.

I told you in New York that Edward was quite a remarkable fellow and would be worth your efforts. He certainly saw this whole thing much clearer than I did. From now on I shall say no more to him of these matters because he has taken back his spiritual pants and I am delighted to see him wear them.

After studying your work for a year I could easily see and really feel that "all out there, and all those people (in bodies) were really illusion – but not me!" Oh I could accept intellectually that I was not the body, but I was not really *operating* on that principle.

Correspondence 1959

The non-reality of birth did it. I had to say, idea leading to idea, that if *that* wasn't real, then neither was this body. Then the thought came, "If I'm not me, then I don't know who I am;" and almost immediately, "Oh, yes I do, I am *that* I am!" And immediately there was restored to me something that has been gone during the last ten years of really hard search – my sense of humor. And I felt as if a 30-pound load had been lifted off my shoulders.

You told us on Oahu that your goal in life had always been freedom. So has mine, and in this striving I have been led into many strange channels which could be explained in a human sense as "freeing the body" – and I now think that I have always known, deep down, that it was a shackle.

Also, I thought in your home that it was Barbara seeing the real Joel – I now know that 'I' was seeing 'him'.

This is the last letter that you will be receiving from me for some time because I have been fed – and feel it is only fair to move over and let someone else in at the feast. I shall be reading, listening, and meditating and being grateful to you, but I will not be taking up your time for awhile – at least until this big bite digests.

I appreciate you,

Dear Barbara –   March 20, 1959

It all adds up to the fact that it is now reaching consciousness that "My Kingdom is not of _this_ world."

All there is to the Infinite Way is the ancient teaching that there is a "_My_ Kingdom" – a "_My_ Peace" – which has *no relationship to earthly harmonies.*

The young student believes that the Infinite Way is a short cut to physical health, harmony, and satisfaction.

The seasoned Traveller has learned that there is another realm – another type of harmony, peace, etc.

Write again.

Aloha to all the family –

Joel

Dear Joel,   May 29th, 1959

I'm so glad to have finally sat down to write you. It helps me almost as much to write you as to hear from you. Sort of solidifies the contact, or something. We aren't dead – as you might have supposed – just been hibernating in the human. I was ill for the first time in over seven years – flu idea – Ed had it, then me, and of course it then ran rampant through the house. We ignored it – but it was time consuming with the babies. Also, Ed and I just returned from a wonderful trip to New York where we saw a lot of really good shows.

I am very conscious of all the help you have been sending me – and it has certainly been needed – because while I have been occupied with seemingly human things – much hurricane stirring has been going on at a deep level and finally came to a head in the last four days and my boat was really rocking. But it spilled up to the surface and out last night and we are finally at rest from this one. I am very glad about this particular one, because I think through it I am now through yelling at my children, and that will be a relief to all of us.[1]

Along with everything else, the two little ones have been asking more and more of me, and I have had one by one to give up my outside activities: singing, guitar, piano, Italian, etc., and can see that with this new one, too, it just seems indicated that I forego the outside points

---

[1]   As it turned out, I had not conquered yelling!

of growth that interest me. This has occasioned quite a
struggle, you may be sure, because I certainly was not
born that unselfish. But I do really consider that their
lives are far more important than mine – just on the basis
of the fact that they have all come in at a far more
advanced level than I did and I consider the world is
going to need this kind of citizen, and I realize I should be
absolutely willing just to serve. But the desire for time to
devote to my own studies and reading dies hard.

My sister,[1] who is so devoted to your principles, had a
very interesting experience recently and I urged her to
write you about it – but time or shyness intervened – and
so I thought I would tell you about it. The yearly drive
for polio shots had come up in the schools and while for
the last several years my feelings had just rubbed off on
her, and she had refused them, this year it seemed that
she had to work it out for herself and really come to a
final decision. Her thinking ran something like this: "I
certainly would not have shots for myself, but each child
is really responsible for his own life, too, and how can I be
sure that there is no thought or acceptance of polio in their
minds, and that therefore they might need that type of
outside help. If something is right for them, it doesn't
seem right for me to impose my own thinking on them."[2]

Of course I'm telescoping the whole argument she gave
herself for over a week. She was trying to be sincere, fair,
and logical. Finally she asked me about it, and wondered
what you would say about the whole thing. I suggested
that she write you and find out. She said she would do
that, and then (she has four children and does all her
own work and is very pressed for time) day after day
went by without her being able to sit down and really
write. Finally she decided to save some time when she

---

[1] My darling sister Virginia McKnight.

[2] Of course today, I know the answer to all of that. Until they are about sixteen, one's
children are under the parents' consciousness – for good or ill. They are either protected or
polluted, depending on the level of spiritual consciousness in the home. At about age sixteen
they move out under their own consciousness and begin to live out their own Karma (see
Glossary). Other such events that occur while rearing children will be explained whenever
I can write my book for parents, *What to do Till the Psychiatrist Comes!*

could write by composing the letter in her mind, which she proceeded to do. This letter (as she tells me) went like this: "Dear Mr. Goldsmith, I have had a problem disturbing me for quite some time in connection with my children and I wondered if you would be good enough to –" and right at that point she said, she got the answer to her letter, just as clearly as if she were reading it off the paper – and you said to her, "The shots are just as unreal as the disease you would be trying to protect them from." Well, of course, that was her answer and she has had her release, and that is the end of it.

The interesting aftermath was that she was asking me how it could be that when you obviously could not know at just what moment she began to write, how the answer could have been received at just that moment. I would like to check with you the accuracy of what I told her. I said there were, as I saw it, two possible explanations. Either the letter was never sent to you, but to her own inner being, and the answer was not received from you but from her own inner being – or, and I prefaced this one by saying that I often – well not often, but sometimes – felt that I was actually making contact with Joel, and that if that were the case I thought the answer would have been that you were doing *that thing* for which I am the most grateful to you – your willingness to maintain that state of consciousness 24 hours a day. And that if that were the case, there would have been no moment in the 24 hours when she could not have turned to your Consciousness for help, and the contact would be instantaneous. What do you think about that?

I really wish it seemed indicated that I could come to Honolulu for the July class, but unless the Father has a plan I don't know about, it looks most unlikely. I do miss your personal charm and your sense of humor. But, of course, all I have to do is walk into my living room and turn on a tape and you are right there. I don't know where you got the idea of these tapes, but it was brilliant.

D.S., the director, and his wife, two highly literate and studious people (but a little dilettantish, also) have become converts to the Infinite Way. D. had gone to Japan on a picture a while back and became interested in Zen and of course he just jumped right into this after hearing the first tape. And, surprise of surprises, my mother's sister-in-law picked up "Lesson to Sammy" (which my mother had taken to her *sister* to read) and now has asked me to loan her everything I have of yours, which I am delighted to do.[1] The sister-in-law, in telling her boss (a buyer at Sears) about the wonderful new philosophy she had stumbled upon, found that the buyer has been coming to Honolulu for years to buy for Sears and never fails to see you when she comes. I don't know her name, but you may find a connection. Talk about a small world.

Also, a very lovely friend of mine, whom I had invited to hear a tape almost a year ago, who was then all caught up with J.M., called me yesterday morning, and after beating around the bush for 20 minutes finally asked me if I were still as interested in Joel Goldsmith as I had been the last time she talked to me. Well, she wanted to talk and talk. And finally I said to her, "This is something that can't be talked about – it has to be lived. You've had two of his books for over a year, and we run tape sessions every week to which you are welcome, or you could subscribe to his *Monthly Letter*, or you can write him and buy the tapes for yourself. Other than that, I can't tell you any more." I just didn't feel like getting into a long philosophical hassle with her, because she really wanted me to, and wanted me to try to convince her of the value of the I.W. and to coax her into coming – but I guess I'm getting to be an old dog, for my crusading days are over. The Infinite Way seemed like such a miracle to me when I first got hold of it, and recognized so practically instantly that it was what I had been looking for all my life, that at first it really surprised me that others I knew who had been searching earnestly, too, didn't take to it the same way. But as you said in

---

[1] My mother was Jacqueline Kean.

Honolulu, it is bound to appeal to very few, by its nature, and now I am only surprised and delighted when I find someone *does* take to it.[1]

Well, that about brings you up to date on the Muhls. I would like to be brought up to date on the Goldsmiths, when you have time.

Please say hello to Emma for us, and give her our kindest wishes, and also ask her to please let me have her recipe for the cottage cheese pancakes she spoke to me about and which I forgot to get from her before we left. I would appreciate this.

Love to all,

Dear Friend Barbara: June 2, 1959

Well, at least when you do sit down to write a letter, you write a letter, and that is the real purpose of writing a letter. I have enjoyed every minute of yours and have equal pleasure in answering you. First of all, it would have meant nothing more than a cable or a telephone call to have had immediate help for those flu conditions in the home, and of course *they came only as a temptation to yield to world belief.*

Thank you sincerely for your most thoughtful and generous enclosure, and I do hope that you know how grateful I am at any time for all of this, or nearly all, goes back into some Infinite Way activity. I corrected myself there because the Infinite Way has two partners who share, and that is – of course you'll recognize our first partner as Uncle Sam, and then our home here at Halekou takes its share.

This is certainly interesting to hear of your sister's experiences, and those of the others who have come to the

---

[1]   Since 1964 the appeal of the Infinite Way has spread over most of the world and today, in 1991, his books are selling better than ever.

Infinite Way through contact with you. It is always good to learn of these experiences of our friends and students because of the assurance and confidence that it gives to others on the Path who may not respond as quickly as these.

Answering your question about your sister's receiving the answer before she wrote the letter, of course you are absolutely correct. No one should come to the public ministry of a spiritual teaching until they have received some measure of "fourth-dimensional consciousness," called in religious circles, Christ-consciousness. It is this higher consciousness which meets the needs of those who turn to us, and it is only because we are avenues or instruments for this Consciousness that the help can be given. *Since this consciousness is omnipresence itself,* anyone may touch it by turning to the consciousness of those who have attained a measure of it. You notice I keep repeating "a measure of it," since even a grain of actual spiritual consciousness does wonders for those who turn to it. As you have observed, except in minor details, I do not live a personal life, and therefore am constantly and consciously in tune with fourth-dimensional consciousness to the extent that in some measure, again, "I live, yet not I, but this which has awakened me lives my life."

Now, to bring you up-to-date on the Goldsmiths. We will leave here the end of July and have a few days in San Francisco with the children, and then we come down to Los Angeles for a few days at the Beverly Hilton Hotel. I am keeping this kind of quiet since there will be so few days there, but of course I shall certainly look forward to a visit from you and Edward.

Will add the recipe for the pancakes when Emma returns home – she is in town at present.

Our united love to you and Edward and the family.

Joel

P.S. Pancakes (for two)

> 4 eggs
> 1/4 cup flour
> 3/4 cup cottage cheese

Blend in blender if you have one, otherwise beat well.

P.S. Along with June letter, study
>   Tapes # 5-6   Maui Advanced Work
>   Tape # 3   Hawaiian Village Open

Dear Barbara: June 8, 1959

By now, you will have received my letter telling you of our coming trip to Los Angeles, and therefore it will not be necessary for you to make the trip to Hawaii.

I wrote you previously that I certainly hoped we would have opportunity for a dinner or a lunch together. You see, the few days that we will be there will make it possible for us to see only a few of the students, and so we had planned on you and Edward. That is why we did not wish it mentioned to anyone else.

Aloha greetings to both of you,

Joel

Dear Joel,   June 19, 1959

How I love the clarity and order you have reached! I was listening to the first side of Reel 16, Kailua Study Group this morning, and was relieved by it of the funny little guilt feeling I had for not having written you yet; it actually had not yet occurred to me that this thing operates also in all the "unvital" areas, matters not life and death, because in the tape you mention having things on your desk for days and days without being "prompted" to do anything about them – and now here this afternoon I see why I was delayed in answering you. Had I written before I couldn't have written anything decisive.

As far as the Muhls are concerned, Edward does want a private session with you and he will come any time at your convenience, morning, afternoon or evening. I would certainly appreciate sharing meditation with you. If it would interest Emma or you to see Edward's "plant" we might arrange a luncheon at the studio and a little trip around the lot to see the sets where "The Big Fisherman" and "Spartacus" were shot, or anything else that might interest you.

And we certainly want to have you up to our house, any time you can come. We do have a very nice view (you'll have to arrange to keep it smog free – although I do pretty good on that score myself!) so it would be nice if you could come while it is daylight, early enough to use the sun and the pool if possible, and then stay to dinner. Well, you just tell us what you can do, and when, because we are holding that week completely open.

Also, if you can come to us, you must tell me whether or not it would be all right for me to have my sister and my mother up to meet you because, of course, they are both alight with the thrill and excitement of your proposed visit – as much as we are, ourselves – and as for us, it just seems like a miracle that we are really going to have you both on our home ground for a while.

I certainly don't want to mastermind Edward's meeting with you, but I do feel prompted to tell you about two things that are troubling him, in case he either forgets, or might be too shy to mention it. His eyesight seems to be failing, and he is urging me to have the children given polio shots – and I am trying to hold the line against either glasses or the shots until you come here and he can talk to you about these two things. Actually, he has to make extraordinary demands on his eyes with all the reading he has had to do in the last 6 years since he has been head of the studio, and much of this reading he does in bad light and lying down, so he does need some kind of help – and maybe he <u>needs</u> glasses – I don't know – I just have such a reluctance, personally, to submit to limitation that I can't help feeling that way for him, too, even at the same time wanting to stay out of the way and leave him free to run his own life.

And also, although I know you'll laugh at this, I can't help feeling that some of his eye problem is that there are still some things he "refuses to see." However, be that as it may, that's your department and I leave it to you.

Sunday I am off to Catalina with the whole brood for two weeks, so will save the extraneous matters I wanted to mention for my next letter.[1]

Mother will be coming over to Catalina on the 29th and will bring any mail, in case there should be a letter from you.

Love to all,

Dear Barbara,   June 25, 1959

First of all, let me clarify this situation about our trip to Los Angeles. Emma was immediately enthusiastic about coming out to your home sometime after 4 p.m. and remaining for dinner, and so we are assuring you of our joy at accepting this invitation, and of course I do believe that it will be wonderful to have your mother and your sister, since they are both so interested in this Message. As you know, I want to utilize every minute, even those which may be accompanied by what seems to be a social activity, to give, share, impart, all that can be accepted.

Now, regarding the matter of Edward's eyesight. *You have been led more by zeal than by wisdom* in your approach to this situation. The first step for you to have

---

[1] I nearly had a miscarriage on this trip, which Joel healed. It is explained later.

taken would have been to undertake to bring healing to Edward for this situation. Then, if within a reasonable time there had been no response, and considering the fact of the inconvenience and probably pain under the circumstances, the second step would have been to suggest that Joel be given the opportunity to meet the situation for him. And then, *if after a reasonable period there had not been a response, the right solution would be to get the eyeglasses,* but as a "suffer it to be so now," with the idea that there would be no relaxing the effort to meet the situation spiritually.

In other words, as we would not deny splints to a person with a broken bone, nor would we deny crutches to the man needing them, so we cannot deny the use of glasses where an acute situation exists which is not being met. And of course this subject of eyes, you know, presents quite a different proposition than almost any other claim, since to be perfectly logical, we should all give up the use of glasses and work spiritually until we are healed, but this would involve, *let us say in my case, a neglect of my students and patients,* since I am under the necessity of reading and writing mail probably eight hours out of twenty-four, and of writing books, articles, arrangements for tours, etc., for some more hours, and then of course, the need for reading, not only my own writings, but Scripture and at least a brief period each day with the mystics of the world. All of this really is a violation of the natural law, since eyes were never made to be used for such purposes under such lights or lack of lights as we do work, and so this particular claim is not always as simple as it may seem.

Actually, at this present moment, I am working with ten cases of cataracts – this is humanly speaking – and am already having the most wonderful results with three of these, and so you see that nothing is really impossible, even with these claims of the eyes, and so the only point that I am making is that where one is suffering discord and pain, and is at the same time compelled to make as much use of the eyes as Edward is or I am, that we must consider it a "suffer it to be so now" if we resort to glasses.

However, be assured that if Edward feels that there is no particular rush within this next week or two for glasses, that I would be very happy to see if we cannot break the situation immediately.[1]

Aloha greetings from both of us to all of you,

Joel

Dear Joel,   July 19, 1959

Well, I don't know where to begin – and it certainly won't be at the beginning – but you seem to be able to make some sense out of my rambling, free-association style so far, so I shall just trust to your high degree of receptivity,   rather   than   to   my   low   degree   of communicability, and plunge into the middle, letting the ideas fall where they may.

Guess now is the time to bring you up to date on our "human" problems. The day before Mama called you about my threatened miscarriage, "Nanny" (Edward's former wife's mother, who has been living with us for the past 8 years, ever since her husband died; who has been helping me with the children and cooking, and who has been the Rock of Gibraltar on whom I have been able to lean in any emergency and for whose love, loyalty and conscientiousness no amount of money could pay) fell at her daughter's house and broke her hip in what they say is a very bad place for a woman of 72 years of age. She has been in the hospital ever since. Tomorrow she goes to a convalescent home for 3 months. I have been holding down the fort in the house, with the cooking, laundry, cleaning, child care, etc., alone. However, that is not a bid for sympathy – because it will turn out to be a

---

[1]   In my own teaching and healing work it has been of inestimable value to have the authority of this sensible and pragmatic letter from Joel. One of the major problems with the beginning student is the pain and guilt they feel because they are not more *spiritual* than they *are*. Sometimes, some things have to be handled *at the level of the problem* until God has taught the student something he needs – and that he does not yet know. Patience is indicated in such cases.

blessing, I think. First of all, my children, for the first time (first because they are only now old enough) have been asked by me to contribute to the care of the house and they have responded wonderfully and I actually think that that part of the experience has served to draw us all together more.

The upshot of my deductions was that Nanny would not be able to work again (all this really is leading up to the miscarriage bit).

After I had concluded that Nanny would not be able to come back I felt the prompting to come home and get the household situation straightened out, and since mother was there at Catalina with me, I asked her if she would stay till the end of the week so as not to shorten her nor the children's vacations, and she agreed to this. This was early morning, and I couldn't get a plane out until 5:20 p.m. At 3 o'clock I went up to the house to pack, and in about 15 minutes I felt a strange contraction. Having had my children without any anaesthetic and having had so *many*, I am very familiar with all the sensations of pregnancy. While sometimes after the 6th month one has *stretching* pains, they are nothing at all like the pains that dilate the uterus just prior to delivering a baby, and this pain definitely felt like the latter. However, I had absolutely no history of this sort of thing with a pregnancy, and my first thought was to ignore it. But shortly after there were 2 more contractions and I began to have the definite feeling that the cervix was dilating. This really alerted me – and at first I thought, "Good Lord, do you suppose all the walking I have been doing since I came here, and all the unaccustomed work, is going to cause me trouble?" Anyway, I was concerned enough that I wanted to be sure – and by then the contractions were becoming "grindings down," and that just wasn't a good sign.

A miscarriage was the last thing in the world I wanted – so I called a Dr. friend of my cousin who lives on the island, and had him come over to examine me. He told me the cervix was definitely dilated, that he was afraid I was going to miscarry, and that at only six months they would not be able to save the baby.

I thought, "Well, we'll see about that!"   And immediately asked mother to call you. The doctor came back in about 45 minutes and gave me another examination and he said with some surprise, "Well, something has happened, the cervix is closing down again." And I knew we were safe. So, I stayed flat for 24 hours and went home the morning after.

Now, I know you're not concerned with the human aspect of things, and I am a little at a loss as to whether I should burden your eyes and your time with all of this human dross by way of explanation – on the other hand – it is the "lifting" of the *human* illusion that reveals the reality of spirit (seems to me I've heard *someone* say something like that, *sometime!*). However, if one doesn't know any Truth, and if error is all he has to deal with, it *is* helpful to discover that it has a pattern, even if subsequently, with spiritual understanding, one comes to realize that error and its patterns are both nothingness.

Anyhow, I don't quite know how to relate the spiritual unfoldment which has come to me, without leading up to it by recounting the pattern of bondage which preceded it. Or else I could simply say, "Have had another great unfoldment" – but then you wouldn't know about what, or how, and I have somehow gathered the idea that while you certainly see none of this as real, even you are interested in the actual steps we take, laboriously, one by one, to awareness.

Well, the morning I came home my obstetrician came to see me, examined me and said there was not, now, the slightest sign of dilation and as far as he could tell everything was absolutely normal. Now I know you say it is not necessary to discover the "why" of any of these things – and I can certainly accept that – but I still have an interest in the "pattern of error." I have found that once I really see the pattern and the thinking that lay behind it, I am freed of it for good and all. So I asked the doctor if he thought that all the work and walking at Catalina could have brought this on, since I had absolutely no history of this kind of thing, and he has delivered me of 2 babies without anything like this ever having come up before. He stated that he thought the thing was psychogenic.

I was flabbergasted and said so. I said that I had had a clean Rorschach Test over 5 years before which stated that I was a "well adjusted human being" – and while I realized I certainly had at one time been a text book neurotic, in the last 10 or 12 years I had lifted out so much junk that I just couldn't think of anything *I* knew about that was troubling me sufficiently to have brought on anything so serious that it would actually endanger another's life. If it were a first baby, perhaps, or if I had had a history of blood spots, or threatened miscarriage, or anything like this, I could understand it – but here we were with my *sixth* child – and why now?!

Well, he said I had better give him a blow by blow account of the whole trip to Catalina which I began to do, and, to make a very long story not quite so long, I remembered an unhappy experience in a waffle shop. Then another unpleasant experience happened with a telephone operator. I really didn't know what was happening until my cousin took the phone from me and told her she was being very unprofessional.[1]

Then Tuesday we had the shock about Nanny.

Tuesday night we had a family picnic and my mother and I were having a discussion about the relationship between parent and child in which I held that a parent must, in a human sense (Goldsmith principles not aside), be willing to accept a good portion of responsibility for a child's psychological problems or philosophical lacks. I said I certainly felt that I was, in a good measure, responsible for my children's balance or

---

[1] "Devil" is what was happening. (See Glossary for our definition of "devil").

lack of it, and that I felt she had to accept that same responsibility. I laid my hand on my mother's arm to emphasize this and she spoke to me very sharply, saying, "Take your hands off me." This triggered the rejection I had always felt from her as a child. (She is a very, very different person today from what she was when I was a child and she is the first to acknowledge this, and that she made many humiliating mistakes, with both my sister and me. But even today, she is the executive rather than the grandmotherly type).

Then, on the way home I had a row with Edward on an old subject. I had from time to time tried to explain to him why I was sometimes difficult or over-sensitive in the area of personal security because I had never had love or understanding as a child. My father had beaten me almost daily and he, himself, never grew past the emotional age of 9, was an alcoholic, etc., and a few other sordid details which I certainly will not bore you with. Edward's answer to me had always been, "You're exaggerating, that is absolutely impossible – no man could be the way you tell me he was, and no woman could possibly have been as callous to her children as you tell me your mother was." Well, his not believing me was a further rejection and my trying to explain this to him in an effort to elicit a greater display of affection from him was never successful and always ended in my defeat. (For good reason we now know, don't we?).[1]

My obstetrician was aware of much of this background including the fact that I came in with a pretty well developed feeling of rejection, which was added to by a very unhappy childhood. He remarked, "All of this adds up to your being pretty full of rejection." Well as

---

[1] It was several years before I really understood this, and had matured enough to accept the *primary* axiom of the I.W., "There is *nothing* that can happen to me that is not an outpicturing of my *own* state of consciousness," i.e. – *I* have made every event, and every experience, of my life. No one has ever done anything to me but read back my own script. Starting in 1986 we had four years of work on this, which turned out to be "The Truth that makes you free." My book covering these lessons, *Script, Kid, and Fantasyland*, will be published when I can get to it. Until then the tapes of these classes are available. You can write to us for the Tape Catalog.

soon as he said that word, "rejection" my solar plexus tied up, the tears started to flood, and I had the understanding and the conviction that this was the key to the whole thing. I still stated that while I knew I had suffered some emotional insecurity, it was very hard for me to believe that there was any kind of trauma still lurking around of sufficient potency to have caused such a serious development. But he explained that usually we lift all the less serious ones first; that the organism has a tendency to want to jam the most serious and painful ones way, way down and just not look at them, that it was probably only *now* that I had evolved to a point where this could be brought to the surface and dealt with, simply because I now had sufficient freedom and balance to face it. Well, he left, and I lay the rest of the day and thought about this. I kept saying the word "rejection" to myself and every time I did the tears flooded out again, until finally after about 3 hours the pain was extracted from the word and I was calm about the whole thing.

Then – oh then! – the *enlightenment!* I realized that this whole experience was *unavoidable* – the rows, the serious and frightening situation, which I immediately decided to have healed spiritually or not at all, the quick turning to you – the fact that mother had with her the May *Letter* which I kept reading and reading while I was lying there waiting for the doctor to come back for the second examination – the emergence to the surface of this old, old, painful, wicked human-bondage belief in rejection, the understanding of it even from a human standpoint – and then, wonder of wonders, the answer to it all contained in the recollection of the May *Letter* where you state, "God realization dissolves human experience." You explained so, so clearly that the human illusion always appears as a personal I – as "I need this or that, I need a job, or a home, or companionship, or *not to be rejected*, or to be understood." And I so clearly saw the old dragon's head of human ego which had lain so quiet and so deadly – and I became thankful, thankful and grateful, for having had so disquieting an experience, so thankful for you for the healing of the threatened miscarriage, so grateful that God had allowed this old bugaboo to come up to the surface and had shown me *really* – not humanly – but *really* how to deal with it once and for all, forever. Because, you see, this longing to be understood by Edward has been a very strong and a very painful thing left lurking around.   And, naturally, since I have been studying the I.W. I have long known that the problem was that I kept insisting that I should have understanding and affection from *him* – that he was the *one* – whereas intellectually I learned long ago from you that we must not look to "person" but to God for all of this. Nonetheless, until this old tired feeling erupted I couldn't seem to come to grips with the thing *emotionally* – and as you say – that is where we really must solve these things – intellectual acceptance won't do the trick.

Well, the outcome was that this *need*, this human need, has been *lifted* from me and it feels as if someone had taken 100 pounds off my shoulders and a knife out of my back!   I believe only you could possibly know the *gratitude* I feel to the Father, to Principle, and to yourself for being the one to lead me to this understanding.

Before this goes too far afield I must quickly explain that when I mean I longed for understanding and affection from Edward, I am separating that from love. Edward loves me – he *proves* that all the time.   But it is kind of an impersonal love – he feels love for all mankind and he is helpful and considerate to all.   Intellectually, I have always understood that it is *easy* for me to show affection, that it is just my nature to be outgoing, and it is difficult for him to do so because his nature is reserved, to the point where he actually almost feels it is bad taste to be demonstrative, except with his children.   Sometimes it has occurred to me that that is part of what I wanted, his Father expression, because a father (humanly) was denied to me.[1]

Anyway – that's all in the past – and done with. Grace God!

---

[1]   Today I would phrase that differently. I would say, "*I* wasn't sufficiently *evolved* to be able to demonstrate that."

Now, the peace that filled up the hole where the rejection was extracted has infiltrated so many other avenues. I'm just not the same person. I just seem to be sitting on a great rock in the middle of the ocean – observing the changes flowing on around me, but with our center ground disturbed not at all. A few days ago there was a bad fire in Laurel Canyon and then one started here in Coldwater not 100 yards from our house, yet there was not one minute where I felt that we were in any danger. I knew where *I* was and that it would "not come nigh our dwelling place." And it didn't. The wind changed and blew the other way, endangering no one, since it went down canyon where there are no houses.

A few days after that April came down with 104 degrees of temperature, and also, for the first time, I felt no emotional involvement (more about this healing bit, which was really started in me when I received your letter about Edward's eyes, but that is another subject and must be dealt with separately). I just went to work, and actually felt *able* to handle it myself without having to yell to you for help – and it resolved, peacefully.

Well – what I am trying to say is that I hardly know myself!

All of this started with the culmination of our heavy correspondence early this year when I wrote you that you had proved the non-existence of "Barbara" – and now there is not a "rejected Barbara." What a relief!

And speaking of relief – I think you must need one, too – and the family is home from the ranch – so I had better stop for now and go into the other subjects – which are not quite so urgent, anyhow, except the matter of healing – but that, too, is a long subject...

Except – while you wrote lengthily and well about the subject of the eyes – you did not mention the polio bit – what about that?

Much love and many thanks to all of you for everything – and especially to you for being you,

Dear Joel,   July 23, 1959

There was a P.S. to my last "book" to you, which I forgot, and haven't had time till now to send another one.

It was that I think certainly part of the healing experience (even if only from a human standpoint) was that when I turned to *you* for help – you did *not* reject me! So that the rejection cycle was certainly broken, and furthermore, I feel certain about your lack of condemnation, correction, or rejection not only for me in this experience, but for me in *any* experience and for anyone else you know, too.

So you see, while I recognize, understand and appreciate the spiritual help, and know that that really is the all in all, I also thank you just for being you.

And I must tell you a rather moving thing about mother, too. After she came back from having talked with you, she was telling me what you had said and she could hardly talk and I could see she was holding back tears, and I laughed and said, "So he makes you cry, too, huh?" – and then she did boo-hoo, and she just kept saying, "Oh, that wonderful, wonderful man."[1]

Now, there is more to this than meets the eye, too, since one of my mother's worst *human* problems has always been a basic disrespect for men. She completely dominated my father, and her second husband, and in not too nice a way – and she has always really wanted to wear the pants. Since she is bright, and executive, she has

---

[1] The experience was a tremendous one for my mother. She had been "hanging loose" from any real contact with Joel, but when she called him she said, "They say Barbara is miscarrying and she wants to know if you will help her?" She told me that Joel answered, "That I will." That was all, but she said love just poured over the phone (Joel was helping *her*, too) and she burst into tears saying, "Oh, that wonderful man!" That was a *lot* for my mother to say about anyone. She had been touched by Love, and it changed her.

always made it stick. Until, that is, she began to grow and recognize that this was a *problem* with her, not a virtue. Of course she does respect Edward, but she has even had reservations about him. So it is a very thrilling thing to me to see her humility about you and your wisdom, and her willingness to sit and learn. Not that I have thought that I had any monopoly of appreciating you – but it does please me when I see others do it, too.

I know you don't fasten people to you, personally. I think that is absolutely right, and it makes you practically unique in my experience, and is just one more thing that makes me know your validity – nonetheless, I feel "fathered" and you *did* it – and that's that.

Love to all,

Dear Barbara,   July 25, 1959

Thank you for this letter from which I gather that you have come to see that the psychological approach to life offers very little in the way of healing or satisfaction.

Regarding the polio bit which you say I did not answer, I am sorry, but I have completely forgotten what I should have answered, and so you had better save it until our arrival.[1]

Aloha greetings,

Joel

---

[1] Joel's answer about the Polio shots was, "When there is a divided household on an issue, the one who is farthest on the Path must yield to the one who has the fear." So I did, saying to Edward, "OK, we'll get the shots, but you must take the children." The first time he heard April yell at the needle, the matter never came up again.

Dear Joel,   July 27, 1959

Just to clean up a lot of odds and ends before your arrival.

Wanted to mention that a while back something was made clear to me that had been troubling me – and in quite an interesting way.   L. mentioned to me in Honolulu that the first time she interviewed you, you asked her who she was and she answered, "A point of God," which is what most of us would say, or would have said, I think; but that you answered her, "You are the *fullness* thereof." She said that while she didn't really deeply understand this, it made her somehow know that you were "the one."

Now this concept has troubled me, too. In other words I have been able to paraphrase this in terms of the electric light, or fingers on a hand, or branches on the vine – but I could never really *see* how one light bulb, or one wave of the ocean, or one finger on a hand or one branch on a vine could express the "allness," or how *each one* would be expressing the allness.

Well, I have a little reading place in my bedroom where I keep all the pamphlets you have written and before the children wake in the morning I do a little reading and just go through each one, one after the other, with what time is available. Except that I had been skipping the one addressed to business people, called *Truth for Business and Professional People*. I skipped this one thinking that since I was neither in business, nor a professional, it would not be pointed at me. However, one day, about 2 months ago, it came up in the sequence and I started to put it behind the next one, when all of a sudden the thought came, "Now, really, every word he says is worth reading or listening to, just go ahead and read this one, anyway."   Which I did – and came upon your wonderful illustration about the diamond – in which every facet expresses the *fullness* of everything the diamond is, all the value, lustre, color, fire, richness – and for the first time I could *see* how a thing which, on the outside looks individual, e.g., an individual facet – was still, each one, expressing the wholeness and the full capacity of the entire diamond. So that one was cleared up.

It seems wonderful that that day (your arrival) is actually only a week away – it makes it seem like Christmas is coming early this year, and how we do look forward to it.

Until then, much love to all,

Dear Joel, August 17, 1959

Just to say "Love and Gratitude" for your visit and for the insight gained while you were here. The effect will go on for a long time.

You meant so much to my sister and she was so grateful for the time she had with you. She is a wonderful girl, and time spent with her will be very fruitful, I can assure you. She is really working on this, and grows by leaps and bounds.

Have sent to Emma in Hawaii for the 4 tapes mentioned in the August *Letter,* but when you were here, you mentioned a total of 10 tapes dealing with this subject. If you get time, would you drop me a note with the list of the other 6 we should have?

Please tell Emma I just love her qualities – and that I have had several warm feelings of appreciation that she told me she had "missed" me when I left Honolulu.

By the way, you were so right in your last letter that there is "no satisfaction nor healing" in the psychological or psychiatric approach. They can restimulate these beliefs, and perhaps bring them to the surface, but there is no getting *rid* of them, until one can see the "nothingness" and, of course, the very psychologists and psychiatrists, themselves, absolutely don't see or believe in the

"nothingness" of these experiences. So there you are –
impasse. Well, I just feel lucky, lucky, lucky.

Love to you and the whole movement,

> *Note:*   *End August, 1959*
> *There is a letter lost, here, in which I told Joel*
> *I had recognized, after his visit, that his*
> *Consciousness had "doubled in power" and*
> *that on his trip "the world might wake up and*
> *find itself at peace."*

Dear Father,   Thursday Sept. ?, 1959

I think part of my problem is that I'm just awestruck
since you've lost your "person." It's wonderful to know
that the Messiah walks the earth again, but I adored Joel,
and I shall miss him.

I guess those of us who have been able to see you at
home were spoiled, and now growing up seems difficult –
but possible, I think.[1]

Aloha,

56 Curzon Street,
London. W.1.
England

Dear Barbara   4th September 1959

I am happy that your sister got so much from our visit
and, of course, this was only a seed planted and the
fruitage will appear in due time.

---

[1]   This was my first experience at "impersonalizing" Joel and seeing him as his Christ-
Consciousness, rather than the human form.

The ten tapes that I mention are: Maui Advanced Work Nos. 5 & 6; Hawaiian Village Open Class Nos 3 & 4; and the six tapes of the Hawaiian Village Closed Class. These are the tapes which eventually will be a book entitled *Advanced Instruction in Spiritual Healing.* As you know, the new book *The Art of Spiritual Healing* will give the principles and the application, and will be presented in such a way that students may start from scratch and develop the consciousness and learn the specific principles of the Infinite Way. However, for those who make the Infinite Way their way of life, there is still a step beyond this, and that is the understanding of those specific principles which constitute the message of the Infinite Way, and which provide the reason that there is an Infinite Way message in the world. You will know what I mean as you study the September *Letter,* and, of course, I will look forward to hearing from you after you have given this letter serious study.

My experience at the Mental Institute in California was another unusual experience, and again indicates how necessary it is for a message such as that of the Infinite Way to come into the world.

Please be sure to keep in touch with me as I will be here throughout the month of September, and soon will be able to give you my October addresses.

Meanwhile, Emma joins me in love to you, to Edward, and to all of the family.

Joel

Dear Joel, November 4th, 1959

I had a nice letter from W. in which he told me that you had changed your reservations. I wanted you to know that I had sent a letter to you at the Buckingham marked "hold for arrival." It contained a little check, so I want to be sure you get it.

I want to specially thank you for the November *Letter.*
I seem to be ready for the paragraph heading, "First be sure
you are in the Spirit." I have that stuck up on the
window in my bedroom where I have been spending all
my time since Erica Joelle joined us – and I find that
remembering that keeps me in a remarkable state of
serenity – and nice signs following – such as that my
milk is coming in nicely, Joelle just sleeps and eats
peacefully, the other children seem in very good order,
and, as Edward said, "The whole house has an air of
calm that is very nice to come home to." Believe me, I am
grateful for this and intend, if I possibly can, to maintain
it – permanently.[1]

There is one problem I wish to discuss with you,
however. A short time ago Edward was rather ruefully
outlining the things he said he had done "for my sake"
and, in saying how he had always tried to go along with
me, mentioned "even studying Goldsmith for your sake."
I told him that *I* had to study Goldsmith for *my* sake, and
that if he were not doing it for *his* sake, he shouldn't be
doing it at all, because he could neither help nor hinder
my evolvement, any more than I could his, since this
was a very individual thing and could no more be done
one for the other than I could digest his food for him.

Although I honestly did not press him on it, merely
stating that our trip to Honolulu last January would
afford him freedom from business pressure and *time* to
break the habit of smoking, he really felt it was
something he had to do to please me.

In any event, he rarely makes it home in time to hear
a tape any more. Now this doesn't particularly worry
me, because first of all, I have immense faith in his basic
spirituality, and certainly in his intelligence, and
smoking has already lost much of its glamour for him

---

[1]   That is easier said than done. The carnal mind, devil, human mind, or whatever
synonym for "ignorance" you like, never sleeps, and pours its poison into the mind twenty-
four hours a day. It took time for me to develop the spiritual muscle that can maintain
peace.

(judging by his complaints about it, saying, "It's a device of the devil," etc.). And I do know that if he is to let all this go once and for all, it has to be because of his *own* desire and unfoldment, and not "for my sake."

However, I would like to be *really* helpful in the situation and this is where you come in. Some time ago when you told me I should first have tried to heal his eyes, I just wouldn't have known how to begin. But on your visit here, you mentioned that there is a specific truth for each problem, and I realize that that is where I bog down. I only know how to work in a very general way, such as meditating on a general truth – "God is" – "My hand in yours, Father" – and things of that nature. And whenever I have tried to work on a specific problem I have always felt inadequate and as if I were not doing it right – such as, before Goldsmith I would *pray* – but always had the feeling I wasn't doing it right – and I wasn't!

So, would you please tell me the specific truth on which I can meditate regarding Edward's eyes, and also for the dissolution of this seeming discord.

In this connection, I can tell you from a human standpoint what his greatest problem is. I have only been able to see this since I have been relieved of the same problem myself (since the big healing of the "rejection" in June). Also (even as you say in general terms that we must not criticize anyone for not giving us more love, or affection, because anyone is giving all of it that he can at any given moment), I can now see that all this time when I have been wishing for succor from Edward for my own feelings of inadequacy, he was always doing the best he could, and *could not* have done any differently all this time. He actually couldn't *see* my needs (human, that is) because of the pressure of his *own*. And since I have been, thank God, relieved of the need to have my feelings of insecurity soothed, I can see that his problem of insecurity is larger than mine ever was. Now I know how this can make one suffer, and I certainly would want to help him in his, except that I know now that just soothing the human ego is not *real* help, and that if *permanent* security and peace are the desired ends, it must be done on a spiritual basis.

So, will you tell me exactly what I can do to be doing the right thing: I will appreciate it. I mean just exactly how I should work, or *not* work, if that is the answer – since I feel very ignorant about this aspect of I.W. (healing, that is).

Well, thank goodness the Closed Class is only a little over two months away. I look for spectacular results from this, in us all.

In fact, in many ways it looks like Edward's current pitching and tossing might be the last gasp of the devil. Certainly I have found, myself, that very often when I am on the verge of a big, new enlightenment, it seems as if the devil pulls all his tricks out of his bag and really throws the book at you. I have experienced this often myself, and have found that this is the very time when we have to be the firmest in resolve and determination to "let go" the human. That is the very reason why I feel a sympathy for what I think Edward is going through right now and why I want to help if I can.

W.'s letter just glowed when he described your and Emma's state of consciousness. I know you are just pumping on all 16 cylinders and I greedily await our own class.

Love to Emma and Joel,

Salisbury Hotel
123 West 57th Street
New York, New York
until November 20th

Dear Barbara: November 6, 1959

To you, to Ed and to Joelle, our united love and

congratulations! Emma and I are thrilled to have your letter of Thursday and to know the great joy and peace that fills your household with another pair of lusty lungs. Be assured that I know of no words with which to express our emotions, but you yourself must understand the nature of our love and of our joy.

Thank you, also, for your very thoughtful enclosure. And, of course, I do look forward with tremendous joy to the experience of telling you all that has happened on this trip since we saw you in California. Actually, it reads like a fairy story, and for this reason could not possibly be put into print, although surely somewhere between the lines those with inner vision can read.

The first week of the new book in New York has been a fine experience. It has been wonderfully well received, and I am pleased with it. The last time I said that was with *The Infinite Way*, and the original manuscript of *Leave Your Nets*. The present *Leave Your Nets* is going to be allowed to disappear, and then I am going to have the original manuscript released for publication under that same title, but that will be at least a year away.[1]

Of course we are going to be in Los Angeles before the first of February, and so there will be further occasion for an opportunity of a visit with you and Ed, and of course, a look at Joelle.

And so, for now, Aloha greetings from Emma and from me,

Joel

Dear Joel, November 11, 1959

Well, *Art of Spiritual Healing* had not yet arrived when I wrote you my last letter regarding Edward. If it

---

[1] This was never done, which was unfortunate, because the original, which I have, is a precious jewel.

had, I wouldn't have had to write, because the answer is contained in the first 40 pages I have read. At least I think I have the answer, I can check it with you. It seems as if one simply must get to the point of "so what" even about those close to one. Particularly, since I have not been *asked* for help. In fact, I am quite sure that Edward doesn't for a moment consider that he is in *need* of help. And perhaps his innocence about some things that would spell trouble to me is the proper evaluation to put on the whole matter.

In any event, unless you should tell me otherwise, it seems as if my effort should be entirely to rid myself of being able to *see* this as anything that *needs* healing. Since I took it to heart that one must "not take a sick or sinning person into one's consciousness."[1]

By the way, I have had the manuscript of C.U.[2] for two years and have been studying in it, but when I found the published book could be purchased I bought it, and I was reading currently in the chapter called "Meditation" and noticed that you have made a few alterations in the book. In particular, you describe the exact manner in which you go about meditation. I think this is wondrously helpful. I find that I, and most of the people I talk to about this work, need things actually spelled out as to techniques, etc. That is the reason why I feel I bog down on healing work – I don't really know how to go about finding the "specific truth" for a problem. Suppose, for instance, the problem seemed to be one of temperature. How would you go about it? When this happened with April last spring, I wasn't excited (as I think I have already told you, I haven't been able to get excited since the big healing last June) and I just held her and tried to "go in" – but all I knew to think about was just "God is." Now, is there a specific truth that I could have meditated on, as well?

---

[1]   My insight was absolutely correct, but achieved, as always, with sweat and, sometimes, tears.
[2]   Goldsmith, Joel, *Consciousness Unfolding.* The Julian Press, Inc.: New York, 1962.

Actually the only problems that seem to come up in my life with any regularity are three; the slight illnesses of children (and thank God they have never been serious), a sense of fatigue coupled with a kind of exasperation when it seems like 6 children are about 5 1/2 too many, and a sort of nagging little drive (that comes up less and less often, but still comes up) of ambition about my music. So if you could give me "S.P."[1] to use on these three, that would be very helpful.

Of course, I haven't finished *Art of Spiritual Healing*, and everything I am wondering about may be contained in there. If so, just say so, and you won't need to bother answering these things specifically in a letter. By the way, I think this new book is absolutely tremendous! It is a marvel of clarity, and the style is so warm that much as I love everything you have ever written, I can't help but feel that this little book will have a special attachment and meaning for everyone who contacts it. I know that already it's the only one I have that I would be reluctant to loan out – not wanting it out of the house for even a minute. (So I guess I'll have to buy some more "loan out" copies).

Joelle continues to be miss "Princess Perfection." And we are all absolutely devoted to her. Oh we look forward, forward, forward to January.

Much love to all,

Salisbury Hotel
123 West 57th St.
New York, New York
until November 20th

Dear Barbara,   November 12, 1959

The words that come to me first of all are "loose him

---

[1] "Specific Principles."

and let him go" and then next follows "what is this to thee; follow thou me."

We give the greatest help to our loved ones in proportion as we are able to loose them and to let them go. *Sometimes, this brings about an immediate release into harmony for them, and at other times, it may seem to leave them without a foundation,* but then they can only be left without a *human* foundation, for the spiritual one is always there. And so, I am going to give you for this week's lessons the chapter "Love Thy Neighbor" in *Practicing The Presence,* and "Relationship of Oneness" in the new book *The Art of Spiritual Healing,* and then after you have had the opportunity of studying these, and at the same time, loosing him from your thought, then write to me at the Congress Hotel, Chicago.[1]

Aloha greetings to you, to Edward and to all of the family.

Joel

Dear Barbara, November 28, 1959

This is our final day in New York, and while Emma is packing, I am trying my best to clear up the mail on my desk.

Answering this last letter of yours, I believe that I will ask you to study well the entire book *The Art of Spiritual Healing,* and the *Monthly Letters* of June, September, and October, 1959, on the subject of healing work and treatments, and when you have thoroughly digested or assimilated all of this material, then if there are any

---

[1] After receiving this letter, I said to myself, "I know you are right, Joel, but if I could *do* that I wouldn't need you!" Of course I didn't say it to him. I wouldn't have dared. Many years later, after I was able to *do* this, I learned how right Joel was! When one can *rush* to *forgiveness,* and reach being able to say and mean, "God Bless – " we are free, and so is the other. Furthermore, that *blessing* touches the Christ of the other one and he, or she, is moved to change!

remaining questions, write to Hawaii, where we arrive December 7th.

And so, until then, our united love to you and to all of that wonderful family. Aloha!

Joel

Dear Joel,   December 20th, 1959

As you will see by the date on the first check, I had by November 15th, read the book, "got the message," and decided on my course; not only in the matter of the tithe, but as to Edward. It has taken me this long to get around to setting it down to you.

Now, you had better prepare yourself for a long session – for I have the feeling another "book" is forthcoming. I seem to want to get finished with all the little tag ends of things I have wanted to tell you about, probably not so much that they would be interesting to you as that they are to me. That is one of the penalties you must suffer for being teacher. We dearly love to report our progress no matter whether it brings forth a pat on the head or a slap on the wrist. (I have had both from you!).

Sometimes it takes a long time to put two and two together. For instance, I have known for years that the experience I was part of in the healing of that little baby that had been given up by the hospital and sent home with less than two weeks to live, was not so much for the baby's welfare, as mine – because it completely changed *my* life, but not his, nor his parents'. It changed mine in that I then *knew*, definitely, that God existed.[1]

---

[1]   The baby was suffering from cystic fibrosis, had pneumonia, and one lung collapsed. Since birth he had gained no weight. We were successful in meeting this and I was sent a picture on his graduation from college. I have recounted the full story in my previous book, *The Royal Road to Reality*, published in 1982.

Just recently I was thinking about that experience (it was almost 12 years ago) and I realized that about a year before that happened I had been walking up and down my room one night cajoling God to let me "know for sure." I remember saying – out loud – "Now, I believe in you, and I know you're out there, somewhere – but after all, in Jesus' time he had to show the disciples miracles in order to be sure that they were convinced. Now why won't you be a good sport and send me a miracle so that I, too, can know beyond a question of doubt? I don't ask for anything spectacular, just a little miracle – but one that will let me *know* that what I believe is true; one in which I will *know* that no human hand could have been involved."

Now, you have taught me well enough that I am appalled, today, at my temerity. But He does protect "fools and drunks" and apparently has a tolerance for ignorance – because, far from striking me dumb on the spot, in less than a year He produced my miracle – and I have "known" ever since.

What brought this to mind was that the other day a cousin of mine came to see Joelle, and we got to talking about you, and I sent her home with *Practicing the Presence.* She has been a student of Christian Science for a long time but is still full of doubts. She asked me how I could be so "sure," so "positive" – and I recounted this experience of the miracle healing as being the thing that turned the trick for me. She then said, "Yes, but you have just said that true prayer is listening, not asking for things, and yet you asked for this miracle – and what's more, you got it." That stopped me for a minute and I had to go inside for the answer, which was that I had not asked for *things* – but "to know him aright" – and since I got the miracle – apparently it was O.K. with the Father to ask for that!

Then I have another funny story to tell you about Tony – you will remember his remark about having proved there was a God, "Because the hour goes by so slow during the school semester and so fast in summer," and,

"There just has to be a God or else He couldn't change the time around like that." He came upstairs the other day while I was reading. I put the book down on my table and he announced that he didn't want to be called Tony any more, he was tired of that name, and from now on he wished to be addressed as "Anthony." "How do you spell it?" So I told him how to spell it and he put his paper down and began practicing the name with many flourishes. He was writing with a ball pen and you know how you can even scar a table top with these and I noticed he was writing on a book. I said, "Hey, move over, you'll scratch my book." And he quickly answered, "Oh, it'll heal up," and I said, "It will not, those ball pens leave permanent marks!" Without another word, he took his finger and underlined the title of the book he was writing on, *Art of Spiritual Healing.* Nuff said.

One thing I have noticed is that the Father is very arbitrary about talking to me. Sometimes I can sit in meditation with a very strong desire to get through and the contact just won't come, as if He's off on some other business. But when *He* wants to talk to me! About last February I was working around the house – a very busy day – and I felt this kind of pressure on my shoulder and I kept shrugging it off. I really wasn't aware what the pressure was until along about 5 o'clock in the afternoon I was in here in my office where I have my meditating chair, and I was literally shoved into it and urged to go into meditation. I said, "Oh, is that what you wanted?" And went into the deepest meditation I have ever had. That wasn't very deep I must admit. But deep for me – I almost lost consciousness – and when I came up out of it – some 15 or 20 minutes later – I had been told that I was supposed to contact the daughter of a musician friend of mine who had died a short time before and that I was to send her a certain sum each month and an additional sum twice a year to take care of her tuition at UCLA and her books, until her education was completed. He actually told me exactly what to do, say, and exactly how much I should send. How do you like that? So I said, "Naturally, I'll do it – and I just think I'll keep this line open, so the next time I want to talk to you you'll have to answer the phone."

Another thing I have wanted to say, is to tell you how wonderful it is to me to be able to go to you for answers. Believe me, in this, like in the learning of every other subject, it's a helluva lot easier to have a teacher who's been there before you, than to try to jumble it out for yourself. It's also very time saving. So, thank you.

Well, that's the end of my notes of things I wanted to mention. There's nothing left but Edward.

I certainly was ready for the answer I received from you on him. It is not only working with him – but about human things in general. I have made up a little "pome" which I recite whenever the picture gets cock-eyed:
> "What is that to thee"
> "Loose it and follow me"
it almost scans. Anyhow – it works.

It has resulted in big – but very subtle changes in Edward. So subtle I won't bother to try to delineate them. You'll no doubt feel it for yourself when you see him. I don't mean it has resulted in any outward difference – but the vibrations are different. The reason I say I was "ready," was because it was so easy to do. I just seemed to have to be told.

Art of Spiritual Healing is a masterpiece. Ginny and I cried all the way through.[1] Naturally it still needs much study – but that is a lifetime, anyway. I am also reading through the new book *God the substance of All form*. I find the footnotes with the New Testament references very distracting – they take my mind off of what you are saying (since it seems impossible not to yield to our habit of dropping the eyes to read footnotes) and I sometimes lose a moment of inspiration thereby. What I am trying to say, I think, is that when *you* write you create a kind

---

[1] Ginny is my sister.

of magic that comes out of the pages and actually creates, within the reader, an atmosphere and a response that is very close and personal – the kind of thing that really exhorts one into practice of the principles, a kind of "meditative presence" – and sometimes just from the very reading one can have a creative or healing experience. I find that having my attention drawn to the references sometimes breaks that circuit.

I don't remember ever noticing this format of footnoting every, or almost every, biblical reference or quotation in any other of your writings and it has always seemed to me that the use of quotation marks is sufficient – they have the quality of emphasis and one realizes that you are quoting without being distracted. It doesn't seem to me to be terribly important just what you are quoting from, so much as to realize the sense of what you are quoting and to recognize how it points up the principle you are explaining.

Also, those numbered and footnoted references seem, to me, to make the book more like a text book which causes it, again for me – perhaps not for anyone else – to lose some of the personal warmth which your writing always contains.

Well, this is certainly none of my business, but since this is the only book of yours I have seen done in this way, I did wonder if this format has some special meaning in *God the Substance of All Form* ?

By the way, you may remember that I asked you in Honolulu last January whether or not you had a Concordance, or were planning one, and you said not now, because your pages were not numbered as to lines and the publisher thought it would not be indicated, or too difficult, or something. I don't remember exactly what you did say. Anyhow – this keeps occurring to me, and I thought I would explain that I had not meant a concordance like *Science and Health*[1] has, with reference to numbered lines. In fact, I find the numbered lines in S.&H. also distracting – and I much prefer the first edition of *Science and Health,* which I have, to the latest one, which may be more scholarly but from which, for me, most of the personal inspiration has been edited out. Also, in using the concordance to S.&H., I find that when one is referred to just specific lines there is a tendency to start and stop reading with just those lines. Whereas, I have often, in years past when I was studying Science, found that there was sometimes a *greater* inspiration to be had by going back and beginning the reading somewhere near where her thought had begun and reading to its conclusion.

The type of thing I had in mind perhaps could not properly, therefore, be called a concordance. I merely meant some kind of reference to a word, such as "healing" and then page reference given where this subject might be taken up in the writings. Or the word "meditation" – in fact, these large subjects have often whole chapters in several of the books. Well, anyhow, I haven't gone through all your writings for the first time, yet. And I am greedy to at least assay them once. Then on my second time round I intend to go slowly and make up such a glossary (or whatchamacallit) for myself, and if it proves interesting I shall show it to you and you may have it for yourself, or others.

The point of it would be I think, that one often has the feeling that study should be done along a certain specific line, such as for instance "meditation." To be able to look through several books, or *Letters,* which dealt with this subject should have, I think, a cumulative good effect. And if only a page reference were given, there wouldn't have to be anything added to the presently published books, at all.

---

[1]   Eddy, Mary Baker, *Science and Health With Key to the Scriptures.* Boston: Christian Scientist Publishing Company.

The Merriest Christmas to you, Emma, Sammy, and all there. We would love to be with you – and we are, in Spirit.

Please excuse the awful typing and the many mistakes. Joelle is yelping to be fed and I'm hurrying.

Love and gratitude, and God bless you all,

Dear Joel,   December 23, 1959

As I am sure you already know – everything is all right.

In about half an hour you had me calm and Phillip[1] began to feel better soon after.

I really do apologize for my condition when I called you, but I was really in over my head and felt absolutely unable to cope with the whole situation. I felt an obligation to nurse the baby, who depends on me, and yet I had to be with Phillip who had apparently hurt himself severely when he fell this morning because he was crying and in pain and kept holding his neck saying it hurt him, and I had all the others home from school and they were fighting and yelling at each other – and I just dissolved when you spoke kindly to me. If I hadn't felt the kindness I think I could have controlled myself but that dissolved me. And I don't mean to indicate that the big children were being bad, they weren't – just kid stuff, and later they washed all the dishes and mopped the kitchen floor and wrapped all the Christmas packages, which were still to be done, and I love them all dearly – but I was just inadequate.

I think the whole thing was my mistake, too. You know last year at Christmas time all my children got sick, and I seemed to feel in the stores and on the streets,

---

[1] My youngest son.

with the drivers, etc., an intense vibration of hysteria. I had the intention of doing protective work and not letting us all get caught up in it this year by being aware before it got started – but I now think that we have all had such growth this last year that that wouldn't have happened to us. And I sort of feel now that putting a reminder card in the calendar was a kind of acceptance (as real) of that very hysteria that I wanted to "rise above." Anyway, I think that was a mistake and that I was wrong there, too.

Also, as you read in my last letter, I had had some wonderful results from my reading of *Art of Spiritual Healing* and I was feeling that everything was in such good order. Boy, I've learned from the past that it's dangerous to feel that things are under control because invariably the rug gets pulled out from under you. I don't know just why – but there must be something wrong with that feeling of security – I don't know what – but there must be, because as soon as I get to feeling it – it is removed! Maybe it's a lack of humility.

Anyhow – I certainly feel humble today. And terribly grateful that you are in the world. But also my own Consciousness must have improved somewhat because I am also getting help and understanding in other directions such as my mother, and my sister, and Edward, which was not forthcoming before. They were all just wonderful today.

I had been intending to send along another thought I had about Edward and that was that I somehow had the feeling I should help him, because when I wrote you about his eyesight last June you had answered me that the first thing I should have done was to try to bring him a healing and, failing that, should have suggested that Joel be asked to handle the situation. So I had the idea that I had an obligation to try to bring a healing here, too. However, I can see that that might have been the correct answer last June, and the answer to "Loose Him and Let Him Go" the correct one for now. Anyhow, Loosing Him is what I have done and it has not only freed him of my thinking – but I, too, feel an increased freedom. I can see clearly that this is the thing to do with all, and with every human situation. I can see it – but I certainly couldn't do it today.

next morning

We had a lovely soft rain last night and my yellow roses are in bloom and I am sitting here typing and looking out at God's wonderful world. A nursing mother is always a kind of an emotional creature – it's pretty hard not to feel a keen sense of responsibility – and, of course, as you say, when *we* feel responsible, we are always inadequate. So I'm emotional, and inadequate, and it's lovely outside, and I love God, and I love what you are, and I love Emma for being a mother, too, and I love Ginny for being understanding to me yesterday, and my mother, and God bless you all.

Merry Christmas,

P.S. Am enclosing a couple of checks for Emma for some tapes. I am looking forward to the "Sunday School" one. We have all the 1959 tapes now, and so I am picking some out of the catalog. Which are the ones that deal with Isaih – how do you spell Isaiah?

Dear Barbara: December 28, 1959

Happy indeed to have your letter of December 20th, and thank you sincerely for both these enclosures.

Regarding experience number one: Of course we often indulge in contacts with God that are not along orthodox lines, and which may not even be scientific, but they have a way of getting through. When you asked for the miracle, actually it was not because you were interested in miracles per se, but rather that you were seeking actual God-realization, and the fact that you phrased it in that particular way did not change the nature of your search. In the same way, when we declare within ourselves "Speak, Lord, thy servant heareth," we are not actually addressing such a statement to God, but rather clearing our own selves for receptivity.

Your experience which had to do with the daughter of your musician friend is certainly a most interesting one, and I am sure that it is going to have far-reaching effects.

Regarding Edward and your changed attitude, you must remember that this is based on another Bible text which is one of the foundational points of the Infinite Way; "Cease ye from man whose breath is in his nostril, for wherein is he to be accounted of?" *You see, as long as you are trying to change, heal or improve a human being, you are working from a psychological standpoint and not a spiritual one.* The moment you let loose of the human being, you *impersonalize* both good and evil, and thereby attain the demonstration of spiritual harmony. I think this will be made clear to you in *The Art of Spiritual Healing.*[1]

Actually, I have not paid attention to the way in which these Bible references are noted in the writings and so did not notice in particular that a different format had been used with *God, the Substance of All Form.* Actually that was arranged by my editor, and I will have to really check into the books to see the way this is handled, and then I might ask her why this change was made.

Now, regarding the concordance as you visualize it – this is something that I have long had in mind, and some day someone will have to do just that very thing. Just take the major subjects, like meditation, God, spiritual healing, treatment, the nature of God, the nature of error, etc., and list the chapters or chapter titles, and book and page. Should you do this in the rough while you are doing your own reading, it could be whipped into shape for publication afterward. If you are led to do this, go ahead.

---

[1] The counsel Joel gave me here is absolute Truth and, after many years of developing my understanding, I have taught it with success to my students.

And so, for now, Aloha greetings to you and to Edward and all of the family, and a joyous New Year to all of you from Emma and me.

Joel

Dear Barbara: December 28, 1959

This morning I dictated a letter to you answering one received last week, and now I am answering your letter of the 23rd. First of all, to thank you sincerely for your Christmas check enclosed. This is indeed thoughtful and generous of you.

I am grateful indeed for your immediate response and also for Phillip's quick response to the work.

Never feel that there is any lack of demonstration in the fact that problems arise, because it is only through these problems that we are compelled to take the higher steps necessary for spiritual demonstration.

Now, as to that matter of last Christmas and the notation this Christmas, of course you were in the wrong, because *all treatments must be given instantly and can never be put off, even for an hour.* The moment that "two times two is five" touches our awareness, it is necessary for us to realize two times two are four. *To postpone this until tonight, to give us time to think it over is, of course, to make ourselves victims of the false beliefs.*[1]

In the spiritual Kingdom, there is no such time as past or future, and therefore the moment Truth is realized *now*, it is eternally manifest. This is the meaning of "To know Him aright is life eternal." To know Him aright – that is, to know Truth aright *this moment*, is eternal harmony.

---

[1]   In later years I discovered a statement of Mary Baker Eddy's which is a wonderful admonition and one which I and my students have put to effective purpose: "Stand *porter* at the door of thought and allow *nothing* to enter that you do not want to see instantly manifest on your body."

In your study of *The Art of Spiritual Healing*, be sure to give a great deal of study to the chapter "Relationship of Oneness."

And so, for now, many, many more Alohas from both of us to you and all of your family,

Joel

CHAPTER 3

CORRESPONDENCE 1960

*Note: The following is a letter I sent to
several friends, letting them know about Joel's
class.*

Dear Friends,   January 20, 1960

Some of you will know his name, others not, but I
wanted to let all of you know that our religious teacher,
Joel Goldsmith, who lives and writes in Honolulu, is
coming to Los Angeles the end of this month and will
give three open lectures: February 1, 2, and 3, 1960, at the
Statler Hilton Hotel starting at 7:45 p.m., each night.

Edward and I feel so sincerely that we owe
everything we have learned, and everything that we
have grown to, in the past two years so completely to
Joel's teaching that we felt almost obligated, out of our
affection for you all, to let you know that a man whom
we consider a great teacher will be in our neighborhood
for the first time in 14 years, and for only a few days.

His viewpoint may be new and even strange to some
of you, and we are in no sense urging any of you to attend
his lectures, but just wanted to advise you of the dates in
case you should feel so prompted.

Love to all,

Ed and Barbara

Monday
Dear Joel,   February 8, 1960

Well, apparently you came to bring to me "not peace
but a sword." At least I feel all cracked to pieces. I hope
this breaking apart is constructive (as I guess it is) – no
"old wine in new bottles," etc. – and that you intend to
make something out of the rubble. I don't really mean
that, either – about making something out of me, I mean.
And, speaking of that, I do hope you knew I was joking
the other day when I said you had to work harder on me.

I have been thrilled to see the size of the audiences here
in Los Angeles, and particularly the size of the Closed
Class. But it has also been very illustrative of the size of
the job you have to do, and all of a sudden you seem too
big for me to bother – and, in fact, I am appalled at having
taken up so much of your time when there are so many
others who need it, too.

I am willing to get off your back, and if you will give
me the name of some of your practitioners and teachers in
this area, I will try to do so. You mentioned the other day
that so many of the students are reluctant to take help or
instruction from anyone but you, but I am not that way
and anyone in whom you had enough confidence to
allow them to be an Infinite Way practitioner or teacher, I
am sure would have something for me.

I thought last night was just a powerhouse, but I am
thunderstruck for fear some of it was occasioned by some
of my practices (although this may just be suffering
delusions of personal reference) – but in case it was, I did
want to try to clear up some of the things.

I will enclose a copy of the letter I sent out to about 25
people, and hope you will feel that I didn't overreach
myself. I had only the intention of "letting them know
you were available," as you mentioned last night. Now
three of them told me they were taking the class. A man
and his wife I haven't actually seen, but I may have

missed them. But one other lady I have seen there every night, and she is so sincere in searching for God that it never occurred to me that you might not have wanted her in the class. Anyhow it's too late now.

Also, as you probably know, I am paying for the *Monthly Letters* for 4 people: Ginny, my mother, Edward, and his secretary. I have been giving this as part of their Christmas present. I haven't seen anything wrong in this, but if you think there is (you mentioned last night that everyone must ask for this for himself), I will stop doing it, because I really do not want to do anything in a way that you would not approve of.

Also, I wanted to further explain our "discussions" of you and your work – I didn't want to take up any more of your time with it the other day. First of all, these discussions take place between me, my mother, my sister, M., E., and K. No others. Oh yes, one other, an old friend of mine who comes to our tape sessions. The discussions are not at the tape sessions but when we meet for lunch, and they never take the form of *opinions* about you or your work, or an interpretation of it or the practice of it. Rather are they *witnessing* sessions when one might mention a healing, or the resolving of a certain kind of problem through the use of these principles – or, and this is most of it, just an expression of the joy and gratitude we feel for being able to study these works. I am sure that none of us would feel able to pass an opinion on your work or how to operate it, such as how to heal, etc.

Well, that's my confessional. I didn't want to be doing anything that you perhaps didn't know about and wouldn't approve of. But I really feel our motivation to be all right.

Gratitude,

Note: The 1960 Los Angeles Closed Class really rocked my boat. When I was a child my father used to slap my face saying, "Stop crying!" So I learned to stop crying while being slapped. It so shut off my ability to shed tears that from the time I was about ten until this Class, no matter how anguished I might have felt, I never shed a tear. This class opened the flood gates and released buckets of restrained misery. I felt much better afterward.

Dear Joel,

Wednesday
February 10, 1960

Edward was held up at the office, and I was still in a state of complete disintegration from the night before. I bawled so all through the whole thing that I was actually afraid I might disturb some of the others and finally stumbled out hardly able to see. You have just killed me, my dear friend.

Anyway, we didn't have the courage to risk walking in late so went to be with some friends who had had a daughter killed last Saturday night in an accident on the freeway. I had intended, anyway, from the beginning, to have these tapes as soon as they become available. But today Mama tells me that I missed the voice and face of God last night, and two of my friends have said they couldn't move for ten minutes after it was over. Ginny is rocked today, too.

I knew the first night that this was going to be the most powerful class I had ever heard, but, even so, I had not calculated its effect on me. Thank God I had made plans to go away, anyway, because if I hadn't they'd have had to cart me off in a basket.

I was going to call you on the phone, but can't because I can't stop crying long enough to talk.

I know you must know of our love and gratitude.

Aloha,

Monday
Dear, dear Joel,   February 29, 1960

Whew! No time to say much but "kill the people." And if it all goes like Los Angeles there'll be corpses of "humanhood" lying all over the West.

I'm better – in spite of being called back from my vacation in 5 days because my nanny had a boy hurt in a construction accident in New Orleans and she left to go to him. She has asked me to write you for help for the boy – and, of course, I told her I would. So I am.

I'm very glad you aren't going to give me up. I was really *noble* and gave you a chance, but you muffed it. I won't give you another one.

If I've told you this story, don't bother to read further:

It's a cartoon I saw that gave me a real 'yuk'. "Brother Sebastian" is a cartoon about a cute, little, fat, priest named Brother Sebastian. In this one he is walking along the monastery walk with another Brother, who is looking down his nose at him, very seriously, and saying, "But I *am* holier than thou!"

Love to all,

Dear Barbara –   March 6, 1960

My heartfelt thanks to you for your tithe check forwarded to me here. Am sure you know my appreciation for your ever thoughtfulness.

Our California experience continued to ripen and deepen as we reached the Pacific Northwest. The subject of Transcendental Consciousness continued to unfold. Yesterday we reached some higher plateau.

The Art of Spiritual Healing continues to make history. Another Religious Science church in NYC has me scheduled in August for a Sunday – and Silent Unity will have about 45 in my class in Kansas City. All due to that book. And the Masonic work is flourishing – so that time does not hang heavy on our hands. (What time?).

Aloha to you & Edward & the family,

Joel & Emma

Dear Barbara,   March 10, 1960

This is answering your letter of February 29 to tell you that the work did continue right from where it left off in Los Angeles. The Seattle class was all on Transcendental and Primal Consciousness,[1] and the message appeared in still a different form than before. And in Vancouver there were two tapes that I am sure will have a deep interest for you, and that is Canadian Class, Reels 2 and 3. While some of the students felt that Reel 1 was fine, I cannot remember what was in the message at all, but both sides of number 2 and the second side of number 3 seem to me not only to be of tremendous importance, but somewhat of startling nature.

Regarding Brother Sebastian and his brother, who says, "But I am holier than thou," I am sure that this is our attitude much of the time, even when we believe that we are being very humble. This is a tricky situation, this one of humility, and one of the tapes of this Pacific Northwest, and I cannot, at the moment, remember which one, is on the subject of true humility, which subject appeared to me in an entirely different light. Oh, yes! I am sure that it is on Reel number 1 of the Canadian Class, and if so, you might as well have 1, 2, and 3, for you won't be sorry.[2]

---

[1] The "Ur-Consciousness," the "Void Consciousness" which exists before the "Spirit of God *moves* on the waters," e.g. the "unknown God before God."

[2] Number 1 is "True Humility." Excellent!

I do not know how much you perceived in Los Angeles of the nature of the work with the other metaphysical movements, and to what extent it came into our work there, but this also continued the entire trip, and I am not only dated ahead with our Infinite Way students, but Religious Science, Unity, and Divine Science are all scheduled for lectures, and 45 students of Silent Unity have enrolled for the class in Kansas City. So you can imagine that there is going to be another experience like Los Angeles, where 91 of that class of 242 were from Religious Science, Mind Science, and Unity.

Of course this sudden break-through is entirely due to the book *The Art of Spiritual Healing*, which has taken the whole field by storm, for this is the first time that a textbook on spiritual healing has been given to the world which *does not embody partly mental and partly spiritual healing*. As a matter of fact, the only three textbooks worthwhile at all have been *Science and Health, Lessons in Truth*, by Emily Cady, and the *Divine Science Textbook*, and all of these are sixty to ninety years of age, and all of these embrace both mental and spiritual aspects of healing, whereas *The Art of Spiritual Healing* is the only modern textbook, and the only one presenting purely spiritual principles, and the proof of it, of course, has been its tremendous acceptance. Already, the Vice-President of Harper and Brothers has written me for the date when the next manuscript will be ready for them. And of course, *The Art of Spiritual Healing* has carried *Practicing The Presence* and *The Art of Meditation* into those centers also, and now they are beginning to start on the other writings of the Infinite Way, so an interesting 1960 still lies before us.

And so, for now, Aloha greetings to you and all of your wonderful family,

Joel

Dear Barbara: March 18, 1960

Well, it would seem that we are not going to spend much time with ourselves in Honolulu, much more with anyone else, as already the middle of the month has gone by, and we are due to fly on April 6th. Actually, the bags aren't all unpacked yet, and it's almost time to start packing – it just seems impossible. (This week the first two invitations came to talk to orthodox churches).

The "Science and Thought Review" in England evidently had a great response from the articles they have run this year, and wrote for us to please rush them a new series, and so this morning I edited a series of four articles on prayer for them. And "Beacon Magazine," which is published in London, but is an international magazine, just ran an Infinite Way article this month, and the Unite' Universale in Paris this month is running the "Lesson to Sam." Also, we have already received the January, February, and March issues of the German Infinite Way magazine. So you see, there are still some things to be done before getting away this next trip.

My sincere thanks to you for your very thoughtful and generous enclosure, and Emma joins me in Aloha greetings to you and all the family,

Joel

Dear Barbara: April 1, 1960

I am so very happy to have your letter here today, and first of all, let me thank you for this thoughtful and generous enclosure.

Between the lines of your letter, I feel a peace and a calmness which is a new note in your consciousness, or rather, a higher note, and I welcome this.

There is nothing so wonderful as the *Is* of the Infinite Way. To be able to relax in the consciousness of "Thank you, Father, I Am," is wonderful. To be able to feel the assurance of the twenty-third Psalm: "The Lord _is_ my shepherd, I shall not want." To relax and to rest in this Is, is immediately to feel the mind be at peace. This is truly a high goal, and _it is possible to live in the constant and continuous assurance that I Am._

Aloha greetings to you and Ed and to all the family and your group of students.

Joel

Dear Barbara: April 21, 1960

Before I forget it, let me remind you that we are to be in Los Angeles the evening of May 23rd, and will remain there about three days, and we will be looking forward to seeing you and Edward while there. We will be at the Beverly Hilton Hotel.

Then, to thank you for your message received today, and for your ever-thoughtful and generous enclosure.

And now to tell you that our class here is of quite a different nature than the one in Los Angeles. Before the class began, I was told that it would be a class on advanced healing work. We are two-thirds through the class, and while I cannot say that there is anything in the class that is not now known to our more serious students, I believe it is safe to say that it is so compact and so concentrated on certain particular facets that it might safely be termed a class in advanced healing work.[1] It may be that this class is especially given to me so as to bring into focus the major principles which must never be forgotten, and which must become part and parcel of our _conscious_ being.

---

[1] Denver 1960 Closed Class

We will look forward with great joy to seeing you again in Los Angles, and for now, Aloha greetings from Emma and me to you and all of the family,

Joel

Dear Joel,   April 25, 1960

This is a letter I am really embarrassed to write but I have been struggling in the grip of false appetite for two months, by myself, and seem to be getting nowhere. In fact, ever since the Class stirred me up so, it seemed to have really opened my "Pandora's Box" and come up with some problems I had thought were long dead. To be brief, I have been drinking, smoking, and overeating. And the worst thing about it all is that they're just little piddling vices – just a little smoking, just a little drinking, and just a little over-eating. Nothing that I couldn't have, in the past, easily handled with willpower. But I don't have any will-power any more (nor any "won't" power either!) and I don't seem to be able to realize sufficient Grace for them to drop off of me, as smoking just dropped off my sister a few months ago.

In fact, I now wonder if this were the real thing behind my strong desire for Edward to stop smoking and drinking, because seeing him do this is a constant temptation for me and I just succumb, instead of being intelligent. Anyhow, I can feel the tentacles of "The Beast" closing in and I both hate and fear the thing in myself (which is probably why I can't stop – but I can't seem to get rid of the hate and fear of it, either).

Well what I mean is Praise the Lord and Please Pass the Grace.

Or in other words,

H E L P !

Note: In re-reading the following letter, while preparing this book, I can re-live the sense of comfort and gratitude I felt when this letter arrived in answer to my plea for help. I had a great and loving teacher!

Dear Barbara –   April 27, 1960

You make mountains out of molehills. You condemn yourself for trifles – but the Master said to the woman taken in adultery, "Neither do I condemn thee."

Error is not personal – and has no person in whom, on whom, or thru whom it can operate – and it isn't even an it since there exists but a belief in two powers.

Let the tares & wheat grow together until the harvest –

Write me soon. Kansas City was a tremendous experience. A public Lecture of 300, of whom 150 were from Unity Farm. A two session class on healing work with 75 ministers, teachers & practitioners of Unity! And a packed Masonic Hall for the lecture on Esoteric Masonry.

Aloha,

Joel

                                                  Monday
Dear Joel,   May 3, 1960

Of course you're right – and nuts to it!

I thought it might please you to know that I have just had a call from a lady, one of three new people (not new to me, but new to the tape group) who have been coming to hear tapes since the Class in Feb.

She said she had been discussing the meetings last night with her husband; and they both wanted me to know how much of a privilege they considered it to be able to "hear that man in that wonderful room where the atmosphere has already been formed and where there is such a presence maintained."

So, you see, there is *some* wheat with the tares.

As a matter of fact, last Monday night was the most tremendous meeting we have had. I have finally prevailed on everyone to come <u>early</u> for meditation before the tapes and last Monday night we were locked in a unity of the Presence such as I had never felt (except in your classes). I was so grateful that He came through so strongly and the lesson has just stayed and stayed with everybody. It was the second half of the last reel of the Haw. Village Open – Nature of God, Nature of Error, and everyone has asked that these two sides be run again, which I think is a very good idea.

Love and gratitude,

B.

I know who you are – you are the "missing link."

Dear Barbara,   May 5, 1960

There is more wheat than you know – but it is also good that you do not realize how much wheat there really is. It doesn't take much encouragement for the ego to rise up again!! Better to know that "I can of mine own self do – and be – nothing" and <u>feel</u> the Father within do the works.

In our opening Open Class last night a major miracle took place. A message came forth of such a nature that for only the second time in my platform career, a spontaneous applause came from the students at the end of the hour. *This is the first side of Reel 1, Chicago 1960 Open.* If this is happening now what can be left for class – or is this the start of the new unfoldment?

Our united love to all of you –
Aloha,

Joel & Emma

Monday
Dear Joel,   May 9, 1960

Thank you for your letter. It was so helpful.

You are very right about it not taking much for the ego to dust itself off and get ready to fight another day. I fell flat on my face last Friday – Thursday night, to be exact – after being careless enough to say that I was an artist, and that I was a good mother.

It was awful, and when I saw on Saturday the colossal ignorance of it, I was only surprised that He didn't just flick me right out of the universe.

However, I suppose it had to happen to show me the danger I was in and I am right now locked in mortal combat with the "adversary." Oddly enough, I have just been reading Dr. Suzuki's book on *Zen in Japanese Culture,* and I now understand the part about swordsmanship, where the true master must reach the point where his survival is of no account. I am not sure that Barbara will survive this battle, *which I did not really ask for* but which seems to be here – but survival is of so little importance that I can't even say "help."[1]

Love and gratitude,

nobody

---
[1] And so humility begins.

Dear Joel,   June 3, 1960

Just a quick note to tell you that the Grace of the Chicago class is still working in me and it has produced, among other things, an interesting result. Four years ago, after the birth of Suzi, I had 2 cavities in my teeth, and it horrified me. I said to myself that I had thought that kind of problem to have been solved in me long ago, and couldn't understand how health of any kind could rise up to plague me again – I thought I had developed beyond that.

Yesterday at the dentist for cleaning, the x-rays showed two small cavities and all I said, and felt, was "patch 'em." I was thinking of course of your statement that health can be health today, and sickness tomorrow, that wholeness can be that today and decay tomorrow, and that righteousness can be that today and sin tomorrow – and I seemed to be proving it. But I had no more feeling about it than if it were a chair with a broken leg, which is also a tool for our use, and realizing that there is no life in the body, I just said, "patch it," and we'll go on using it till we get a better one.

I must also, in honesty, say that there is still a little sadness in letting go of this, much the same as I have when I see a dress of which I have been very fond wear out. If I like them, I do wear mine until they fall apart. I seem to have a bad capacity of being able to become attached to things I am used to, and which have served me well.

I am starting on the Concordance.[1] I know, only too well, that this is years and years of work, that it must be an inspired and inwardly taught activity – I also know that the deep study and concentration that will be necessary to do a good job will make me the recipient of

---

[1]   See my letter of 12/20/59 where I suggested this Concordance to Joel. He answered, in his letter of 12/28/59, "Go ahead."

more good than anyone who may later use it. And I look forward both to the challenge and the activity.

I am beginning with the small pamphlets – the first one being "The Fourth Dimension of Life." I shall do these one at a time – and they can all be coordinated into a single volume later, but I see no reason for not making available each one as it comes along, for there is an infinite possibility of study in each little pamphlet, and in each book, in itself, if a person really wants to dig. Also, I want to do one small thing at a time and then send the results to you for your ideas and corrections or additions, until I am sure the pattern is what you want.

Now, in this connection, I cannot do the job right unless I understand every word and every sentence, so where I come upon a blank, I shall have to write you for clarification. And the first one has already arisen.

In "Fourth Dimension" you mention, "I and the Father are One but the Father is greater than I." This seems paradoxical to me – which, of course, only means I don't understand it. You may remember my telling you that I had had great difficulty in comprehending your statement, "You are the *fullness* of the Godhead," or L.'s saying that when she went to see you and you asked her who she was, and she said, "A point of God," you corrected her with, "No, you *are all* of it." Then I read your illustration about the diamond – in which you pointed out that each facet showed forth *all* of everything the diamond was – and that seemed to make it clear to me how *each* was *all*. But now comes along this – we are one, but the Father is greater. Now, how can that be, and one be one?[1]

I know it's just a blind spot, but I would appreciate further light on this.

---

[1] This is answered in his letter to me of July 2, 1960. In 1990 an explanation of this was brought through in a class, which was the clearest insight we have ever had. But it was an hour class, so it must wait for a subsequent book.

Love and gratitude from

X9 (the anonymous worker)

Note: There is a lost letter of Joel's here, in which he told me he thought that a little more serious study on my part would have revealed the answer to me, without my having had to write him for clarification. (Not my first slap on the wrist!).

Dear Joel,   June 12, 1960

I think I sense from your letter that you are trying to put me on my own feet. Well, if you think I am ready to try that, I must be, so I'll jump in and get wet, anyway.

I have learned that the only sin man can commit is the belief in a life separate and apart from God. (How long have I been hearing this from you?). But what it has cost me to learn that, I cannot tell even <u>you</u>.

There is one point which I have felt all along that you understood – but I seem to have the urge to put it into words – so I will. It has to do with paying you.

I think the most important reason that I tithe is that I find I am absolutely incapable of putting a price on anything you do for us. How much is Joelle worth, for instance? Now I have no distaste for money, nor for fiscal things, and your concept of money was one of the easiest for me to grasp. Nonetheless, I find it emotionally necessary to me – at this point, at least – that what I send you shall be a gift of love – and so must what you do for me. This may not – and probably will not – be the final unfoldment on this subject for me but that is the status right now.

Love and gratitude,

Note: Joel answered the above letter on July 24, 1960.

56 Curzon Street
London W.1.
England

Dear Barbara,   2nd July, 1960

The work you saw started in Chicago at the level of Transcendental Consciousness, has continued and there are two tapes of Grand Rapids, Michigan, of importance. And we have already had four sessions of the 1st London Closed Class and here again I have no words. Throughout these four sessions I have been completely in the Spirit and this will be evident to you when you hear these tapes. And of course they will carry you a step further than our Chicago work, not because the message is any greater, but because our consciousness yields with each class of this nature and becomes a clearer transparency for Truth, so that we attain more and more of the essence of the message we are hearing.

You ask how can it be possible for "I and the Father" to be one, and yet the Father greater than I? And I will return you to the very example you used, that of the diamond and its many facets. Even though the allness of the diamond is expressed through every facet, and this must necessarily be so, nevertheless the *withinness* of the diamond is greater than any one of its facets. Because whereas the facet is a facet, and does show forth all that is within the diamond, yet the diamond itself is greater than the sum total of all of the facets. Let us see if a little meditation does not reveal the fullness of this message to you.

Emma joins me in love to you and to all of the family, and aloha greetings to all of our students,

Joel

Dear Joel   July 19, 1960

Love and gratitude,

A special kiss to Emma. Please tell her I received a note from Susie – who said she had really enjoyed the book I sent her.

You gave me the Christ in Chicago. Some days I think I'll give it back!

B.

56 Curzon Street
London W.1.
England

Dear Barbara,   24th July, 1960

Answering your letter of June 12th, I do not quite understand your statement that I am trying to put you on your own feet. If that is meant to indicate in any way that I want to separate you from any help from me, then this is incorrect. On the other hand, every action of the Infinite Way is intended to reveal to us our true identity and the nature of our spiritual being, so that ultimately we are brought either to Paul's statement, "I live, yet not I. Christ liveth my life," or to the Master's final revelation: "Thou seest me, Thou seest the Father that sent me, for I and the Father are one." However, while we are on this journey to these final revelations, let no one ever believe that there is anything wrong in turning to a Practitioner or Teacher for help over the temporary situations we meet on the path.

I have no hesitancy in turning to Emma, and asking for a lift. I see nothing inconsistent in this, or anything in the nature of lack of demonstration. After all, "Where two or more are gathered in My name," must have some real significance.

And certainly I do not believe that anyone should permit a belief to intrude into their consciousness that there is any self-sufficiency except that final demonstration in which self is spelt with a capital S.[1]

I would also like to speak to you for a moment about this subject that often arises in spiritual work, and this is that one of price and payment. Actually in my personal ministry I have never put a price on my work since 1931. Nor have I ever asked for money for any purpose. The one exception to this rule came with the Closed Class work when it became apparent that everybody that attended a Public Lecture also wanted to attend a Class, as long as it cost them nothing, or as long as they could put ten cents, or twenty-five cents into the collection. And *this, of course, prevented my developing a body of serious students.* As soon as a price was put on the Class, we found that only those serious enough to feel that they could be benefited by such an outlay of money would enter the Classes. And those who could not afford at the moment to pay for the Classes could make this known to us, and we would gladly admit them without fee, or with any contribution they wished to make. In other words, *money was not the object of the Class fee*, but merely making it possible to arrive in some measure at the drawing together of a group who could be developed into serious students. But no other phase of our ministry has ever had a price on it, and for this reason the Infinite Way has demonstrated beyond all doubt that it could maintain a world-wide activity, and do it without asking for a body of supporters or membership dues, or specific fees for specific services, with an expense that is

---

[1]   In 1990, it came through in our classwork that the transition is from self, to Self, to SELF.

now above $75,000 a year. In fact, without in any way putting anyone under an obligation.

Aloha greetings to you and to all of the family,

Joel

P.S. Just as I said "Aloha greeting," the mail came in and with it a letter from you enclosing your gift of gratitude and your message to Emma. And of course the message on the back regarding the Christ. This is just to let you know of the arrival of this letter, and of course my deep and sincere thanks for all that the message contained in words and in between the lines, and of course in your gift. Aloha again.

Dear, dear Boy,   August 10, 1960

Of course I know that *your* attitude and concept of money and prices, etc., would be exactly right – and I was only trying to clarify my own.

Also, since writing to you last I have had another realization – and thank God this one didn't come with so much pain as the last one. I have realized that "I" am the substance of all form. And the nicest thing about this realization is the increase in the sense of "oneness" – because I realize more than ever that this makes me one with you.

Of course you understood what I meant about the Christ. It does seem to bring with it rather large responsibilities – or opportunities – or however would be the correct way to say it. I am sure you know exactly what I mean.

I am spending hours in meditation, and now have a small recorder by my bed and am listening to four and five tapes a day. And as you can well imagine – this is bringing about great changes daily. Too many to write about, except to say that my gratitude and appreciation of you also grows daily.

Love to Emma,

Dear Barbara,   August 11, 1960

So you have been peeking in on us in Europe! When you hear these tapes you will know why you have received "I am the substance of all form."

Never before has "I" been given such complete expression.

From Los Angeles to Chicago to London to Holland we had Transcendental Consciousness. In Switzerland, Manchester, and now London, we have "Prayer – individual and world." And always – "I."

Our united love to all of you,

Joel

Dear Illusion,   Friday
                                        the 26th August, 1960

We won't be coming to San Francisco. I decided it wouldn't be fair to take up your time when you could be enjoying your family.

Love and gratitude,

smoke

P.S. *Metaphysical Notes* is left off the list in the new catalog.

Dear Joel,   August 31, 1960

I hardly know where to begin – probably in Chicago. As you may remember, I heard "Thunder of Silence" in the Chicago Reading Room and was absolutely stunned. I ordered the entire Honolulu Series One as soon as I got home and since it arrived, about 4 weeks ago, I have heard the whole series innumerable times, but especially haven't let more than one or two days go by without hearing "Thunder of Silence."

As I have already told you, the few minutes I had alone with you prepared me for this, and it has had the most thunderous effect on me. As I told you over the phone, this is *my* tape – of everything I have ever heard. It's like *Art of Spiritual Healing* seems to be *my* book – to the extent that they have had the most tremendous effect on me of all the writings and tapes.

But I also feel that I wouldn't have been prepared for this without those few minutes with you – and this must be my excuse for importuning you for opportunities to be in your presence. You mention on one of the tapes that personal contact with you is valuable – and this has certainly been proved to me – and as you say on one of the tapes in this Series, "Demonstrating God," that you realize that when one of your students reaches out to you he is reaching out to the Christ Consciousness – and this is the case with me. But I must also confess that having had a little of it, I just seem to be starving for more and more. I do not mean, either, that I am not making my own contact every day – I am (and more of that in a minute), but I am greedy for the "giant steps" – and I feel sure you can both understand and forgive me for that.

Now as to the personal contact with my own Christ. As I told you on the phone, I am not using "God" as the anchor word any more, but "I." This transition just seemed to come of its own accord. Since then I am able to make contact at any time. Grace be to God![1]

And this is what I meant when I said that I thought I would have something to contribute to the "Closed Class" which we held last week-end. I meant that I would have "contact" to contribute.

Now – to the Closed Class. I have been thinking about holding one for a long time, but was waiting for an "ooch" as to just what to use. When the Honolulu Series came in I got the "ooch" the minute I heard it – but didn't set any time for it, because of waiting for an "ooch" on that, too. Finally, after four weeks of hearing "Thunder of Silence" – I felt it was the time, and set the class.

I remember Emma telling me in Honolulu that there was a very good result obtainable from such an "intensive" session – and I was sure this was the case – but I had a *wonder* about whether or not we would all be able to create the *mood* – be properly receptive – maintain sufficient Presence – I don't mean in any active sense – but rather in a receptive sense.

I am happy to report that the Closed Class was for one and all a sacred and dynamic experience. One night we really had a Thunder of Silence that lasted for about ten minutes. In fact, the class *was* an interesting experience. I sent out an announcement of it and suggested that everyone who might want to attend be seated by 7:45 for meditation, before the class started at 8 o'clock. The first night no one but me was there at that time – two even came late. The second night every one was there about ten minutes before 8. The third night some were there at 7:30 and *everyone* was in meditation by 7:40. Cute, huh? I was pleased with all my chickens.

---

[1]   A happy experience, but then came more "Dark Nights of the Soul," followed by more Enlightenment, etc. I have learned that it is often two steps forward and one step back – but always marching on.

And I am sure the class was a success, because they were all shaken up by it. After the last night when I ran "Thunder of Silence" Edward said, "Boy, that is really a powerful expression." Frankly, it is still over their heads a bit, in varying degrees depending, naturally, on their previous preparation. I, of course, had the great advantage of having already heard the tape eighteen or twenty times. Since the class, Edward has been having a tremendous back problem – he says he feels like he is being pulled apart – and I am reminded of my feeling after the February class that I had been "cracked apart." I asked him this morning to go within and examine himself and see if he thought his back had anything to do with the Closed Class. He did so, and said, "Yes, interesting." I am thrilled with him for some things, too, such as that he was meditating a bit the other day in preparation for his meeting with Adela Rogers St. Johns (which you will know about). Before she arrived one of his men came in, a brilliant man from Germany, who lived there all through Hitler, etc., and saw some horrible things. He came to this country full of idealism (I'm trying to be brief here) but has been disappointed by the materialism he has seen, and other things. Anyway, Ed said, "The whole thing just poured out to Walter." Also, more and more of the vocabulary of spiritual living is beginning to come out of Edward. But then I think he intends to write you one day, and I will not tell these things for him as he may want to describe them himself.

Well, I guess that's all – except that I am enclosing the checks from the Closed Class.

I cannot tell you in words what it means to me to have found the Infinite Way. The love and gratitude I have for you will bless you, and it, I hope.

Sincerely,

Dear Barbara,   August 31, 1960

1) Heartfelt thanks for your ever thoughtful gift.

2) *Metaphysical Notes* is now a book – *Conscious Union with God,* edited and pre-arranged. Available October in Bev. Hills.

3) Sorry you did not jump up here. Weather is delightful and we would have been happy to see you.

Have I called your attention to the following – and if so – please excuse repetition:

Only for "25" Groups:[1]

> N Y 1959 – "25" Tape
> London 1960 "25" Half Tape
> N Y 1960 – Prac. class – Tape

You have some dedicated ones around you to share these with – and to practice.

Our united love to you and the family,

Joel & Emma

Dear Joel,   September 2, 1960

I forgot to tell you in my last letter that the $25.00 check from L. was for both her and her husband.

Joel, I have the urge again to put my nose in where it is none of my business – and I really may not be too sound in what I am saying, but I bought a new book of the *Letters* the other day and of course was interested to see that in the new printing the lines are numbered, and this might be a good thing. But am I correct in thinking that the book has been considerably altered from the old one? I couldn't tell exactly how, except that the thing does not seem to read so much like you – and that brings

---

[1] See Glossary for explanation of the "25 Groups."

me to a very delicate point – but one I have mentioned to you before, and one I, personally, consider so vital – so absolutely vital – that I am going to risk your displeasure and bring it up.

You may remember I wrote you that when I read the book, *God, the Substance of All form*, I compared it in several places with the manuscript, which I also had, and found there that considerable re-arranging had been done and some of the language altered.

Now these alterations seem to be correct from the standpoint of strict literary style or grammar, but they change in some measure the actual *flavor* and style of your own speaking and/or writing, and I think they lose in the process. Some of what might be called your "meandering style" was sharpened up, and tightened up – condensed and capsulized, if you will – but I think it loses by that very thing.

I think that it is the very manner – every word – by which you bring up and illuminate a point – that is the exact rate of speed at which one should be reading and digesting it.

I am again reminded of what they did to *Science and Health* when the biblical scholars and grammarians got hold of it and edited it to death, so that it has become a text book, yes, and there are absolutely no errors in it of quotation from scripture, etc. It has become, in other words, absolutely incapable of scholastic criticism, and I am sure that is why they did it – but it has also become a very, very different book from her first book, which I have, and which is full of inspiration and warmth. *Science and Health* is now so correct – and so cold and clinical – that there is no inspiration to be found in it for me. Naturally, I realize that others do find inspiration there. I feel they would find more in the first edition, but simply don't read that one.

What I am trying to say, Joel, is this. How can a human mind be put to work to edit inspiration? How can we humanly tamper with anything that flows through as the word of God? Naturally, I don't mean that there couldn't be some slight "cleaning up" of a tape or tapes in preparing them for publishing as a book. But should the flow, the form, the arrangement, the *order* be altered?

To be specific – in one place in *God the Substance* in the old manuscript you just logically say something like (and I must naturally paraphrase here a bit since I don't have it in front of me – this is only illustrative), "I picked up the *Bible* today and read in Jeremiah the statement that..." and then you go on to read the statement and make your point about it after that. In the new book, this is changed and the statement from Jeremiah, or whatever it was, is put at the *head* of the chapter, *all by itself*, and then the chapter is delineated to explain it. Now to me, this destroys some of the warmth, and the feeling that we are really *listening* to you, personally, which the other way has. To me it is the very ability to *follow* along with the logical process of your own human actions and footsteps, as it were, that provides the greatest solace to those of us who are still struggling mightily with the human picture. It is those times when you tell us of your own struggles with the human pitfalls that provide the encouragement to keep on with the struggle. If the thing becomes at all cold or clinical – then it and you become so far above us that there is obviously no point in trying to make it – we just can't.

I can feel that you may be thinking about me at this point – as you have told me before – that I am carried away more by zeal than by wisdom. But, if so, then I just must plead guilty to zeal – but it is the very zeal that you, yourself, have taught me: too much organization (or even *any*) is a destructive thing to the purity of this kind of message.

I might say it another way. Who could possibly edit you, but you? If there are changes that *you* want to make then it could certainly be construed as a *new* inspiration. But, frankly, I should not relish the thought of any one else tampering with your expressions. If the inspiration could have come through anyone else, it would have, wouldn't it?

Well, dammit, I guess this is more than enough on the subject – and I'm not at all sure that I have made myself clear. But, Joel, in the first New York Class you really sold me on the concept you expressed when you told the class they knew that you were dedicated to maintaining the *purity* of the Infinite Way. That statement struck right through to the core of me – because it was my recognition that "any kind of organization killed the spirit of a religious message" that had kept me a seeker for my teacher for 40 years – and it was that very statement that told me *you* were it. And I, in my turn, have become so dedicated to the maintenance of that purity (as you would know if you saw our tape sessions, which we run exactly as Emma outlined to me in New York) that I don't see how any *human* hand could do anything but adulterate it.[1]

If you are laughing at me – it's all right. I've learned enough the last two years to know how silly some of my letters of two years ago must have seemed to you – and two years from now I may laugh at me, too. But it all seems deadly serious now. I just don't want you tampered with. I don't want your inspiration filtered through someone else – no matter how inspired or advanced that person, or persons, may be. And I am sure, from what you have told me, that there are some very, very advanced ones in the Infinite Way. But if they are – let them write their own books and let us judge them for ourselves by what they write, but let us not have Goldsmith *"and"* man.

Oh, dear, I know how bold this is. And if you are

---

[1]   When I asked Emma how to conduct the tape meetings she was *very* succinct: "Meditate fifteen minutes before the tape, meditate after it and go home. Don't serve coffee!"

angry with me I don't blame you (of course I know you won't be – but I wouldn't blame you).

Zealous

Note: In re-reading this in 1991, I feel more strongly about the subject than ever, and more convinced that I was right. In a number of the books that were published after Joel made his transition I found, after checking, that a lot of his down-to-earth way of communicating had been "cleaned up" – euphemized, which caused it to "lose its salt." It made me sad – for Joel, and for those who hadn't had the blessing of experiencing his wonderful sense of humor.

Dear Barbara,   September 6, 1960

Your letter of August 31st reached me here yesterday, and I am certainly thrilled with every bit of it. First of all, to know that the tape, "Thunder of Silence" has done so much for you, and secondly, because Eugene Exman, Vice-President and religious book editor of Harper and Brothers, told me in New York that our new book, *Thunder of Silence*, is not only the best of the Infinite Way writings, but constitutes a unique religious literature. He was so thrilled with it that he kept the manuscript and would not even return it to us for the minor corrections that are necessary in re-typing, and said he wanted to put it into immediate work, without a moment's delay. The reason this will be of interest to you is that the first half of the book concerns the subjects of Karmic Law and God, and then the origin of evil, Genesis II; and the second half of the book is made up entirely of the *Sermon on the Mount*.

The subject of my work with individual students is, of course, one that is never spoken about, but since you have already experienced it, *I will merely assure you that there is far more to it than you have already experienced, and that you are welcome to the rest of it.*

As to your unfoldment on the nature of God as "I" you will, of course, receive your full answer in the London tape for the "Twenty-Five group" and in the New York Closed Class. We also had a two-session Practitioner Class, and this tape also is only for the members of the "Twenty-Five groups."

Your class, of course, went wonderfully, and I know it must have been a tremendous experience for all of them. The seven tapes of the Chicago Class could be divided into two such classes, and I am sure that these would be great experiences, and more especially, a solid foundation for the New York Closed Class, which should, by all means, be given in this same way.

You are certainly thoughtful and generous in sending these checks here from that class, and there are no better words for such a generous spirit than just "thank you," and a thank you that comes from the bottom of the heart.

Will be happy for you to keep in touch with me constantly while I am here at home, and I will be consciously with you in my meditations.

Emma joins me in love to you, Edward, and all of the family,

Joel

Dear Barbara,   September 7, 1960

You tune in all too well, and sometimes pick up things that were not to be picked up. Meaning that this particular subject of the editing has been under deep discussion in the past week, to such an extent that I do not wish to comment on it by mail, so please, for the sake of peace, let us forget about this for the time being.

The Letters has never been edited or touched from its first printing. As you have it in your copy, so it was in the original edition. This is likewise true of *The Infinite Way* and *Spiritual Interpretation of Scripture*. None of these have been touched, and are exactly as I turned them out. At the present moment, this is also true of *First, Second,* and *Third San Francisco Lectures*, which, of course, is still in manuscript form. All of the others have been edited for publication by first-line publishers, but we will say no more about that now.

No other news now except Aloha greetings from all of us to all of you,

Joel

Dear Joel,   September 9, 1960

Just received your wonderful letter of the 6th and want to answer it in a hurry while I am sure you're still talking to me.

First of all, as to the individual work – I really know, very deep down, that there is a world yet to come and that I have only scratched the surface of you and it – and while I am very eager for it to come as it will – what I have already had is producing such alternate periods of elation and depression that if the human ego could be cut out with a knife I would gladly submit to surgery – and you know how I feel about doctors and medicine. To me this ego seems the most insidious and treacherous thing imaginable.

By the way – I was in such a blue funk the other day that I just wanted some easy reading and having heard about Starr Daily, got his book called *Release* and read it. Do you know about him? I almost had the feeling that he might have been in one of the prisons you visited because the preface to his book, where he talks about practicing the presence and the mystical experience, etc., is almost pure Goldsmith. The rest of the book does not

quite measure up to the preface and yet one has the feeling
that he certainly had a valid conversion experience.

One of the women friends (part of our group) who took
the class with you last February, in a desperate state, is
just coming along by leaps and bounds. I don't know
whether or not I have mentioned to you her particular
problem, but her husband is here at the studio. He is
Edward's oldest friend and has turned out to have all the
symptoms described in the book *Alcoholics Anonymous*.
He is filled with resentment, and an unwillingness to
face any kind of reality or grow up. It has been
fascinating to me to see what has happened to his wife
since she started with the Infinite Way. She is just
handling the thing completely from the standpoint of
principle, and Edward has talked to her frequently and,
together, I believe they may bring about a healing in this
man, although at this point he is still really jerking,
giving her a great deal of trouble about coming up to the
meetings, calling Edward the "Little Tin God in the
White Shroud," etc. If it weren't so serious for his career
and his children, etc., we would laugh at him because of
the really childlike degree of his jerking around.

I am so very grateful for the help I had from you
when I was struggling with my attachment to Edward
and you finally brought me to the place where I could
"loose him and follow Me" – because I am able to
encourage her from my own personal experience to just
be steadfast in this viewpoint and let God handle it.

Speaking of Edward, I want to tell you one cute story
about him. The other day Suzi and April (8 years and 4
years, respectively) were having a row and Suzi said to
April, "April, I just can't stand you." Edward heard this
and just hurled himself into the kitchen and roared at
Suzi – "Don't you talk like that to her, she's a
manifestation of God the same as you are!" The lack of
perspective in *what* he was saying vs. *the way* he was
roaring it was terribly funny.

Do you know that I am seeing indicia that Edward may want to teach this one day, or be a practitioner, or something constructive. I don't mean outside of his own work, but perhaps within it. Have you felt this at all? Of course he knows that he is still a tiny beginner but people have always gravitated to him for counsel, and now he has something better than human advice to give them.

As for me – I walk pretty good one day – and limp the next, but I expect that will go on for ages, maybe forever.[1]

Edward and I are currently enjoying the biography of Robert Frost and reading the poetry aloud to each other. How *that* man can see and hear!

Love to all,

P.S. It's almost too good to be true that we shall have you for 6 whole weeks next year. Can't wait. Edw. and I are off for 3 weeks in Italy on the 20th and I am studying Italian like mad.

Dear Joel,   September 14, 1960

Anent your letter re the "editing" –

"O.K. Boss"

Love & gratitude,

B

Dear Barbara: September 14, 1960

Every time I sit down to dictate a letter to you, I get so interested in the subject of the letter that I forget to tell you of our deep and sincere thanks for your

---

[1]   It certainly went on for a long time.

thoughtfulness. The tea arrived, and it is delicious. The record arrived, and that man really is a comedian,[1] and of a new school. He is unlike anything that has gone before him, even though I am sure that many would like to think of him alongside of Will Rogers. We have already played this record three times for guests, and each time made a fan for him.

Yes, I know Starr Daily, and I am happy to tell you that almost from the beginning of the Message of the Infinite Way, he has had a very deep regard for me and for my work. Recently, he stated publicly that he felt that Joel was the only spiritual Teacher functioning in the western world today, which, of course, is mighty sweet from a man who knows me principally only through the writings.

His own experience, however, was many, many many years before *The Infinite Way* was in print, and the experience was entirely one within his own being.[2]

I am sure that Ed's friend at the studio will respond to the work his wife is doing and that you are doing, and it is only necessary to continue to abide in *the realization of God as individual being*, and of the nature of hypnotism and malpractice.

Of course you must realize that I recognized the depths of Edward when I sent to him one of my patients, and you can be assured I would send others to him if it would not be taking advantage of a man already as busy as he can comfortably be. However, at the least sign from him, I would gladly send some of our students to him, because I do recognize what he has got.

Do I understand that you are going to Italy this month? If so, it will really be a most wonderful season

---

[1] Bob Newhart.

[2] Starr Daily also wrote a wonderful, inspirational book from prison, *Love Unlocks Prison Doors*. It may be out of print but available in libraries. It is well worth a reading.

of the year for Rome and Venice. My favorite spot in Sicily will probably be too warm.

Aloha greetings from both of us to all of you,

Joel

Dear Barbara: September 19, 1960

Just a line of thanks to you for your letter of the 14th, and for your ever-thoughtful and generous enclosure. I assume that there will be a letter in my mail today telling me if you are leaving for Italy this month. I was not sure whether or not I correctly understood. If you are, of course, a wonderful, wonderful trip to both of you.

Aloha greetings from Emma and from me,

Joel

Thank you for the "near beer" which just arrived. Very tasty!

Dear Joel,   October 17, 1960

Well I assume you have had my letter by now telling you we were going to Italy. And here we are home, after a wonderful but hectic two weeks, including stopping back by New York and attending the "Spartacus" premiere. The Universal Newsreel that came out this week carries pictures of us attending – papa looks like an actor!

Boy, if chastening is evidence of love, then He must love me "real good." The chastening comes so fast – for even an incorrect thought – and particularly if I admit a thought of criticism of another – it seems that I have to go and do the very thing I was criticizing them for, within 24 hours. It has me so scared that the other day I was walking along behind a woman and noticed that her

heels were run over. "Oh, no, Father, didn't mean it –
honest, I didn't see a thing!"

On the other fronts we are progressing, but oh, so
slowly – still have this nagging, small drinking and
small smoking – and I'm determined not to fight it – and
just keep saying, "My Kingdom is not of this world" as I
pick up the cigarette. But oh, dear heaven, I wish it
would fall off me – and so does Edward – and says so.
We are both so *bored* with these sorties into the "all too
human" – and both of us would like to be relieved of
them – just these two things (please!) and we'll struggle
along with the other vices, ourselves.[1]

I have a wonderful thing to report. Edward had a
long talk with his friend here (the one I told you about
who was having the trouble with drinking) and he is
coming to the tape session tonight. We'll see what
happens. But something else – his ex-wife – whom Ed
and I have known for a long time (she is not the present
wife who took your class and who comes faithfully to
all the tape groups) has been a "poor mixed-up kid" for a
number of years – and his present wife (see parenthesis
above) called me today; asked for another copy of "23rd
Psalm," and asked me if I wanted her to tell me what
had happened to her other one. Naturally I said yes and,
to be as brief as possible, she had given it to the first wife,
who read it – called her psychiatrist and told him she
wouldn't be back (she has been going to him for 6 years),
got herself a fine, full time job at UCLA and has just
spent the last week in Catalina in connection with this
new job (which is just up her alley). This woman has a
fine mind, but the psychiatrists have kept her in a stew
for all this time and she had just become fat and sat at
home all the time brooding about her miseries. She has
become reconciled with her sister to whom she has not
spoken for 5 years, etc.

---

[1] Oh, Barbara, what a beginner you were! But all that made it easier for me to be patient
with *my* beginning students.

Now the present wife said she just couldn't understand how the reading of one pamphlet could do so much – but I told her that that was just an indication of how ready the person was, and that, actually it would be conceivable to have a *total* healing in an instant – of every human error – if the organism were that receptive. (Correct me if I am wrong).

Needless to say, I am thrilled and gratified at this good fortune for my old friend (the previous wife) but I am also thrilled that, to me, it is further evidence of how much of the Christ the present wife is permitting to flow through her. She had said for many years that she wanted to help the previous wife – but this was the first time everything seemed to open up. She also told her about our tape meetings – but she seemed not too responsive to that. However, we shall see.

I am anxious to hear what is going on in the orient so write me a long letter when you get the time.

Love and gratitude for what you are,

Dear Barbara,   October 25, 1960

Your letter starts off as if one of my letters failed to reach you. Indeed I received your letter telling of your trip to Italy and I answered with two letters. However, that is water under the bridge and gone by. Happy to hear this one of Oct 17 on our arrival here to-day and first of all my deep thanks for your everthoughtful enclosure. Hope you had as good a time in Italy as I always do – and as Emma had on her one trip. She keeps wanting to go back.

Hope your picture went over well. Have seen no reports.

Do not accept these experiences as chastening as there is no one to chasten. These are the very opportunities which will lift us into the higher consciousness – and without these we would stand still in ease in 'matter'.

Now for the remaining trivialities – smoking, etc. – I give you a sacred and secret mantram: – "Be not afraid, it is I." Keep this on your forehead; bind it on your arm and nail it to your door!   But sacredly & secretly remember it always.

Heartfelt thanks for sharing with me the experiences of this couple and ex-wife.   It is a soulstirring story. (Incidentally, using the word story reminds me that for the first time in my life I think I have a story for films. Not religious – but with immigration as its theme – from the commercial & national side of the picture.   Will inflict it on Edward when I see him as it exists only in my mind).

Now, our trip to the Orient.   We had three weeks in Japan.   It was not enough.   We placed several hundred copies of Japanese translation of *Art of Meditation.* in the hands of serious thinkers.   The subject & its handling proved startling to them as a whole.   And spiritual healing was difficult for them even to think about.   We spent four days in the Cultural, Religious Art centers, and around Fuji.   Nice experiences – worth while.   I talked thru interpreters in church, college & Govt. offices.   The seed is planted.

Hong Kong is a story in itself.   A whole new Hong Kong & Kowloon has been built since my visits there in 1955 & 1956.   This is a story Edward could do.   In my more than 50 years of travel I have seen no equal to this city of 600,000 become a state of 3 1/2 to 4 million.   No other city has come out of the war like this – and there is a sequel not yet made public.

A member of the Dutch Embassy at Burma has come over to see me here – a student.   The Romance of a Religion in embryo!!   Think of the dozens of cities in which I have introduced Infinite Way in the U.S – Canada – Europe – India – Africa & now the Orient.   O,

yes – Australia & New Zealand & Puerto Rico!   An
unpublished, unfinished, and impossible story!

Emma joins me in love to you & all the family.

Joel

Dear Papa Bear,   November 10, 1960

My God – I've learned non-reaction![1]

Can't figure why all the steps leading up to this should
interest you particularly, so won't bother – but they were
fantastic.

Love and kisses to Mama Bear – love and gratitude to
you,

threadbear

Dear Barbara   November 27, 1960

Our last city – three more days – 8 sessions – and then
the Big Hop home.

Just a piece of news I discovered over 25 years ago: it
doesn't cost money to travel. If it did, these journeys of
mine never would have happened.

Will write again when my feet are settled under my
new desk – in my new office – in the home Emma has

---

[1]   Well – not quite, as it happened. After thirty years of teaching and continuing to be a
"learner" myself, I know that when we have a *Realization*, a stroke of *Enlightenment*, it
really only means that we have reached a new plateau, but the mountain is still to be
climbed and growth must still continue, perhaps to Infinity. That is why I call the
"mountain" the "Spiral Road to Infinity." Occasionally the clouds part and we get a glimpse
of the "City of God," but they close down again, and we must just go marching on. But
nothing can ever take away from us the reality of that glimpse. That is what gives us the
courage to continue.

just done over – inside and out. Or – come see it.

Aloha to all of you,

Joel & Emma

Dear Joel,   November 30, 1960

Well, here comes another "book." One part about me, and the other another unwarranted invasion into your private business. I hope you know me well enough by now to know that I am not motivated by anything petty, but by a sincere respect and regard for you and the Infinite Way.

It has to do with the handling of the tapes and the correspondence about the tapes. It used to be that the tapes one ordered would arrive at the latest within 2 weeks of the time of ordering. Then about last January or February I noticed that it seemed to take considerably longer to get them. I didn't have any idea of the reason – and still may not know it – but this is what I wish to ask you about.

During the class last February, here in L.A., some of the other students mentioned to me that their tapes were a very long time in coming. That was the first inkling I had that the problem was not singular with me. The "grapevine" also said that you made it a practice never to *hire* anyone to work for the Infinite Way. And you mentioned something to me in Chicago about, "After all I'm not going to hire those people, they must make their own demonstration – I am not their supply." I easily understand the reasoning behind this and I am sure that anyone would agree with the principle.

However (and in no way construe this as a criticism of *anyone*), last February in talking to B. she mentioned to me that she was having a sound-recording studio added on to her home. Naturally I construed from this that she had been put in charge of getting out the tapes.

Also, in asking her whom I should bother about the *Monthly Letter*, she wrote me that she was the one.

About a year ago I wrote her and enclosed a check for the *Letter* to be sent to a friend of mine in Germany, in the German edition, which you had told me was then available. Two or three months later I learned that the *Letter* had never arrived.

I have also ordered other tapes months ago which have never arrived, nor no correspondence about them.

Now, I want to say again, that I in no way mean this as a criticism. I simply construe that she has far too much to do. But it does seem to me that these matters are not being handled in a business-like way. And while I understand your feeling about not hiring people for the I.W., nonetheless, in the matter of sending out tapes, sending out the *Letter*, your correspondence, sending out books, etc., it would in no way interfere with your avowed purpose of "no organization" to have capable, professional people, and enough of them, to handle with dispatch these matters for a spreading student body.

I feel sure you would agree with this principle, since you, yourself, almost bend over backward to be exceedingly prompt in answering each and every letter sent to you.

You realize, of course, that I am very aware that I really know none of the facts surrounding these things – and have only heard some rumors, and a chance remark of yours, to cause this speculation of mine. If I have misinterpreted the facts, please excuse me. If not, perhaps you are not aware of this situation and, if not, may welcome my calling it to your attention.

Well, this seems enough of a burden for you for one letter, so I guess I will withhold my problem for another time.

Am enclosing love and gratitude for November.

Always,

Dear Barbara,   December 5, 1960

First of all, thank you for your good letter of November 30th and for your ever-thoughtful and generous enclosure.

Next, you really did misunderstand me, and it is surprising that you would have misunderstood this point, but since you have, let me explain it to you. When I said that I do not hire people just because they want to work for the Infinite Way, I meant exactly that; that those who are active in the Infinite Way have all demonstrated their way in spiritually, and some circumstance has brought about their being in whatever position they hold; that is, some circumstance beyond that of merely the human activity of engaging them. There is no one who works in any capacity at all for the Infinite Way without receiving remuneration, and that rate of remuneration is always based on a figure higher than that which is normal in regular business channels. Recognizing the infinite Source of supply, it is possible for us to be more liberal in payment to those who are in any way called to our activity.

Now, everyone who works for us is handicapped to some extent by the fact that I will not organize. As you know, it would cost only $200 to form a religious or educational corporation to receive tax-free contributions, and it would then be a simple matter to set up a headquarters building and as many employees as the situation may call for. However, this means that when my period of retirement comes, regardless of what form it may come in, there would be an organization left behind me, and this, of course, is strictly out as far as the Infinite Way is concerned. Therefore, regardless of what handicaps we work under, we will continue to do it rather than organize.

First let me tell you how this has worked out in regard to the incident you describe in the Letter Department. To begin with, our Letter Department in Honolulu has absolutely nothing to do with our activity in Germany, and therefore the most that B. could do would be to send your request to the publisher in Germany, and any remittance along with it that was necessary. Beyond this, Barbara, she would have no way of knowing whether or not the order was filled or even whether it was received in Germany, since they do not communicate with her.

Practicing The Presence was due for release January 1, 1960, and up to this moment I do not even have a date of release for it, since as you probably know, it has not yet appeared in print. Also, five of my books are in translation in Germany, and up to this moment I do not even get word of when to expect the publication of the first one. Of course you can see that if we had an international organization setup that we could have, perhaps, a secretary acting as intermediary between the various departments over here and in England, Germany, etc. But this we do not have, and therefore I am the central figure that keeps my fingers in every department in every country.

Regarding the Tape Department we have an entirely different situation, and let me explain here some of the difficulties under which we operate. First we built a studio for Emma attached to her home which, of course, was outgrown, and when she began traveling with me, the work had to be turned over to Mr. Hughes, who was her assistant, and a larger studio was built on his home grounds. Evidently his other business activities grew, even while the tape business was growing, and so the tape business was neglected and had to be taken away from him, and during this period the department was in a position where it could not possibly operate perfectly. Meanwhile, a new studio had to be built, and since B. was taking over this work, it had to be built on her property, and a beautiful studio has been built there, and while this was being done, a bookkeeping department had to be set up; and so a long period elapsed in which students had to be very, very patient with us while this reorganization was taking place.

Then, just as this department was beginning to function, the Father sent me out on ten months of travel with more lecture and classwork in one year than we have had in any previous three years, and she had the full responsibility of turning out this work.   In Manchester, England I now have a Tape Department functioning with the most modern tape recording and tape duplicating machinery with two electronic engineers in charge of the work, and now capable, beginning January 1st, of turning out the tapes for England, the continent of Europe, South Africa, Australia, and New Zealand.   So that we are just beginning to ease up on B. in the demand for tapes for abroad, so that as of January 1st, she will have only the United States and Canada.

It is in this same way that I will never forget that there could not be a Tape Department or a Letter Department if it had not been for Emma, who also put in eighteen and twenty-hour days so that I could travel and carry my Message out into the world while she built this Tape Department from the beginning of a $90 tape recorder to what it is now in two countries.   Some of these things can never be paid for in money, and yet this is no excuse to underpay, and therefore I try to do the best I can in sharing as liberally as the circumstances permit.

Now, as to the specific tapes that are behind in delivery, or the unanswered letters, please let me assure you that we do require all of the patience you can give us, because there is only so much that can be done in the way in which we are working.

In spite of the fact that in my last stop, Auckland, New Zealand, I answered nearly two hundred letters by hand, when I returned home my desk was completely covered with mail. How many letters were here I have no way of knowing, but dictating constantly since I am home, and in between, writing as many by hand that had to be gotten off immediately for one reason or another, my desk is just as full as when I came home, if not more so, including Saturday's mail. Students must be patient with me, because I am dictating up to the limit of the hours available, and I am writing by hand as many as must be answered on the date of receipt, and trying to give the attention to the healing work that must be given, and then of course, all of the other details of the work in manuscripts, editing, etc., which are a part of a work which no one in the world would believe unless they were here to witness it.

This little band of assistants is working far beyond anything, I am sure, that has ever been asked of a small group of people before. Oh, yes! We are at the beginning of a whole new world era, and we are probably the little band that is sparking this entire new era, and the recognition that is coming to us is beyond our ability to handle, and only time and patience will be able to show us how this work can be conducted.

Well, Barbara, love to you and all the family, and Emma joins me in every good wish for a joyous Holiday Season and a new dispensation in the new year.

Aloha to all of you!

Joel

Dear Joel,   December 12, 1960

Thy Grace is my sufficiency.

Happy Holiday to all.

CHAPTER 4

CORRESPONDENCE 1961

Dear Friend –   January 9, 1961

Will be in Los Angeles next week for three nights.

If you would like me to talk to your group in my hotel suite or at your home – it will be my pleasure.

Probably arrive Bev. Hilton sometime Monday.

Aloha,

Joel

Dear Sweet Friend,   Monday
                                                       January 23, 1961

Well, I told you on the phone that I had written you a long letter which had not as yet been put to paper, and now that I am settled here I wonder why I think all this rigamarole should be interesting to you – but then there is no one else to whom I should care, or dare, to mention it, and so I take advantage of your spiritual generosity.

First of all, the other night again, as I left, I felt such loving kindness coming from you. That is the second time I have felt this – the other being when I called you in Honolulu the time Phillip was hurt. I am just not used to being treated with kindness and understanding and it has an absolutely dissolving effect on me. As far back as I can remember I have been kind of a rebel, and a fighter – determined not to be beaten by all this human mess – and having such a rigorous, blunt honesty, I know that my personality has nearly always been very difficult for other people to stomach, and it has resulted in everyone thinking that I am strong and powerful enough to stand alone – and you and one other person in my life (who is long dead) are the only ones who have seemed to realize how very weak and inadequate I am and who have not held back on kindness with me. This other man was humanly kind to me and, of course, yours is universal and even, if anything, more effective. In any event, I appreciate it.

> *Note: In a personal interview I had discussed the place of sex in the life of one who wanted to walk the spiritual path. Joel had said, "In marriage we are entitled to experience and enjoy anything that comes to us naturally and lovingly." He also said, "Some of us do not come down from the level of spiritual consciousness for long enough to indulge in it." I, perhaps mistakenly, took that as a spiritual challenge, hence the following letter. However, in April, 1964, Joel said to me, "I must take a new look at sex, I have discovered that I have been the victim of my Jewish conditioning." I took that to mean that he had then a more liberal view.*

I left a lot unsaid the other night – most of which can easily remain unsaid, but there is one point which I feel I want to explain. That is that it is not, and never has been, the physical act of love to which I have been attached but rather to *lovemaking*; and not even necessarily with the desire to receive love, but rather needing the opportunity to express love to another. I realize that it's been on the human level, but it is a similar feeling (only, of course, different) to the way I have loved the feeling being brought up in me of loving my children. I am by nature passionate and intense – about everything, even spirituality – and I have loved the feeling in me of feeling love and affection for a child. Likewise I have wallowed gloriously in this feeling of pouring myself out to another person. I just loved the feeling of being that intensely involved – if you can understand   what I mean. And it was the thought that I might never again feel that feeling in myself that made me so reluctant, for it is a kind of glory. But, so be it, it's human – and I feel that you must be right that I was somehow holding it as a thing separate and apart from God and therefore it must be given up. And I am willing to give it up, though I must confess it makes me feel like ashes inside. The physical act, itself, would never have meant anything to me without this feeling of love. But with this growing impasse with Edward wherein our rates of vibration have become so different that we have lost our rapport, and are more like strangers, I suppose the whole thing will, even humanly, just boil itself off into nothingness.

The last two or three weeks I have been seeing things a lot clearer anyway, even from a human standpoint, and have had to do a lot of growing up about my marital situation. You see, I have been passionate about Edward for more than three lifetimes and, as I wrote you before, this one seemed to me to be the culmination and fulmination of them all and I brought to Edward (though only humanly, I realize now) a passionate worship and devotion that used up my whole being and, in my concept of him, he returned this. Certainly he has evidenced in the past a great need for me and I, in seeing just what I wanted to see, construed this as being "in love" with me. As my human vision has been clearing it has seemed to me that he was loving me less and less – but now I know that he hasn't changed at all. He still has the same amount of love and the same attitude toward me that he has always had (and I do think he loves me as much as, and in whatever way, he has the capacity for, or the desire to do) and it is just that his nature is very different from what I have kept insisting that it be all of these years. I have the feeling that I have kept writing a script but he has kept refusing to play the role.[1] Now, of course, this is no fault or lack in him – nor is he responsible for the fact that I have been writing my own script. There is nothing that says that he has to read the

---

[1]   It was my "fantasy script" that he refused to read. "Fantasy script" is explained in my forthcoming book, *Script, Kid and Fantasyland.*

lines. And if the situation were reversed I don't suppose I'd have wanted anyone else writing my lines for me.[1]

I have been seeing that this is a situation that just must be faced, and grown up to. Again, I am willing to do this. So perhaps it's all part and parcel of the same thing, culminating in my talk with you and your definitive counsel, which I accept wholeheartedly and shall do my best to act upon it.

A human is really nothing isn't he? And all these joys and woes, triumphs and failures are, as Shakespeare said, "...tales told by an idiot."

I probably placed Edward, too, in place of God (with a kind of worship) and that is undoubtedly why I have to change. Although I have also been realizing fully in the past weeks that one can't lose what he has never had. And that's part of growing up, too, I guess.

Well, next week *East Lynne*.

So "Let the dead bury the dead," and back to the subject of my gratitude to you for your kindness and understanding. I know what prompts it in you, and where it really comes from – partly because I have felt something like it flow through me for other people – but nonetheless, I am grateful that you do permit it to flow through you to me and others and in return, please take this as a warm, personal hug from me to you. Something I would never do in person for fear of embarrassing you or being misunderstood. However, if you don't wish people to love you, you must cease being lovable.

---

[1]   In 1986 I was still having some rare experiences of frustration in my relationship with Edward, even though it had been 80 per cent purged of human ignorance, when, in answer to my question, "Why can Edward still have this effect on me?" the Father answered, "He is a perfect reader of your script and you cannot forgive him for that." For the next three hours God unfolded to my vision the cause of the misery in human relationships – and *the way out*. That became the foundation of our next four years of work. The fruitage of this "hidden script" will be published someday as *Script, Kid, and Fantasyland: "The Truth That Makes You Free."*

I'm saying to myself, "You're not really going to send him this silly letter," at the very moment I know damned well I am. Well, if the screws are loose you'll just have to take your spiritual wrench and tighten them up. In fact, I could probably do with a good spiritual valve-grinding. And will no doubt get just that in April.

Enclose small check in love and gratitude,

the earthling

Dear Joel,   January 24th, 1961

Well, I was so absorbed with the personal matter that I forgot to tell you about what is really far more important, and that is the reaction of our group to the wonderful opportunity of having you with us in intimate session. They are fully aware of what an extraordinary privilege it was and are thoroughly grateful.

There was one interesting little sidelight. Mrs. D., who sat on the couch at your right, is the wife of the man I wrote you about, who works at the studio and who has been having the problem with excessive drinking (which is just another way of saying excessive ego). Now I don't think I had written to you that after Edward's long talk with him he had been coming faithfully to every Monday night's tape session and while his progress was slow (he had no previous metaphysical background at all, but rather was very bitter against religion even to the point of being very cruel to his wife about her going to church or coming up here to meetings), she reported that he had, nonetheless, made giant strides in the last few months, certainly compared to the level at which he was previously operating.

We were all interested to notice that he found himself unable to make the meeting with you personally, even though he had known about it for days. Of course you know why he couldn't, and so do I – and he really *couldn't*, I am sure. But he was back again last night to the tape meeting, and his wife says he might as well have attended last Monday because the difference in him since Monday is unbelievable. I don't know just exactly what these differences are because I don't inquire into details on these things – but there is the story.

There was one other thing I wanted to say to you; you have taught me this well, at least, that while I know it will never happen that you could fall from Grace, show feet of clay, or make mistakes with me, I would never criticize you but only hold out my hand in continuing love and gratitude. My loyalty to you is unequivocal. This may be kind of a silly thing to' say, but I felt like it, so here it is.

Love and gratitude, and I am trying to be obedient, and while I can feel the wings sprouting I am afraid my halo will always be a little crooked.

                              still the earthling

Dear Barbara,   February 2, 1961

It was truly a joy, being with you and Ed on this last trip, and I am happy to see by your skill in drawing, the spiritual fruitage of that visit. Looking at your drawing, I was certain of three things: One, I was looking at a tree; two, I was looking at the male figure; and three, I was looking at the female figure, and believe me, I have seen many, many paintings lately that made none of these things clear, and as a matter of fact, gave no evidence of what the artist had in mind, and so I enjoyed looking at your drawing for a change.[1]

Aloha greetings from Emma and from me to all of you at home,

                              Joel

---

[1]   I didn't keep a copy of the drawing so I must join with Robert Browning: "once God and I knew what the meaning ('drawing') was, now only God knows."

Dear Joel,   February 15, 1961

Since you said my cartooning amuses you – this is
how I see people:

"States and stages of consciousness"

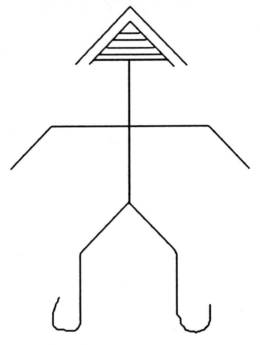

<u>L & G</u>

Barbara

*Note: Following are Joel's letter and
instructions to the Tape Group Leaders.*

Dear Friend,   February 20, 1961

I have just completed one tape, Waikiki 1961, Reel 2, for use as a text tape in your instruction work on the quotations from Scripture, and the application of these quotations.

If I am any judge at all, this tape makes the teaching of this subject very clear. In other words, while I have outlined the way in which Scriptural quotations and passages may be embodied in our daily living, I have left the fullest scope to the individual to select their own quotations and present the application of these in the way that the teacher has himself or herself found practical and fruitful.

Should there be any questions at all, now or at any time while you are teaching, do not hesitate to call upon me.

Aloha greetings,

Joel

Dear Friend,

I would very much like you to start a class one night a week, but only four times a month, for the specific purpose of teaching the major Scriptural quotations used in the Message of the Infinite Way, and their application to our daily experience.

I would like the class conducted as follows: The first, second, and third meetings of the month, the students to be given two of our major quotations, and then an explanation of them, and the manner of applying them to our daily experience. The fourth meeting in the month to be used as a review period, during which time the students will tell whether they have memorized these six passages, and if they have developed any facility in applying them to their daily problems.

Every week thereafter, one outstanding quotation of Scripture to be taught, and its use and application, and of course, bring into the period of the class some of the quotations from previous months, so that there is a continuity of the teaching of these quotations *and their practical application to daily experience.* And always the fourth meeting in the month should be a review period, during which the students review, not only the quotations of that particular month, but those of previous months, and of course, again explaining the degree of facility that they are developing in the application of these principles.

Naturally, this is only the outline of the subject and function of the class, but actually each teacher will have to be individually guided as to how to conduct the class to bring out the fullest measure of good.

We might take, "He performeth that which is given me to do," and here, of course, you realize *how many problems every person faces in the course of a day that bring to thought a fear that we may not be equal to it, or a concern that we may not be up to it,* or that we cannot financially meet it, or that we do not have the understanding to resolve it; and here, of course, the application would be the immediate realization that the responsibility is not mine, since He performeth that which is given me to do.

In the first three weeks of the next month, we again take one or two passages of Scripture each week, and then the fourth week again review, and this review must include not only all that has gone on in the second month, but that which took place in the first month, also, because here the teacher must ascertain to what degree the students are able to make themselves proficient in memorizing these passages, and then in the application of them; and should the teacher feel that sufficient progress has not been made, there is no reason why the third month cannot be used for taking up the same Scriptural passages as were used in the first and second months, and noting how the students become even more proficient when this is done in this way; or if suitable progress has been made, the third month can go right on being a continuation, taking again six new passages during the three weeks, and a review period the fourth.

I have merely outlined the procedure, but of course the teacher has the widest latitude, keeping in mind always that, "By their fruits ye shall know them," and the teacher is only succeeding if the students are revealing wonderful changes in their consciousness, and eventually in their affairs.[1]

If there is any way in which I can make this entire subject clearer to you, do not hesitate to call upon me.

This letter is being sent to about a dozen of our students, each one of whom is certainly ready for this experience, else I would not have written it to you.

I will be very pleased to hear from you as to your reaction to this letter.

Aloha greetings,

Joel

Dear Barbara: Febrary 20, 1961

This is just to let you know that we have set our arrival date in Los Angeles at Monday, March 20th, and we will be arriving about dinner time, and therefore would be happy to hear from you any time from March 21st on.

This means that we have about a week in Los Angeles before our work begins, and so if you would like to

---

[1] We began this study immediately following Joel's suggestions. The "practical application" is explained thoroughly in my book *The Royal Road to Reality*, in the chapters on "Flashcard Work." This procedure developed naturally into a workshop class. This method works!

arrange for a group at your home and invite any others that you feel you would like to have there, I would be very happy to set aside an evening for you and your group and your guests. As we will have a suite, should you prefer the meeting to be held at the hotel, this will be equally agreeable with us.

Aloha greetings to all of you from both of us.

Joel

Riverside Mission Inn
Friday Morning
May, 1961

Dear Boss,

My conscience has been bothering me because I was not wholly honest with you yesterday morning when you asked me where I had been that you hadn't seen me, and I answered that I had been working. The question caught me unawares and I didn't just want to blurt out anything.

However, I have duly thought about it and decided that I do want to clarify things.

I suppose a certain amount of politicking and jockeying for position is inevitable around any kind of leader, at least among a goodly portion of the people. I had really never seen this before but there has been a certain amount of it evident during this class – and since it would be entirely foreign to my nature to enter into any such competition, but rather to back away from it, that is what I have been doing. I simply cannot enter the conversations that are seemingly held for the purpose of proving "how close I am to Joel" or "how he needs me and depends on me for support." It's more comfortable for me to be alone. Well, so much for the human picture.[1]

---

[1] Joel called together the students who had been having these ego problems, and straightened them out. Ego problems can adulterate a class. He told me that once, in

For the spiritual picture – I am very anxious that you know how I feel. As you know, I never hesitate to bother you or yell for help whenever I am in trouble, or need a spiritual principle to be clarified, I am almost conscienceless when it comes to those things – for two reasons: 1) I am *determined* to learn, and 2) I feel that you have drawn me to you as a student and therefore you have voluntarily taken on the obligation to teach me, so that I am entitled to whatever of your time is necessary to accomplish this. But, as right now, for instance, when nothing is troubling me and when I seem to be growing at a nice easy pace, I would not think it would be fair for me to take up your time when there are so many others that may be needing it more than I do right now – that is the other reason I have not asked to see you.

However, all these other things – real and unreal – aside, there is one thing I have been wanting to say to you since Chicago, and I guess now is the time.

I am constantly desirous of sharing meditation with you whenever there is the opportunity of being in your physical presence. Of course I share in it often when you are thousands of miles away, but there seems to me to be an added something from being in the same room with you and that is something that I am always, consistently hungry for. But during this class I am not going to *ask* for that because I do not want to impose on you or your own need for privacy. I just do want you to know that I would be happy to just come in at any time, when you are alone, or with Emma, or meditating with others, and just be a silent– not social – mouse in the corner, and bask in the sunshine. But I will wait to be invited and I will not press you for this but will leave it entirely as it may unfold itself to you.

Chicago, his Closed Class "...almost didn't get off the ground." I have experienced these problems in my classes. It is up to the teacher to heal them.

I am your friend and remain full of

Love and gratitude,

B.

Dear Barbara –   New York
                                             June 1, 1961

Everything happened so fast – my head still says, "Which way north?"

Sent you a wire of thanks from Washington D.C. – then back to N.Y. for Tues. and Thurs. talks. Got a temporary hotel room and our own flat will be ready June 7th newly decorated. Will remain all month and will have four weekly meetings.

We are having a peaceful week until the work starts. Weather just June beautiful. Fruits, berries, and vegetables coming in fresh and delicious.

Our united love,

Joel & Emma

Dear Boss,   June 15, 1961

Well, as soon as you told me it was my consciousness holding things together, the whole thing collapsed. Nobody comes any more. Edward's two secretaries haven't come since they took the L.A. Class.

Mrs. D.'s husband is not drinking (much) and seems to be behaving. She has dropped the divorce proceedings against him. But the price of all this seems to be that she shall not put herself under *my* influence. This is the second man who has considered me a witch. The other was Ron Hubbard of Dianetics fame, or infame, whichever way one's opinion runs.[1]

However, Mother, Ginny (my sister) and I still have ourselves a wonderful time every Monday night at 8 p.m. Altho' I am running a tape every day (or almost every day) in the daytime right now, they will be running alone for the summer, because beginning last night I have started rehearsals with a student opera workshop to do a "Mme. Butterfly."

In other words, everything seems to be in a state of much flux – but very cheerful.

As to me – the growth that has taken place since March 31st is too much even to bore you with (point by point – or rather blow by blow, that is) – suffice it to say that last week I realized that *this is a spiritual universe* – and, *after* that, I became *aware* of being hypnotized. Now, again, this sequence amazes me – that the awareness of being hypnotized should *follow* the recognition of the spiritual universe. It would seem as tho' that would come first – but there it is – and I can't argue with it. But it's like I couldn't see why sex could come *after* fear and death – but there that was, too.[2]

I should adore being in London with you and Emma – but have a wonderful time (even without me) and be sure to let me know when you will be through here again.

Joel, why don't you do as your next book a clarification of the difference between Cosmic and

---

[1] Edward and I had gone to Elizabeth, New Jersey, to take the first class Ron taught. Actually, Ron called me a "super clear with power." He wasn't being exactly complimentary, since he thought power should be his exclusive domain.

[2] It is, of course, perfectly clear to me now. One cannot *see/recognize* the spiritual universe until he is out of the hypnotism. Only then can he "look back" and see from what he has been freed.

Being freed from the fear of fear and the fear of death was being freed from human *evil*. It is relatively easy to be freed from evil – we cooperate in that. We see sex as human *good*. It is much harder to let go of concepts of, and attachments to, human good. One has to be well along on the Path for that.

Spiritual Consciousness; in the same manner that you clarified mental vs. spiritual healing in *Art of Spiritual Healing*?

I have very much enjoyed Dr. Bucke's *Cosmic Consciousness*[1] but he obviously was not aware that Cosmic C. and Spiritual C. are two different things. He lumped them together, and sometimes got them mixed up.

Also, this is a matter on which you have been asked questions many times (I have heard the question both on tapes and in classes) and it would bear, I think, a whole writing to itself.

Love and kisses to you both (I'm feeling *very* expansive tonite!).

B.

6/26/61

P.S. Well, as you can see, there was some delay between writing this letter and shipping it off and I look back (in re-reading it) and remember with awe how peaceful and cheerful I was when I wrote it – for in the meantime, apparently, I have been given another "opportunity" for growth and am currently in the midst of a very hard and dispiriting struggle, working on the latest phrase which was given me by the Voice which is, "To depart from love is a sin." Oh hell!

London
June 28, 1961

Dear Barbara –

Came over here without a program or arrangements – and we have been having a full schedule in halls wherever and whenever available. Have already had

---

[1]   Bucke, Richard, *Cosmic Consciousness: a study in the evolution of the human mind.* New York: E.P, Dutton and Co., 1960.

over two weeks in London, five days in Manchester, and now finishing in London. Then July 1-8 Beau Rivage Palace, Lausanne, Switzerland.

Will keep travelling until God catches up with me! Then we will take a rest!

Jesus asked, "For which of these things do you stone me?" and then related the good He had done. Do you wonder that some who "feel" the influence of the Christ – rush away from it? The Light is too bright!

I have witnessed four who reached Initiation, afterward tear the Christ out of their hearts! [1]

You do not actually get hypnotized – you are past that. But – even after you receive an unfoldment – *you still must think* – and thinking spoils it. The correct procedure after illumination in any degree – is rest.

Well you have done it again – last week, maybe while you were writing – I did a tape on the difference between Cosmic Consciousness & Spiritual Consc. It will show up on one of the recent tapes.

Do not take the human scene too big. It doesn't rate it!

Thank you for your everthoughtful and generous enclosure. And be sure to take our love and pass it along to all who would welcome it.

Lovingly,

Joel & Emma

Dear Joel,   July 26th, 1961

Great Gadfrey – where does the time go!

---

[1] Initiation into the Fourth Dimensional Consciousness.

First, I didn't mean that I was hypnotized, or being hypnotized – thank God, yes, I am past that. What I meant was that I had become aware of having been (previously) hypnotized. It is a strange feeling, like not being quite awake, and sometimes there actually seems to be a sort of film over my eyes – but I have the feeling not that these things are "becoming" but are dissolving – and that, when the film is completely dissolved, and when the sleepy hypnosis lifts off, I shall be really awake and see things as they *are*. Oh happy day!

Happy day because I feel sure that *any* attachment to the human picture will lift off with it, and then it will not matter that I seem to be very much alone in the world. In fact, when you write about those who rush away from the influence of the Christ it touches quite a chord in me, because it really seems to me right now that the only ones in the world who can stand me are my three little children (not the three big ones) and you and Emma. My very nature seems to cause the hair to rise on practically everyone else. (Naturally I'm exaggerating).

You are so right about my *having* to think. My singing teacher said that to me just yesterday, also. He said, "You think too much." So I'm just trying to be a vegetable for both of you. I fancy I'm rather like a parsnip. And I must learn how to rest.

I just love these evidences of my oneness with your consciousness. It's such a big help, when I am morose, to know that, even so, I am "linked." However, I still think that the material of Cosmic vs. Spiritual Consciousness should be written in a book.

I send you the July 2nd program from the church where I am teaching Sunday School. A time for silent prayer is actually written in the program. This is just 4 weeks after I first discussed the subject with the young minister. He learns fast! Also, the Sunday previous they had *Silent* Communion; the first time in their history. Also, we have meditation in my Sunday School class.

Not long – yet – but silent prayer, just the same, and they know what it is, and why.

I have just received Reel No. 4 of the 1961 Maui tapes. It is the most!

Bless you. I'm so glad you're around.

Love to Emma,

Dear Barbara –   July 30, 1961

The attainment of the conscious awareness is the full demonstration. From here on in, It will fulfill Itself and *you will be the travelling salesman showing forth the samples!*

You need make no decision. It will announce Itself without "taking thought" on your part.

And so happy you are all with us.

Lovingly

Joel

Dear Barbara   London
                                                    August 1, 1961

Talk about the passing of time: – we left Hawaii early March for a 7 week trip – and we are still travelling! The story reads like New York to Brooklyn via Tokyo and Seattle! You will hear it all in L.A. as we will stop there en route home. Will have a group in our suite.

The Aug & Sept *Letters*, together with 2 tapes, London 1961 Closed Class constitute a lesson. And there are two tapes in the Open Class with new Scriptural Quotation lessons.

Heartfelt thanks for the thoughtful gift enclosed. Greetings to your group.

Emma joins me in love to you and the family –

Joel

Friday
August 25, 1961
Dear Boss,

Well, so much has been going on that I feel the need to really touch base, and bring you up to date on me. What I mean is that I want to check some evaluations and be sure that I am not off the track, and just suffering some sort of self-hypnosis.

First of all, and most important, I am at rest. I do not mean that this is a full demonstration nor that I can maintain it all the time. But that awareness, which I really never thought to accomplish, began about three weeks ago and has moved into an understanding of what it means to be at rest. This means to me that I have stopped the struggle. I know what it means to abide in the word and let it abide in me, and have that be enough.

At the same time, however, I feel that I do not have an awareness of a State of Grace. I know it's out there somewhere, or *in* there somewhere, but I do not have it. I do have the feeling that there is a big revelation sitting and waiting to come through. But I also feel that I have not been able to achieve sufficient purification, or dedication (or what have you) to let it come through.

I have a strong desire for this purification and want to explain something else that troubles me a little. (I know that I am not being too coherent, but I have not fully thought this out and so am just writing as it comes to me and know that you will try to make sense out of it). You see, Joel, I know who you *are* – and therefore – as much as I love both you and Emma socially I sometimes feel that it is a terrible waste of time (of which I have all too little with you) to just let the conversation take the mundane channels which Edward seems to prefer, or enjoy, when we are with you. Not that I don't get spiritual benefit from just being in your presence, because I simply put in the plug (somewhere around your forehead) and let the current run between us unhindered, no matter what the conversation seems to be. And yet, I know there is a better and more dedicated way to be taught, spiralling right up to where no words are necessary at all. So I am always left with the feeling that I have wasted both your time and mine when we are not "working." (I don't mean struggling!).

Anyhow, this is all leading up to a request I want to make of you if you can find the time for it, that when we come to Honolulu you try to find at least a couple of times a week when I can come to you alone. Edward does not seem to feel the need to work in the way I seem to need – and I don't want to get in his way. But I don't want him to get in my way, either. So I would like to come alone just for the specific purpose of being taught – in any way you are led to teach me.

So much for that. Now there is another matter I want to take up with you. As you will remember, it shocked me when you said to me that it was my Consciousness holding our group together. That was very hard for me to accept, or understand. And I had certainly always consciously felt that it was *your* consciousness that held the thing. Now, I still feel that way, and more so since I see the results of that statement.

As I have already written you, practically no one comes any more – and now even Ginny and Mother don't come. So it is usually just Edward and I alone, although the last three weeks Mrs. D. has come back. Also, at the time you suggested I start the class on Scriptural Quotations I told you that I didn't think anyone in the group would accept me in that capacity and in order to test it, I put out the feeler with my sister and mother by just telling them frankly what you had said about my Consciousness in the matter and that you had asked me to start this class. It met with a complete blank in both of them, and I was confirmed in my opinion that not only could they not see me in this capacity but somehow found the idea offensive to their own conceptions of their state of advancement.

Just by way of putting the record straight, even as I know that you – from your advanced position – can look back at the rest of us and gauge accurately just where we are on the Path (because you have already covered the ground) so do I know that their understanding, at this time, is different from mine. However, they are just as dedicated as I am, just as sincere, just as hard working and serious. They are both accomplishing growth at a very fast rate, and they may both grow beyond my understanding at any moment. At the same time, however, I have nothing but sympathy with their viewpoint about me, because in our human lives together for many years they were both intellectually dominated by me, and I know that they have both inwardly yearned to be able to stand on their own feet and not be led by me. And I, too, wish this for them.

Anyhow, at the time I started the tape group I did it because the Reading Room in Hollywood had been closed and there was no other place available for them to hear tapes and I wanted to make them available. But now there are many groups going in Los Angeles, some of them even closer to them than my house, or as close; and S. now has a functioning reading room where they can even go at their own convenience so that they no longer need to depend on me for this.

I am having the very strong feeling to close out my tape group entirely. I am actually feeling a spiritual urge to do this – as if it were a kind of complete emptying of the bottle. But there is a human reason, too, and that is that no one is taking advantage of having the tapes available, and I, myself, hear them daily (most always) by myself, and this is very satisfactory to me.

If you have any thoughts on this matter I would be anxious to have them. I don't want to do anything rash, nor arbitrary, but I have the feeling that since I don't know "how to go out or come in," the sooner I reduce to nothing, the better. In other words, maybe my tape nights have been sort of a crutch for me, too (like people who can tell themselves they are good because they go to church on Sundays), and without them I'll be thrown more inward. I feel a terrible need to get empty of everything and everybody, and I feel maybe we need to cut even this tie between my sister, my mother, and me.

Well, dear boy, give me the benefit of your wisdom.

We'll be arriving on September 15th for 2 weeks. See you then.

Love,

Dear Barbara: August 26, 1961

Number one, of course there will be plenty of time made available for you for these sessions at Halekou, so do not limit yourself too much. Number two, regarding your tape meetings. I think you probably emptied out those meetings yourself by indiscretions, but with the realization of Truth there will be still a new unfoldment. I know that C. is looking forward to coming to you for tape meetings, because he told me that immediately that you mentioned it to him he felt the rightness of it so much, and such a bond, that he really wants to attend.

When I explained to you that it was your consciousness holding the group, I was not speaking personally in the sense of any personal virtues, but that it was your attained state of spiritual consciousness that was responsible. Now, this is absolute truth. Nothing can rise higher than the consciousness of the individual, nor can a demonstration ever be less than that of the consciousness of the individual, although the nature of the demonstration may change. If I point out to you that in New York there were two people who tried to make a go of tape meetings, and neither one succeeded in holding a group more than a few weeks, and then along comes L., and beyond all question, hers are the largest tape groups in the United States, and not only this, but her work, is deep and continuous, and progressively larger, and even more fruitful financially. The answer, of course, is the attained consciousness. In San Francisco, where I certainly had more students than even in Los Angeles, no one has been able to hold a tape group together, even up to this time, and so you can see that it isn't the Message alone, nor the author alone, but there must be the attained *consciousness* of the individual in charge of the work.

However, where you made your mistake was you *told* it, and that is fatal in this work.[1] The only value there is to what we know is in *keeping it sacred and secret*, and the minute we voice the deep things of the Spirit, they are lost. The only exception to this is in teaching, and that is because the teacher has enough discernment to reveal these things only to those who can receive them.

So on this score, do not trouble yourself at the present time, but we will take it up when you are here.

Aloha to all of you,

Joel

Note: Following are Joel's Letters to the Tape Group Leaders.

Dear Friend: September, 1961

The best answer to the subject of bomb-proof shelters is a joke recently to the effect that, on the subject of bomb-proof shelters, this man says that he is not going to have one, because he wouldn't like to find himself above with the kind of people who buy shelters. And I do think it would be a pretty terrible thing to come out of a shelter

---

1   Joel is referring to my previous statement that I just "...frankly told them what you had suggested to me." He meant I should have found a better way to handle it.

above, if such a thing is possible, and find that practically all the rest of our world was gone.

When this Berlin situation came up,[1] I did my work, and I did it with a few hundred students around the world in groups while traveling, and finally came to a complete sense of peace on the subject. I do not believe that a major catastrophe could take place, and my inner Soul be so completely at peace.

And regardless of what eventualities must come, or should come, be assured that I will stand on the first verse of the Ninety-first Psalm, and the fifteenth chapter of John. And on top of this, of course, I always have the major principle of the Infinite Way, which tells me that there are neither good appearances nor bad appearances, because *the nature of all appearance is illusory*, and how can there be a good illusion or a bad illusion? An illusion is an illusion, and that settles it!

In 1948 I met a religious fanatic who feared the coming of the end of the world and who had quite some means, and so he bought himself a piece of property that had a natural stone cave on it, and he kept it stocked with six months' food supply, and also a stock of underwear and outer clothing, overcoats, gloves, etc. Owing to the perishable nature of the food, he had to destroy this food every six months and put in a new stock, and I guess every so often he had to change the clothes, too. And for all I know, he may still be doing it. The question I would like to know is this, what difference does it make to the world whether this man lives or dies? What is he contributing to the world? What does that sniveling life amount to; that scared, frightened, cowardly existence?

Personally, I think we can make a greater contribution to this world if we spend an hour every single day in spiritually knowing the Truth that might prevent such a catastrophe, because remember, there is *nothing* to the

---

[1] This was the time of the Berlin "air-lift."

belief of incurable disease, or impossible situations. All things are possible to God, and for as long a life span as I have on earth, *I am going to spend it in the realization of the non-power of the world of effect, and the non-power of the carnal mind.*[1] And at least I'll make a little contribution to bringing heaven to earth, even if a bomb snuffs my life out two, or three, or five, or ten years sooner than nature would take me from the scene in any event.

One who is on the Spiritual Path is constantly being confronted with the terms (spelled with small s's) self-preservation, self-protection, self-maintenance, and safety and security from the standpoint of self. On the other hand, the same words, can be spelled with capital S. Now, what is the meaning of Self-protection with a capital S, or Self-maintenance with capital S, or Self-preservation with a capital S? Of course the answer is that if God is our Selfhood, we have an in-built preservation, protection, maintenance. If God is individual Self, that is, if God is the Self of the individual, then we have an in-built safety and security, all of which makes clear the Master's words, "I have meat the world knows not of." Just ponder that statement for a few days, "I have meat the world knows not of," and see if it doesn't reveal to you that I have a protection, I have a safety, I have security, I have a peace, I have supply, I have an inner grace, and the world knows nothing of these, because the world is seeking these outside of Self. The world is seeking safety and security outside of itself, and it is seeking supply, and name, and fame, and riches outside of itself, and yet all the time "I have meat the world knows not of."

Yes, not only I, but *the group of students I have placed all around the globe and around the clock, are working daily,* specifically, consciously, and constantly. Before the Labor Day holiday, when the papers were telling how many accidents there would be over that long holiday, and how many deaths, etc., our group in Chicago took up specific

---

[1]   See Glossary, "carnal mind."

work on this problem, with the result that throughout the entire period of the long Labor Day holiday there was not one fatality in Chicago, and only one fatality in all of Cook County. And what is even more remarkable, yesterday we had word from Canada that over that same long holiday, from west coast to east coast in Canada, the accidents were at the lowest rate of any year in the past seven years. This is a remarkable showing, but it indicates what can be done when we face the threat of death, accident, limitation *without fear*, and with the conviction that *since the carnal mind is not of God, it is not ordained with power.*

Let us never fear to look death in the face, because *neither life nor death can separate us from the love of God*, and only as we face it in the conviction that since it is not of God, it is not Power or Presence, can we meet the issue successfully. To fear "man whose breath is in his nostrils," or to fear what princes can do unto us, or to fear what mortal man can do, is certainly not to take a spiritual stand.

I know that you will remember that 1959 work on the subject of *impersonalization and nothingization*. Only the constant remembrance of these will enable you to be of spiritual help to the world in its present situation.

Please believe that all over the world there are millions of people who humanly would like to do something about this international situation, and I am sure that you must know that no one in the world wants to do more about it than the President of the United States and the heads of state in the western world. On their shoulders rests so much responsibility, and I am sure that they are praying to God morning, noon, and night for strength, for wisdom, for judgment, and decision. And you know that this is not sufficient, because you know that it is *only in proportion as spiritual power is brought to light* that this entire cold war and threat of a hot war will come to an end.

Now, who is able to give this spiritual help? Surely not those who are frightened by it, or who permit the situation to overcome their emotions. *Those who are capable of giving spiritual help will be those who do not minimize the human danger, but at the same time are not fearing "man whose breath is in his nostrils,"* and certainly not fearing what mortal man can do.

We are really doing something serious about this situation, and we are doing it every day of the week. One thing we are not doing, I can assure you, is this: we are not *fearing* the situation. We are not fearing what mortal man can do, nor are we minimizing the human danger. But neither do we fear death. We have come to understand the eternality of life, and that no one is going to remain on this plane forever, and so we shall not fear if we are called upon to lay down our lives in upholding freedom, justice, equity.

We might actually fear to live if our government should prove to be one of those that reneges on its promises and on its commitments, but we will never be afraid to die if we are called upon to do so in upholding our government in maintaining its word and its commitments. I would not be afraid to die, but I would certainly be afraid to live in fear of temporal power.

To pray for world peace, it is necessary to face each moment with *no fear of temporal power since Spirit is the all and only power.*

Aloha greeting,

Joel

Note: Following is Joel's letter to the Tape Group Leaders.

Dear Friend: October, 1961

I think that during your Scriptural quotation series you could set aside one lesson for the subject of grace at mealtimes, and the subject of blessing every home we enter.

In Psalm 72, verse 19, there is the statement, "Let the whole earth be filled with His glory," and of course it would be a wonderful thing, on sitting down at a table where there is already food on it, to consciously remember, "and let the whole earth be filled with His glory," meaning that our prayer and benediction is that just as our own table has the abundance of God's grace, so is it the desire of our hearts that all of the earth, unto the ends of the earth, shall be filled in like manner with His glory. Then there is that other that we use so frequently, "The earth is the Lord's and the fullness thereof," and, "Son, all that I have is thine." This, of course, should be addressed universally, as if the one saying grace were looking out upon the world and realizing that since the earth is the Lord's and the fullness thereof, God is saying to all of the world, "Son, all that I have is thine." Of course the main thing shall be that the object of grace is the giving of thanks that the earth is filled with God's glory, and that the motive of prayer of the one saying grace is that this glory be made manifest universally, impersonally, and impartially.

There are, of course, many other passages which students can look up for themselves, just so that they go to their meals or snacks with the conscious realization of the Omnipresence of infinite abundance.

The question must often arise in the thoughts of thinkers, "Why was I born, and to what end am I here on earth, and am I fulfilling that which I have come to do?" The answer, of course, is always in the negative, especially since we all know that we are not fulfilling ourselves to the highest of our capacities. Therefore, it is inevitable that we are eager to seek to learn how we may glorify God on earth, *how we may be a transparency* through which God reaches the earth.

We in the Infinite Way have learned that the human scene is devoid of God, *except where an individual becomes a transparency through which, and as which, God is made manifest.* Or putting it into other words, Paul says that, "We are creatures, not under the law of God, neither indeed can be, except the Spirit of God dwell in us." We know that the human being living separate and apart from conscious awareness of the Presence of God is this gross creature, whereas the individual consciously filling himself with the Spirit of God, consciously living, moving and having his being in the awareness of God's Presence, becomes actually the living Presence of God, and that wherever he is, God is, and wherever he is, the blessing and benediction of God is shining through. It is for this reason that the Master said to his disciples, in the tenth chapter of Luke, fifth verse: "And into whatsoever house ye enter, first say, 'Peace be to this house'."

This must bring up in the student the immediate awareness that the only reason he can say, upon entering a home, "Peace be to this house," is because the grace of God is with him, and the Peace of God is with him, and therefore his very presence, or hers, becomes a blessing and a benediction. This brings to mind also that, "The place whereon I stand is holy ground," and that even to bring this passage to conscious remembrance is a blessing and a benediction, whether we are standing in a home, on the street, in an airplane, or on a bus: "The place whereon thou standest is holy ground," and "Peace be to this house."

Both with the remembrance of grace at meals, and with this Peace in every home, or business, or shop we visit, we are consciously declaring the Presence and Power of God, and releasing grace into the consciousness of all those present. With this practice, *if the intent of the heart is pure,* miracles must follow in the experience of the student and into the homes and businesses where the student visits.[1]

You see how it is that with no organization, no sermons, no edifices to build, or support, and no special laws to obey, here we are, each a temple of God, each a transparency through which God's grace flows, and *everyone can perform this without interfering with his obligations to his home, his family, his business, his church;* but on the contrary, with each remembrance of this work, add an additional blessing onto his own household.

It would be interesting to start teaching these two points to children, and let us witness the fruitage in their experience.

Peace, be still,

Joel

Note: In the Introduction to this book I acknowledged that in twenty-nine years of my teaching ministry I have never had a student come to me with any kind of problem that I have not had to overcome in my own life. Relationships was one of them. By the Grace of God in 1976 I had classes come through which gave us rules to live by, and they moved us fifty to seventy per cent forward in being able to handle our relationships at an adult level.

I was tempted not to include this letter, but the whole purpose of this book is to give an

---

1   While I was still in Christian Science I was one day wrestling with the statement, "Blessed are the pure in heart, for they shall see God." I really sweat with it, not understanding the real meaning of *pure.* At long last I turned to Webster where the definition was: Pure: "to be *free* of anything unlike itself." Then the revelation came, "Ah, you will see God when you *can't see anything else.*" <u>That</u> is to be "pure in heart."

honest account of my progress. Today, there are, for me, no relationship problems, and there have not been for a long time. But this book is entitled This Pilgrim's <u>Progress</u>, *not* This Pilgrim's <u>Leap to Perfection.</u> *It just didn't happen that way for me, nor for my students. We took one step at a time. The following letter is how I saw it then. Little by little I saw that all that had happened was that my feelings had been hurt and that, despite my declarations about being "grown up," it was "kid stuff." I grew up, gradually, but it was not until 1986, with the classes on Script, that I found the "Truth that made me Free" and, consequently, was able to help others to their Freedom. Hurt feelings and relationships are serious human problems. They are not resolved overnight. And it seems they are never resolved unless one is led, by Grace, to the right methods. We were graced with these.*

Dear Joel,   October 4, 1961

Well, I think most of the pieces are in place, so here comes another book of evaluation. This may be the last letter I write about all this human nonsense, because as you certainly know, after receiving Grace, no words are necessary. In fact all the words are now inside of me as bright, shiny tools and it only remains to keep them working.

I haven't been writing you all the processes of growth during the past two years, mostly because I feel your mail is heavy and that there was not much point in just recounting to you each forward step I took since you, certainly, already knew all the steps and had been through them all yourself, and it couldn't be very interesting just to have thousands of students sending in daily profit and loss statements – so I tried to confine mine to just those which were the most important.

However, in between the three big ones there were countless small ones. I now, however, feel that perhaps I should have kept you current since you mentioned in your house when I was there that polite students kept in contact with you. I suppose it's a matter of degree – and if I have seemed remiss in degree – I hope you now understand why.

As to the growth – from ignorance to Grace in four years is not a bad record, I think. And I want to thank you for the steadfast help you have been to me in achieving this. And help you have been, although there have been times when I wished I might have had more direct contact with your Consciousness. In fact there have been a few times when my feelings have been a little babyish in the thought that you were giving others more than me. For instance I was a little rueful in Chicago when I knew that you were giving E. a session almost every day and mine was held down to one – of five minute's duration. However, I told myself that perhaps that was because you felt I needed less – and since you were able to give me conscious awareness of the presence of the Christ in that 5 minutes – I certainly didn't feel like complaining. And then in the Los Angeles Class when I was able to get the realization of the risen Christ and the fact that "I" was a *temple undefiled* – and always had been – from the first class – I again had no reason to complain about progress. Grace, in Honolulu, took a little longer – didn't it? Two quiet sessions and one stormy one – but even so it was accomplished.

So much for the spiritual things – and after that it possibly shouldn't be even necessary to write about any of the human ones – but I still feel within me that the record isn't complete – so I want to clear the record and then we can forget about the human.

I have learned many, many lessons from the Honolulu episode – all of them important. First of all, I made my original mistake by outlining. I haven't outlined consciously for ten years. In fact, since I received my humility experience ten years ago, my life has

consciously been turned over to the government of God.[1]
It was at that time a sort of blind surrender and is in no
way comparable to what I have learned from you.
Unconscious outlining, however, is quite another matter
and I have been guilty of this from time to time; none
more so than when I unconsciously outlined just how
my Grace would come to me in Honolulu. (That it *would*
come, I knew). I realize that, in the back of my mind, I
had a nice, neat little picture of some wonderful quiet
sessions with you for two weeks, then coming home, and
then a quiet unfoldment sometime after. That, obviously,
wasn't what God had in mind at all, because, while come
it did, it came in 5 days, after a hard lesson and 2 days of
desperation.

Of course, I can now see that the whole thing was
necessary just as it did unfold. For one thing, while
Edward has often criticized me in the past for many
things, they have all been in the line of my
insufficiencies as a woman, a mother, or a human being.
Neither he, nor anyone else, for that matter, had criticized
me – or to use scripture – "persecuted me and reviled me"
for trying to know God aright.

Now, the human criticism hasn't done me any harm,
nor much good – but criticism of my spiritual search
finally showed me that that was the proof that I had
entered the company of the blessed. My conscious
awareness of Grace followed that revelation.

Just in passing, and to witness to the infinite way in
which God works, I received in Honolulu a letter from
Mrs. D. (the one who has been having the husband
trouble) telling me of the newest revilings she had been
subjected to by her husband – including tearing the *Bible*
she was reading out of her hand and throwing it at her
and telling her that she couldn't read that in his house,
and that she wasn't going to bring his children up as

---

[1]   What I call the "humility experience" is that moment when the pilgrim *realizes* he is at
the end of his human resources, drops to his knees, and cries out, "God help me. I *can't* help
myself." Actually, we are not worth much until we have passed that milestone.

Christians; that Jesus was just a dirty man in an old bathrobe who didn't even wear shoes, etc. Now I had told her before I left for Honolulu that the time would come when she would be able to look on him as her blessing, but that was just my intellect which told me that must be true. After my experience in Honolulu (and just at the moment when she needed it) I was able to write her that because of my own enlightenment on that subject I was able to tell her that what I had told her was "revealed truth," and that the passage of time would also reveal to her that she was in the company of the chosen. So it worked for her good as well as mine.

One thing I never bothered to write you, by the way, was the miraculous working out of the problem which my relative (who was in the psychiatric ward of General Hospital, you remember) was involved in. But it was a wonderful experience and out of it I learned once and for all not only the necessity for "getting out of the way" – for "resting in the word," for "being still and beholding the salvation of the Lord" – but how to do it.

As to the problem with Edward. First of all, in the human picture he has never seemed to want me to be very close to anyone else but him, and time after time he has (probably unconsciously) found some way of throwing a wedge in between me and other people so that they are required to choose between him and me. Without exception they have chosen him and his way. This is undoubtedly because he ·has seemed more important to them than I have. One of the reasons for this is that his manner is reserved and austere, and this causes people to want to please him, whereas I am very outgoing and have always been "very easy to get." From the human standpoint, his manner arises out of a strong desire to preserve himself; whereas mine arises out of what is an actual inner security and a lack of concern about preserving myself.

Also in the human scene Edward is somewhat anti-social. Social contacts have never interested him. He is, in that way, truly self-sufficient. However, he also has a

concern about what people think about him. I have
served this in the way of always having been a social
buffer. I have maintained the social contacts, I have
returned the dinners and the courtesies given to us by
others. Ignoring it would have embarrassed me (so
perhaps I did it selfishly). He has both the baronial
attitude of being entirely willing to support everybody, or
take care of them; but fealty, subordination, and high
respect he expects as if it were his divine right. Not God's
divine right, but Edward's.

Now, the problem came up in Honolulu, and that was
part of the problem about my coming to you for lessons.
After the second day he was very put out and told me
that he had not come to Honolulu to spend all his time
with the Infinite Way and that if I *had*, I should tell him,
and he would go home. After the first night he would
not go back to the Study Center, saying he "had been." He
did not intend to invite any of the Infinite Way people,
although we had to spend two days with some of the
men from his office who happened to arrive in Honolulu
at the same time.

The third day he said, "Now Joel tells us that he
doesn't even need to know your name, or where you live
– and you know that as well as I do. Then why is it
necessary for you to go to see him to get help?"

I tried to explain that what he said was true but that
there certainly was an added something that a student
could get from being in the actual presence of your
Consciousness. He didn't understand that at all. He said
it wasn't necessary for him, that he could get all the help
and instruction he needed from your books, or from
listening to the tapes, and I should be able to do so, too.

Now that was what I was trying to explain to you the
last time I had a lesson – when you shut me off. I did not
intend to complain about or criticize Edward because
certainly I know that this is not the true "he" and I do not
fasten it to him (and in this particular case he had no
choice because he was simply being a necessary

instrument for my own growth. If it hadn't been he it would have been someone else). Even in a human way it is not my nature to criticize – I observe and evaluate – but I do not condemn.

And I must say that for a couple of days this really hurt my feelings because while I know that when you shut me off you were simply seeing the whole thing as hypnotism, you, yourself, in a human way did immediately act to succor, not me, but Edward. When I sat down on the same couch with you at A.'s house you moved over near Edward. You spent a long time talking with him at the Tea House – and I knew that while you were also being "at one" with him, you were salving what were his wounded feelings. And my feeling was that while Edward could never have done *anything* that would have caused me to shut you out, he was able to make you shut me out. Of course, that is all in the human picture – and right while I was feeling rejected something very deep was saying, "You know that Joel not only would not reject you, but could not, for you are one." So that finally dissolved into the Grace experience, too.

Now I feel sure that you told both D. and M. not to discuss the matter with me. First of all, because M. had at first mentioned to me how sharp Edward's manner was with me, but when I saw her later she was very tense and "clammed up" and D. said that she couldn't get involved in any personal conflicts with the students, that her students were always trying to get her down into the human with them and she just couldn't do that. Well, I had certainly not asked her to – and wouldn't have asked her to – because, again, that's kid stuff – and I'm no child. But since I hadn't asked her to, nor even mentioned it, her saying that to me was an indication that you had said something to her.

You see, Edward feels completely your equal, I am sure – and he expresses this by saying that while he has not needed to come to you for help, you have come to him for help.[1]

Now, I *don't* feel your equal – and that is because I *know* you. And I *do* know you, but do you know me? I think perhaps you do not know me as well as I know you.

In that regard, you will remember that some time ago I wrote you that my loyalty to you was unequivocal. That you could make mistakes with me and I would not criticize you but would continue to hold out my hand in love and gratitude for all you had done for me in the past, and for just being what you were. Now that statement was not the emotional outrushing of an immature "fan" of yours. It was not made until after three years of being a student and after mature consideration as to whether I could back up that statement. Because I surely knew when I made it, that the day would come when I would be asked to prove it and I felt ready to assume that responsibility.

And the time has come – because I do feel that in this episode with Edward you did not evaluate me correctly – from a human standpoint only (because, certainly you have never made a spiritual mistake with me – and I am sure you never will).[2]

As to the matter of the church, last Saturday the problem came up which I knew would come up one day – that of my becoming a member. I explained to the Minister why I was not, and never could be a member. I explained that my life had been turned over to the government of the indwelling Christ and that while that very Christ had led me into his church in order to serve the children there, it might tomorrow lead me somewhere else, and that if I were inwardly told to go, I

---

[1]   Joel had had a copyright problem. One of the lawyers who worked for Edward was an expert on copyright and he solved the problem for Joel.

[2]   Sometime after this incident Joel said to me, "I have only been personally attached to two people in my life. Edward is one of them." Life is as it is, and that is just the way it was.

would go. I explained that I was not there serving an institution, nor even humans, but was there serving God, and that if in that service others were benefited, it was only proof that He was, indeed, a God of infinite love, that in serving my own spiritual growth I would also serve others. This he accepted and said that the issue would never be raised again, that they were very grateful to have me there on any terms which I found acceptable. So that's over.[1]

Now as to the Center.[2] I have a question to ask. If you ask people to support this, isn't that acting as a kind of crutch to the consciousness which you tell me should maintain and sustain it? And if it is, isn't that just what you tell us you will not do? I can see how you might want to pass along any checks which people send *you*, personally, for the help or maintenance of the Center – but, again, I wonder how inspired they might be to do that if B. had not given the impression that you had asked her to do this. My only point in asking the question is that, even while I do not want ever to "fool" myself about any demonstration, I don't think you, or anyone else, should "fool" himself about whose consciousness is at work. In other words, if you *want* a center, yourself, and want it supported by your students – fine – just ask for it and I'm sure everyone would want to do it. On the other hand, if you really feel yourself disassociated with its demonstration – then it isn't being disassociated to ask people to contribute to it, is it?

As for myself, I find that I do not feel any closer to this proposed center than I do to others, and perhaps not quite so close. Therefore, if it meets with your approval, I

---

[1] It turned out that it was *not* over. Organization was creeping in and, as always, bringing trouble with it.

[2] Joel had agreed to let someone run a Center, for profit, who would not, herself, teach, but who would provide a "place" where the "teachers" could teach; in other words, a "group" activity. Emma had demurred with him when he told us about it saying, "Don't you remember when we tried to do this in Washington as a group activity and it just fell apart? I think that if there is to be a Center it must be raised up by the Consciousness of one person – and maintained by that person." Emma was right because misunderstandings arose and a lack of harmony.

should like to increase my tithe and split it among the three centers.

As I told you recently in your house, I do tithe, over all, more than ten percent of my gross income – but I do not send it all to the Infinite Way.

And so again I say in a small way, but with absolute sincerity.

Love and Gratitude,

Dear Joel,   October 6, 1961

Well, at least I have two cheerful things to write you about before one uncheerful one.

First of all, I think the October *Letter* is absolutely the most wonderful thing I have ever read. It is even, for me, greater than the Lausanne articles. I think that if one could only have one thing, this would be it. There is such *joy* that comes out of it that I cannot read it without tears. Also, it is very close to me because Grace has been my recent experience. It never will cease to amaze me, the infinite degree of the operation of this message, because I know that the October *Letter* was prepared some time ago, and yet here it comes, a letter on Grace, just as it comes to me. Thank you.

Secondly, you may remember that I told you that I had given Bob Arthur, the producer of *Spiral Road* and Rock Hudson, the star, each a copy of *Thunder of Silence* with the suggestion that they read it before starting shooting on the picture, since *Spiral Road* deals with an atheist who has a "conversion experience," and I knew they were trying to do an honest job and thought this would be of great help. It may interest you to know that two nights ago Arthur told me that he was holding up revisions on the script until he could finish *Thunder* and until John Lee Mahin (the writer on the screenplay), to whom he had given a copy, could read it. I think this is terribly exciting. Furthermore, Arthur has used the phrase "thunder of silence" in the dialogue and actually would like to change the title of the picture to "Thunder of Silence." This thought has come up to him while Edward has been in Munich and he hasn't had a chance to speak to Edward about it. If he does, and if Edward, also, would be drawn to this, what would your feeling be about letting them use the title?

Now, as to the uncheerful thing. I want to write you something from my heart, Joel – although I always do write from my heart, anyway. But this is something about which I seem to feel as keenly as I did when I felt compelled to explain to the minister at the church my attitude about not becoming a member.

It has to do with the "25 group" here. At the meeting M. brought up a problem which she said she wanted advice on. She said that she had had a telephone call that morning from a student of hers who had apparently received the form letter you had sent out about bomb shelters in which you mentioned something about the groups who were meeting to do world work. M. mentioned that you have in the past asked that this "25 group" be kept secret and said that she did not know just how to answer her student and what did we all intend to do if we were asked similar questions, since probably students of ours might also receive the letter. It apparently was being sent to all those who are receiving the *Monthly Letter*. Now I made no comment. Some of the others made no comment. And some of them said that they thought the matter could be got around in some general way without admitting that they actually attended such a group. M.'s student had asked her if she were part of such a group.

Now M. said she had dissembled with her student and I feel that anything that could cause a teacher to have to be even in the slightest equivocal with a student could only result in an adulteration of their relationship. So I made no comment at all. On the other hand, M., herself, was uncomfortable and not sure that she had done just the right thing.

B. said right out, "I think we should keep this thing exclusive, after all we are advanced students and they are not." This answer did not sit comfortably with me and above all for the reason that you, in this last form letter had, yourself, mentioned the existence of such groups, and I have noticed before, for instance, in the matter of allowing people to take Closed Classes, that while you recommend for their own sakes that people who have not prepared themselves with the writings should wait for a Closed Class, still you have never, to my knowledge, excluded from a class anyone whom you felt was sincere. Also, I remember that at the Los Angeles private class, which you held in your room, you had invited a Mrs. L., and P. somebody or the other, both of whom were actual beginners, but whom you said you felt were dedicated.

Now, therefore, it has seemed to me that there has been no hard and fast rule set down by you as to just exactly who was eligible for this private work and certainly the people who attend in Los Angeles (those whom I have seen at these private sessions) are, at varying degrees of consciousness, all the way from being able to draw students and do healing work down to having to have "detachment" explained to them.

B. indicated that she felt we should not add anyone else to the group and this just seems altogether too much like an exclusive *club* to me, with a fence around it, holding out other people even though at any given time others might reach the level of consciousness of anyone who was then present. It smacks of organization to me and I can no more be a member of an "exclusive" Infinite Way club than I could join the Presbyterian church. As I told the minister there, "By the very act of signing a paper stating that I am joining your group I have indicated my separateness from all others, and my awareness of oneness will not allow me to do that."

If you wanted to lay down a rule of thumb as to who is really eligible for such a group, such as you lay down for eligibility for teacher or practitioner, in other words, if the "25 groups" consisted of people who have actually demonstrated that they not only understand the principles of the Infinite Way but practice them to the extent that they can heal, or draw and maintain students, or in other words, teach, then I feel that the consciousness would automatically be of such a level that human ego would be held at a minimum. Such a consciousness could obviously maintain itself in a group activity without dissension.

Or, if you, yourself, whenever you were in a town wanted to call together a group of students whom you felt were "dedicated" even though they may not have quite reached the healing or teaching consciousness, your own consciousness would maintain the purity in such a gathering and all would benefit from it.

As it is, now, it seems either too loose, or too exclusive, suffering from the problems of both, and this inhibits the quality of the work being done. I feel that such an arrangement can only result in friction and the eventual disintegration of such a group.

Of course, my experience is only with the Los Angeles group – other groups around the world may all be composed of individuals on relatively the same level of consciousness, and then these problems would not arise.

You, yourself, have not been entirely consistent with your instructions about the "25 groups." First of all, you have mentioned on practically all the "25" tapes that the "25" work must be kept secret, sacred, and private, and then you mention that you have set up such groups in a letter to which you are apparently giving fairly universal circulation. In other words, M.'s student is not a part of this "25 group," but she did receive the form letter in which you mention that such a group exists. Naturally, she would ask M. if she were part of such a group and M. was put to an embarrassment to explain.

I myself can completely subscribe to a policy of purity and sacredness, and I don't know but that a stringent rule of thumb for participation in a true "25 group" would automatically exclude me. I have, so far, drawn only one student and I have been party to a few healings. (One silly one being that my dog has had 3 litters of puppies. On the first two at least 3 dogs were either dead or died immediately, whereas, 2 days before she had this last litter I crawled into the dog house with her and meditated with her for about 1 hour and 13 puppies were all born alive and healthy). Also, I am able to keep my own home free of illness. However, if those things would not qualify me I would be perfectly happy to be excluded from a truly "inner circle," providing that "inner circle" were open to *anyone* who could fulfill the requirements for participation.

But when there are *no* definite requirements for participation, but a group meets as an esoteric group simply because they have been fortunate enough to have been included by you in private sessions based, not on a common level of consciousness, but simply because they were more or less dedicated – and when the leader of that group expresses herself as thinking, "We should keep this exclusive because, after all, *we* are advanced students and they are not" (and I quote directly) then to me the whole thing takes on the aspect of a private club, and takes on what, for me, is the unsavory odor of organization. And I must say, as I said to D. in Riverside, "Joel said to the class in New York which I first attended that he was dedicated to maintaining the purity of this message and to that end he would never permit organization of any kind, because he had seen that any kind of organization was an adulterant." I said I had subscribed to that concept completely because I, myself, had become disgusted with the human element I had found in all the churches I had frequented, and that was the reason why I had continued to search until I found something that seemed based on my own concept of freedom – that if there were to be, as she expressed it, "ins" and "outs" – I would have to take my place with the "outs."

I am open to your comments and unfoldment on all of this.

Continuing love and continuing gratitude,

Dear Barbara: October 7, 1961

I am sure that this is all water that has gone under the dam, and so we can let yesterday's manna take care of itself, while we turn to today.

I am sorry I have not had a tape recording machine in the house since you left here, and a new one is on order, and as soon as it comes in, your tape is on my desk, and will be heard and immediately returned to you.[1]

Regarding the matter of your tithe, you misunderstood the motive of my speaking to you, and we can let that matter ride also. I should add, also, that you misunderstood several other things, and so it is far better that we permit all of this to flow under the bridge.

The weeks roll around here so fast that I realize it won't be long until we'll be back in Los Angeles again.

Aloha greetings to you and to all of the family,

Joel

Dear Barbara   October 8, 1961

There are no words to tell you how fine a work you have done here. I won't try. Your material and your presentation are beautiful and perfect Infinite Way.

---

[1]   I had sent Joel a tape of my Sunday School class, asking for his comments.

Your Sunday School work is headed in the right direction.

You have one personal problem which must eventually be met – that of relationships.[1] It is a weak link in your chain of spiritual armour.

My Peace – be unto your Household,

Joel

Dear Joel,   October 11, 1961

Well, you almost have me speechless. And thank you for that. Also, the signals you have been sending out have been received. Thank you for that.

However, I feel I have one last gasp left, and here it is.

God has forgiven me many an indiscretion in the past, due, apparently, to the fact that I have been for the most part correctly motivated. For this and other reasons, to be correctly motivated has become of first importance with me. This is why I have bombarded you during the past four years with so many words outlining my feelings and conclusions about matters human – so that if you found me incorrectly motivated you could correct it – but also so that you would understand me and the reasons why I did things. I don't know why it seemed important that you understand me, but it was. But then it has always, for some reason, seemed important to me that the few people whom I really cared about should understand and really know me. I should add that I have always been just as concerned to understand and really know them.

I am reminded of a time when, apparently, you expected me to read your mind. Last year (or perhaps

---

[1] How right he was, and how long it took me to see it. But students must *learn*, and I did.

earlier, I can't remember for sure) when I had had tapes on order for months and had had absolutely no word from B., when I mentioned it in a letter to you, you wrote me rather sharply that the students just had to be patient with you, that you were completely re-organizing the tape department, building a new recording room, etc., and that naturally such things took time. Now wouldn't it have been a simple matter just to have inserted a note to this effect in the *Monthly Letter*, in which case, I am sure, anyone would have been willing to wait as long as would be necessary. But as it was we (and I say we because apparently there were others who also had had tapes on order for a long time and who did not know what was happening) were just left in the dark.

As you say – that is certainly water over the dam and I do not mention it for the past, but only for the future in case some other similar thing should come up. Or, perhaps, you just don't feel it is necessary to explain these things and if that is the case, I accept what I consider is your higher evaluation in the matter.

Anyhow, I know the human is all nonsense – and since I learned that from you I certainly know that *you* know the human is all nonsense. Still, what will one talk about, since, in the absolute, words are not only unnecessary but undesirable.

Well, I told you I was ready to be taught silently and I can't complain if you took me at my word!

So, dear great Silence, I am friends with you again. You notice I did not say "we" are friends, because I know you have never moved from your immutable place. But it feels nice within me to not feel estranged.

I am looking forward more than I can say to seeing you next week. Tell Emma I didn't mail the present I have for her because I thought to see her so soon.

Love and Gratitude,

Dear Barbara   October 11, 1961

I can accept the fact that all may not be in complete agreement with what is given me and so can accept your withdrawal from the "25" group. Will inform B. at once that you will not attend our Oct. 21 meeting.

In the back of my mind I probably knew from the beginning that someone would later withdraw, but since you are the first, this is my first experience of meeting the situation.

Withdrew from the family and students and found my peace in about 18 hours. This I know will also make it easier for you because it clears the entire atmosphere.

Actually, you are now a member of the most exclusive club in the world – the only member of the "Voluntary Withdrawal from the '25 Club'!!!"   "Man proposes but God disposes!"[1]

Blessings & Peace,

Joel

Dear Barbara: October 12, 1961

I am happy indeed that the October *Letter* has touched you so deeply. I am sure that if you will now go back to the *Letters* of January and April, 1960, you will also find that a high spot was touched in the unfolding of the subject of Grace.

I am certainly happy that the producer and the star of *Spiral Road* are so pleased with *The Thunder of Silence.* I am sure that with such a picture in the making, this book

---

[1] Joel was angry, and he clobbered me. I still am not sure where the Truth in the matter lies, but by Spring 1962 I was able to "drop all concern" about it.

will surely provide inspiration and ideas. As to the use of the title, of course I have no jurisdiction in these matters.

Regarding the subject of the "Twenty-five group" and these meetings, evidently you have not quite caught my viewpoint, and it is possible from your letter that others may also not be quite clear on this subject. I am sure, however, that whatever questions are open will be answered at our meeting of the "Twenty-five group" on October 21st.

Time is rolling around, and we will soon be in Los Angeles.

Peace be to this house,

Joel

Dear Joel,   October 12, 1961

Well, I never in a million years expected nor hoped for such a wonderful reaction to my Sunday School class as that. As I told you in Honolulu, I realize that I sound just like a parrot, but that is not because the words are not part of my Consciousness, I know you know they are, but there just doesn't seem to be a better way to say it than the way you do.

I feel, personally, that the two big defects in my character are an intense – no, a *too* intense faculty to "care," and impatience; with impatience far out in front.

There is, however, too much evidence to the contrary for me to feel that relationships are a big problem for me. Any more than, for instance, I would consider it a problem in relationships for you to have closed the Hollywood Reading Room. It simply was that she would not meet you at your level. And as you have said, there are people you can't deal with. Also with me, there are some who won't meet me at my level – but that does not produce any problem in relationship, one simply withdraws, without condemnation, and waits for their unfoldment.[1]

Actually, the only person I can think of with whom I have any problem of relationship is Edward, but God seems not to want us to relax into just a comfortable humanhood – so he is "Cleopatra's Needle" – and Cleopatra is his needle.

Love and gratitude,

Cleopatra.

> *Note: Sometimes my determination to be honest has a sting to it. It is most embarrassing to include this letter, which exposes the ego and arrogance I was still suffering from. But, as already mentioned, God wasn't finished with me. (He still isn't). I later learned that humility is learned through humiliation.*

Dear Joel,   October 14, 1961

I have just heard the 1956 Sydney Tape No. 1, and it has unfolded to me that it would be greater wisdom for me to simply accept your statement that I have a problem in relationships, even though at the moment I can't exactly see it. Perhaps it will unfold. Certainly, if it is a serious problem, not seeing it won't help me meet it.

I do know that I seem to have more and more trouble just living in the world. But you mention on this Sydney tape that as we progress spiritually, *"We find that we just can't get along any more with those who have not begun their spiritual awareness and we just have to let them go and wait for new associations to be brought to us on the*

---

1 Oh, Barbara. How *spiritual* we are!

Path." Now this is what I have thought was happening. Certainly, I have had to let go of many of my old friends, because we no longer have anything in common in the human picture.

On the other hand, my awareness of oneness with just everybody, even Edward – has grown by leaps and bounds. Even when I pass total strangers on the street the fact of our "oneness" leaps out at me. So I don't know just how to judge this relationships thing. However, I do know that you can see deeper into me than I can see into myself, so I just accept it, if you say so. Perhaps you will work for me on this. I will appreciate it.[1]

See you soon – am really glad,

Love and gratitude,

Dear Joel,   October 16, 1961

Thank you for your letters. I shall go to work immediately to try to put your instructions as to the Grace at mealtimes, and blessing each home which we enter, into effect.

We both seem to be doing a bang-up job of missing each other's points. I would like to ask you, in this regard, to please read again all my letters on the subject of the "25" group in about two or three months. I wrote so seriously and so earnestly that I can't believe that I absolutely failed to get across my willingness and gratitude at any time, for any reason, to be able to be in your presence and that I would only feel blessed thereby. That has nothing to do with my lack of feeling of comfort with those who do not handle it at your level.

However, I accept your edict about the October 21st meeting. As a matter of fact, I wouldn't have been there

---

[1] In 1984 my inner Voice said to me, "Relationships are what *living* is all about." So this subject was larger than I knew. No wonder it took so long!

anyway, since B. has not informed me that there was going to be such a meeting.

One thing that never fails to astonish me about the working out of the I. W., and that is how absolutely immediately we are asked to put to work any new unfoldment we receive – and I suppose I'll never get over the expectation of being able to "coast" a little while after going through the seemingly desperate struggle that, for me, so far, has preceded each large step of growth. I no sooner received my Grace than I was called on to be the channel for healings. Oddly enough, which greatly surprised me since it is such a change in my feelings, I feel no qualms about it at all. That is, of course, because I realize that Barbara not only couldn't do anything about it, but that she doesn't have to. Just has to get out of the way.

In this connection, it seems to me that the most wonderful, awe-inspiring miracle of all is the fact of *omnipresence*. Of course it's silly to compare things in infinity, but it's more impressive to me, right now at least, than the concept of omniscience or omnipotence – although I naturally realize that they are mutually existent and could not be absent one from the other.

But in this concept of healing, it is so obvious that we couldn't do it at all without the miracle of omnipresence. And speaking of omnipresence, the place whereon you stand is my holy ground. I love you, dear friend, forever.

You will never be rid of me, Joel. You drew me long before I ever met you in this lifetime, and you are stuck with me – so you'll just have to put up with me and wait for *my* unfoldment.

By the way, I think now that I was actually wanting out of the situation with Edward, but I have had a lot of growth in the last week and realize that that is impossible, and therefore not even desirable, and that in order to be rid of my "gad-fly" I must heal him. Since the healing consciousness has been opened up to me this last week, I find *that* not at all a difficult thing to do – to get out of the way, that is, and be the hole in the fence for Papa Muhl.

So you see, growth does continue and I don't feel discouraged with me, so you shouldn't either.

L. & G. (and I don't mean bourbon!),

Barbara

P.S. You are probably not aware that "L. & G." is the name of a quality American Bourbon.

Dear Barbara –   October 21, 1961

I am sure one could not have your experience with the Infinite Way or with me – and think of separating. And the other way around.

Last night's lesson was a deep inspiration to me. And it was a happy event afterwards.

Tomorrow (Sunday) I complete the mail – and then off to Tulsa and the northwest.

Love to all of you,

Joel

Note: Whew! That was a tough one. Early in 1962 I was in his hotel room with Joel and Emma when Joel said to me, "Well, I'm glad we have recovered from our estrangement." I answered, "What estrangement?" (I had forgotten!). He said, "That business about the '25 group'."

My answer was, "That was not an estrangement, I never really felt estranged.

In fact, I see our relationship as stronger than ever. One never really knows how <u>real</u> a relationship is until it has stood the test of trouble. With a lot of the students who have never been except on 'cloud 9' with you – you don't know what would happen if the relationship were strained. On the contrary, we have been through trouble and misunderstanding and you have found out that I would never leave you, no matter what. Our relationship is solid."

We then had a meditation, after which Joel said to me, "I have been told to call you daughter."

You can imagine my joy, and relief!

Dear Barbara:　　　　　　　　November 22, 1961

Thank you for your brief message just received, and please know that it is my joy to be consciously with you regarding Susie.

The phraseology doesn't matter a whit. As long as we understand each other, it would make no difference how we worded our request. As a matter of fact, some of the recent work that I have done with students has been on this very subject of prayer without words and thoughts, since *the only part of prayer that is ever answered is the motive, never under any circumstances the form.*

When we pray there is something in our heart which forms the reason for prayer, and *if this that is in our heart is in attunement with spiritual purpose*, then we may be assured of answered prayer.

The trip through the northwest continued to be as fruitful as the start in Los Angeles, and the work since our return has been on a continuing fruitful scale. I would like to call your especial attention to the tape just completed on Maui, the November 1961 Maui tape. You will find it to be of an unusual nature, and certainly an interesting one.

Please keep me closely informed until we have attained full and complete realization of freedom for Susie. Emma joins me in love to you and to all of the family,

Joel

Note: I had asked Joel for help for my daughter, Suzanne, who had developed a cyst on her temple. I worked, and worked, because I had such a strong distaste for doctors. However, it was not met, and we had to take her to a surgeon. He was a splendid surgeon and was able to perform a technique of removing it and tying off two tiny blood-vessels without even leaving a scar.

During the waiting period in the hospital my healing consciousness came through with a physical experience. Ever since then, whenever that phenomenon appears I have known the healing was complete.

It was a great lesson for me not to be absolute, but to be obedient.

Joel has said, "If you don't meet it spiritually just meet it at the level of the problem and get the mind back on God." That was sound and practical advice.

Dear Barbara: December 30, 1961

The fruit cake arrived this morning. It was mailed by air Dec. 12 but was shipped by sea. Therefore the delay in our thanks to you for your everthoughtful remembrance.

Christmas here was "different" this year. For the first time in 17 years Emma had her entire family in Hawaii: Geri & her Clark & Sue; Bill and his wife and Heidi; and Sam.

From the tapes Maui 1961 Adv. # 3 and Haw. Village 4-5-6 you can see the fruitage of the years work and the forecast of things to come.

Then we had the most wonderful tributes from Dr. Frank Lauback, Dr. Norman V. Peale, Starr Daily and Hudson Strode. (Incidentally, if the time ever comes when the Truth can be told about Lincoln, Davis & the Civil War – Hudson Strode's two books on President of the Confederacy, Davis, are shockers). And he is an authority – recently decorated for literary achievement by the King of Sweden.

You have not kept me well posted on health at home so I do not know of the response there. Answered Ed's call immediately – and continued since.

Our love to all of you and a joyous New Year,

Joel

CHAPTER 5

CORRESPONDENCE 1962

Note: In early January 1962 I sent Joel a further letter about the "25 Group." Then I had an accident. I wondered if the two situations were connected (of course they weren't, but that is where my thinking was at the time). So I called Joel and told him that I had sent him what might be construed as a "smart-alecky" letter and that if it had been, I was sorry.

He sent the letter back without opening it. I could leave it out, but that wouldn't be honest about this pilgrim's progress.

Written on the outside of the envelope was the following message.

Dear Barbara –   January 24, 1962

Since we are going to forget – why have anything to forget or remember?

Greetings,

Joel

Note: Following is the unread letter.

Okay, dear Boss,   January 24th, 1962

Settle down for a long winter's nap, because so much has been going on I think it will take me a year just to write it.

First of all, just to round off and finish up the matter of the LA Study Center. There's no point in your taking the time to re-read my letters about this, but I do want to point out to you that at *no* time did I ever mention anything about withdrawing from the World Work, nor would I ever, and even though I do not attend that particular group meeting, I have continued my world work.

My uncomfortable response was due to a concept of exclusiveness. I felt that our consciousnesses were very much out of tune on that issue, and that I could not be part of a group with which I was out of tune.

But, there was much, much more at work than met the eye. I can now tell you that all along when we were corresponding on this, I knew that I was just being used as an instrument to make it necessary for you to take another look at the whole thing, re-evaluate it, and make a definite statement about how you wanted the thing run. This you did in the way which I knew it would come from you, in the, either October or November, *Letter.* I am sure you can see now that a clarifying statement needed to be made by you to clear the air everywhere, and to leave *no one* in any possible doubt about what the guiding spirit in such groups should be. This you did, perfectly, as only you could do, and I think the whole atmosphere will be healthier as a result of this.

Now, why I was chosen as the instrument for this, God alone only knows. Perhaps I was the only one who, at that time, would risk estrangement from you for a principle – or perhaps I was the only one who was sure enough inside that when it was a matter of principle there *was no risk,* nor danger of estrangement from you. Somehow, I was given the feeling that you had come close to *caring* whether or not anyone bought or read *Thunder of Silence,* or whether or not there was a Study Center in Los Angeles, or whether or not there were world-work groups meeting over the world. I, of course, could have been wrong – but I did get this feeling. And if it were the case, certainly you don't need me to remind you that it is more important for you to maintain detachment than for all of the rest of us put together. [1]

Well, whatever it was, you made a perfect expression in the monthly *Letter* and no one now could possibly find any justification in making these meetings a personal expression or a matter for personal pride or exclusiveness, and by this public statement by you the whole work of the Infinite Way has been helped and purified.

Well, that is the end of that, and I certainly hope that the Study Center is proving to be all the things you would hope for it.

Now, my personal relationship with Edward has been completely resolved[2] – and, naturally, in the last way I would have expected. Honestly, living the life of the Infinite Way is like living in a perpetual detective story; one never knows what's around the next corner – and as surely as one falls into the trap of deciding how a thing will work out, God pulls the rug out and up comes the unexpected – always better and more perfect than one had outlined.

And what happened was this – it was at the time we were corresponding about the "25 group," and it was impossible for me to keep from Edward the fact that I was very distressed and I had to tell him a little of the nature of what was disturbing me. His reaction was unexpected. He said, "Well, frankly, I have never been entirely comfortable with the fact that the groups have a *name*, or a label, I don't much cotton to labels of any kind, and particularly a label such as the "25 group" because it seems to have such a limiting connotation – limiting in the sense of numbers and limiting in the sense that it seems to set up the idea of exclusivity. Why doesn't Joel just call

---

[1] Of course, Joel didn't *pay* me for this lesson I gave him! I wonder how he put up with me. In fact, I know why he did, because I have done the same with my over-zealous students. His patience taught me a necessary lesson since, while impatience has always been my worst defect of character, I have worked *hard* on it.

[2] I was born a "cock-eyed optimist." Foolish girl. It was years before my relationship with Edward was resolved.

these groups 'World-Work Groups', which designates a *function*, but not the idea of a membership?"

Now I'm going to butt into your business again. I don't know why I have such a compulsion that you must know everything I am thinking – but I have it – and if it's a defect in my character there's no use fighting it. So here goes. When you announced at the big, one-night class, when you were last here, that there would be a study center in Los Angeles, and indicated what its function would be – why didn't you also mention that there was a study center in Santa Monica which had been functioning for a long time? After all, S. had been the first one, and was maintaining it with her own consciousness and it was a very good and useful thing, and I thought the students would have wanted to know about its existence.

Well, I guess I'm running down. There's just one other thing – you know I have struggled with this smoking thing – and the real basis for my struggle was not being able to reconcile the scriptural teaching with what I felt within me was a deleterious effect on the body. I am referring to the statement, "There is nothing that goeth in the mouth of a man that can defile him." So I kept saying to myself, "If that be true then what one eats, drinks, or smokes simply doesn't make any difference." Yet I knew that any indulgence in these things not only seemed to hurt my body, but actually gave me a sense of loss of God contact – and I just couldn't see how that was not hurtful.

Well, you know how long I wrestled and had absolutely no light on the situation. I am happy to report that that has been corrected. Last Christmas Eve, I was wakened in the middle of the night and those words appeared before me in writing, and a voice reading them, but with an entirely different inflection from the one I had been using (I am reminded of what it did for my life when I heard you on a tape say, "I am THAT I am" when all my life I had been reading it, "I am *what* I am," and wasn't getting anywhere).¹ This voice said, "There is nothing that goeth into the mouth of man that can defile HIM!" And then I understood. Of course nothing could defile HIM, because HE was undefiled, had within him that which never had been defiled, and never could be defiled – but the body can be defiled, in the same way that one can dig in the dirt with a pair of gloves and they will get dirty. It, therefore, remains a simple matter of choice as to what kind of an instrument one wants to live with, a dirty one, or a clean one. I am not going to say that this gave me a healing (although I have not been able to smoke since then) because I have thought at times in the past that it had fallen off me, only to return. But we shall see. Certainly I am grateful for the light.²

Much love, much gratitude, much looking forward to your arrival which is, gloriously, not too far off, now.

One last thing, since, I repeat, I at no time mentioned anything about withdrawing from world-work, nor from your activity – I want you to be sure and invite me to any meetings which you hold in Los Angeles. Besides, you won't have as much fun without me.

Love to Emma,

HeavenSent
Holiday
Oh, dear man, it wasn't that bad!³   February 22, 1962

I couldn't write anything to you that would be so bad

---

¹   1957 Kailua Advanced Class.

²   That was a complete healing, with no withdrawal symptom, no struggle and never a temptation to smoke since then. I just woke up a non-smoker. Many years later, in recounting this story to some, I remembered a luncheon Edward and I had had at the Studio with Joel and Emma. Jokingly I said, "Well I wish I didn't smoke, but I guess I'll just have to blow smoke until Joel gives me a healing." He snapped back, "How much more spiritual do you think you would be if you didn't smoke?" I was thunderstruck because I saw, instantly, "Not a drop." I had received my healing right then, although several months passed before it was manifested.

³   Reference is to the unread letter.

that you couldn't read it! It was just that I was, in one instance, butting into your business again and I thought that what I meant to be only straightforward might be construed by you as rude.

However, I'm sure your instinct was right, even though you shouldn't go around throwing away hundred dollar checks like that – there was one in that letter.

There were also many other little stories of my development and of considerable development in Edward's and my situation which I thought might be of interest – and yet – oh that "water under the bridge."

What a great blessing my accident was. The world might find that a strange statement – in fact I have found that I simply will not talk to anyone about the accident because I cannot tell them the truth about it, and the story as it would "appear" just bores me so I don't want to even talk about it.

The greatest of all, of course, was that you wiped out my sense of guilt (which I know you realize has always plagued me) and my complete memory of any past life or lives, insofar as they contained any karma, with five well-chosen words, "Remember, now, there's no past."

So, love for *now,*

P.S. If you have time for a private session with me when you get in town, I do have several things I would like to check with you.

I am enclosing a check. If you want to pass it to LA Study Center that is fine with me.

Tuesday
Dear Barbara –   February 27, 1962

Picked up your letter at the P. O. Box on the way to the Lurline yesterday. Arrive LA March 3 and remain through the 8th.

Am sure you know I meant only to wipe out any previous misunderstandings and start fresh.

I will be happy to see you at the hotel 5-6-7 or 8. Why not a lunch also? Please phone Statler Hilton & we will set the day and time.

My sincere thanks for your generous enclosures.

Our united love to you and all the family,

Joel & Emma

Dear Joel,   April 17, 1962

You are *so* good for me! So is Emma!

Am enclosing check for my lessons. Am also enclosing tithe check for April.

By the way Joel, B. came up to me last Friday after the Palisades class and said to me that she thought my sister was rather upset with her because she hadn't let her know that there would be a "25 group" meeting in April. I told her that you had indicated to all the students, I thought, that notification as to your activities would be sent out from the Center by her. She said she was too busy to call everybody and that we couldn't expect her to call us. Therefore, I just wanted to ask you, whenever there will be anything in the future at which you would want us to be present, if you will please let me know, I will notify the others. We don't want to be a burden on B. and perhaps we misunderstood the situation.

Don't forget our dinner and picture, Friday, May 5th.

Love to Emma – and some for you, too,

Dear Barbara –   Easter 7 a.m.

This letter is a long list of thank yous – covering quite a page of items. But it can be summed up with a thank you because you are you.

Arrangements have been made to purchase addressing machine & have mimeographing so that notices will go out.

Resurrection is an experience which does not come to many. It cannot take place before there is a death – and who wants to volunteer for that?

We are more apt to hug the tatters of our self – rather than be unclothed first – and then clothed upon with immortality. Oh – here is the point – being unclothed – releasing those items that constitute our self – many of which we have prided ourselves upon!

I am not raised up from the tomb until Joel is dead. *The process of dying is not accomplished with one crucifixion. It is an experience of dying daily for a long time* – and even then it is good to thrust in a dagger to make assurance doubly sure.

There is Resurrection or rebirth possible.

Greetings,

Joel

Dear, dear Joel,   April 24, 1962

Thank you for your beautiful letter. I have already known that this class will be the Resurrection.

As to death – I have already had that – Barbara died in an automobile accident last January and since then there has been no past, no karma for me, and very little memory that even goes back as far as the last five or ten minutes – and if it seems desirable to do so I can even loose the last five minutes.[1]

In fact, the result of that is the dissolving of my last resistance to teaching. I have long been willing to "go for God" 85% of the time, but there was certainly 15% of desire left to "do something with Barbara." That is gone and along with the dissolving of resistance there is a growing interest in teaching, or in other ways helping to disseminate this message to the world. (I love the word "disseminate" because it contains the concept of "sowing").

However, (if I understand your letter correctly) it is good to be reminded that Barbara, too, might be resurrected at any moment (I had forgotten that!) and that the process of dying is not accomplished with one crucifixion. (I had fallen into that error, too, I think).

If your statement about loosing those things of self "on which we have prided ourselves" was directly for me, I would appreciate it if you would tell me specifically what you might have reference to – that it may be considered and worked on. In considering me as objectively as possible, it truly seems to me that I have never had much pride – in anything. If you have reference to my love of study – that is simply a natural facet of my character as others love to dance or play golf. It is never done with any desire to use it or display it, only for the joy of growing.

If, on the other hand, you have reference to mind, or intellect – please know that I have never taken any pride in intellect since my Alanon days when I got my humility through hearing the halting, ungrammatical

---

[1] This, too, turned out to be a temporary experience of Grace. After a time, humanhood reared its head again, and again.

speech of a truck driver, who taught me that he had more
spirituality in a few badly constructed sentences than I
had with all my four syllable words.

Furthermore, my mind is not *my* mind – and never
has been. My mind is a gift, an instrument of God and I
have known that there was this "other mind" in me ever
since I was a child. There have been many times, for
instance, when I was quite small, when I would be given
a conviction and I would ask myself, "Now, how do I
know that? There is nothing in my experience that
should enable me to know that – and yet I do know it – –
it must be that *somebody* is knowing it for me." Of course,
I did not know that "somebody" was God – but I have
always known it wasn't Barbara.

On the other hand, if it isn't any of these things, but
something else – I will be grateful if you will give me
some light on it.

I have heard from a couple of different sources in the
last 3 weeks (and you must have heard something like it
because you spoke on the same subject the first Sunday at
the Center) about people being a little disappointed (this is
not many, just a couple of individuals) that the work
seemed so "basic," that they had hoped for some more
"advanced" work. You should hear my little lecture that I
give on this whenever I hear this statement. I won't bore
you with the whole thing – but it begins with asking a
few pertinent questions about their lives, such as, are they
satisfied with their present demonstrations in every
department of their lives, etc. (of course you know what
they answer!).

Then it goes on to point out (as you did that Sunday)
that the very message of the Infinite Way, in its entirety,
is the most advanced study on the face of the globe; that
its basic goal is one and the same at all times (increasing,
unfolding God Consciousness); that all the words and all
the lectures are just different paths for going the same
place, but that the paths must be provided to care for the
various states and stages of consciousness of the students –

some of whom are drawn in one way, others in another; that in essence the whole message can be reduced to two words: "God is" – and then if they want more advanced work they can reduce it to one word: "God" – and then when they want still more advanced work they can reduce the entire message to no words at all – just a smile – – so that the proper question is not, "Why doesn't Joel give us more advanced work?" – but, rather – "How are *we* advancing *in* the work?" This little talk seems to straighten them out a bit.

Then, too, I noticed last night that there were quite a few attending the Closed Class who had not come to the open classes. This is just further evidence that they have not yet reached the stage where they can understand that there is no difference between classes except sometimes a slight rise in Consciousness – just as the sun is always the sun – although it *feels* hotter to us some days than others, but that is our reaction to it and has nothing to do with the *amount* of warmth *it* is sending out. I am grateful that I have been shown that it is a matter of *being in the Presence,* and not the words.

On this point – I am going to pat myself on the back a bit – I *can* be taught. And I feel I can be taught rather easily and rather quickly. However, I feel no pride in this – just gratitude. But I am noticing how quickly what is in your Consciousness transmits itself to mine. For instance, this "love kick" you're on – the first two days of the class it entered – and, as usual, I was immediately given the opportunity to prove whether it had stuck or not. The temptation arose, with two people very close to me, to fall into a pattern of being distressed by them when they did a certain thing which had caused me a lot of pain in the past – but I am grateful to report that I saw very quickly who the "Adversary" was and was able to say, "You can't fool me, you're not after her – or him – you're after *me* – but I know you for what you are" – and immediately in both cases the words came, "Neither do I condemn thee – thy sins be forgiven thee" – and Abracadabra, Presto change-o! The devil went up in smoke (till the next time!).

Anyhow it is wonderful to have this continuing proof that you *are* my teacher and that you *do* teach me Consciousness to Consciousness. That's evidence of a pretty good oneness. I know Resurrection is possible – and I am willing – as far as I know *consciously* – to pay the price. I can't speak for my subconscious because we're currently "not speaking to each other." So I don't know how *she* feels about it. We'll have to wait and see.

Pride has never really bothered me – Fame long ago lost its luster along with Name – Achievement has turned from "drive" to "unfoldment" – there has been progress. But, like Paul, there is still the thorn in the flesh. A sometimes all too unspiritual interest in the opposite sex lets me know that I am still in the flesh. Oh I don't *do* anything. But I think!

Love (spiritual type) and Gratitude!

Dear Barbara –   April 25, 1962

There is one mistake in your letter which you must correct in order that you *consciously* remember to carry this out in your IW work:

Nothing in my correspondence is personal. I am always revealing the spiritual self and/or impersonalizing and nothingizing.[1]

Regardless of what form of error you discern in a person – instantly relegate it to the carnal mind – & then *unsee* it.

This class is the Resurrection experience in which I

---

[1]   I never really understood this statement until I began my own teaching ministry. Then I learned that transcendental consciousness (i.e. the *teaching* consciousness) is always impersonal, and imparting, not to a *person*, but to *his* Christ Consciousness.

am being raised from the tomb and My presence, My peace, My grace is being revealed.

Greetings,

Joel

Note: This Closed Class at the Princess Kaiulani Hotel was my first great gut-breaking, ego-breaking experience. It was not exclusive with me. It was a comfort when one of his oldest students said, "Don't be upset, he only does that to the ones he thinks can really make it." And, of course, we all survived.

Honolulu
Sunday Morning
July, 1962

Dear Joel,

A few months ago the "impersonal" nature of my relationship with Edward was revealed to me. As you can imagine, this came to me not only as a surprise, but even as a shock – and yet I could easily see that the real root of our conflict was that I had not operated correctly in this relationship – certainly not with the objectivity that it would demand.

This was revealed to me at the same time that sonship was revealed to me (about which I told you in Los Angeles), which was later apparently revealed to you when you said you were to call me daughter.

When sonship was first revealed to me I intended, at first, to write you about it and claim it – but something held me back – and then I was glad it had because it was subsequently revealed to you, independently, and I was happy to have that confirmation. After that session in your hotel suite, on the same afternoon on which you called me daughter, there was another thing revealed to me which I again heard with intense surprise, even disbelief. I will not write you this, because if it is valid, as my revealed sonship was, it will also, in due course, be revealed to you.

Everything that I have learned of *Truth* I have learned at your feet. I will always remember this, and you will always have my continuing love and gratitude,

Dear Barbara –   July 3, 1962

We cannot be anyone's Teacher until they invite us. The Teacher-student relationship is more sacred than the marriage tie – and therefore there must be mutual recognition; and *above all, the students yielding to the Teacher*, – that is yielding in the sense of spiritual cognition.[1]

It would be well to forget students in order that you may be so established spiritually that the need to be a Teacher is dissolved.

The opening session of P.K.[2] Class last night, opens a wide vista.

Greetings of Peace,

Joel

                                             Thursday afternoon
Dear Joel,   July, 1962

Unfoldment never fails to fascinate and amaze me. I have had very few inward revelations in this lifetime, but quite a few hunches. One of these hunches came when B., just before I left, asked me to teach a class to

---

[1] He was, of course, entirely correct, and later, in my own ministry it was revealed that it is the *student* who must declare who is his teacher. That is revealed to him as: "Your teacher is the one by whom *you* have been *taught*, and *you* are the only expert on that."

[2] The Princess Kaiulani Hotel, Waikiki.

parents at the Study Center beginning in September. I told her I could not give her an answer. I said, first, that I would like to discuss it with you – and that in any event I felt that my answer would be given to me during the Honolulu class – and today here is your letter doing just that.

You use the words "...the need to be a teacher." If you think I have a need to be a teacher you know something about me that I do not know about myself. Not only do I not now feel a need to be a teacher, I have *never* felt a need to be a teacher, and have always considered myself a student, not a teacher. I enjoy the role of a student and have all my life, whereas the role of a teacher is one I would never choose for myself.

However, when you mentioned it to me, and when B. mentioned it to me, and when I received a request, in writing, from the Session of Elders of the Presbyterian Church where I had taught Sunday School, asking me to teach their adult class beginning in September, I did have to entertain the idea that it might be indicated for me, and to make myself willing to do whatever the Father wanted.

Now your letter has freed me of that, and makes it very clear that my answer to B. must be, "No."

As to the teacher-student relationship. Of course we cannot be anyone's teacher until we are asked. But that asking does not have to be in words. The "I Am" revealed to me that you are my teacher. I have not governed my own life for a long time now – in fact since the Los Angeles Class a year ago – Barbara whose breath is in her nostrils has been of no account to me. I have just been a hole in the fence with no life nor activity of my own. In fact, at that time, you wrote me, "From now on you will just be the salesman setting forth the samples" – and that has been so.

I certainly do not mean that I have dissolved all my humanhood – but as to running my own life or making my own decisions – no. I am past the point of no return on that.

In the classes you are unfolding beauty daily. I thank you for that – and for my freedom.

As ever,

Friday morning
July 1962

Since you gave us permission Monday and Wednesday night to use the jargon of the world, I will resume with

"Dear Joel,"

And by the way, I am very grateful for those nights. If I had gone home without them I don't really know what might have happened. Those nights you put us back in the world and showed us how to live in it. Without that, I don't know what might have happened in my home.   It is an unbelievable, completely uncommunicable experience to be taken apart and then put back together again.[1]

Thank you for your wonderful letter. How I wish my life and our relationship might just have rested at that point. But I have not been allowed to stand still. I have been faced with something which I could never have even conceived until it was presented to me – and, again, I must try to tell you the untellable, communicate the uncommunicable. I know you already know what I am going to try to tell you – so I ask you to please read behind and between my lines and give me the help for which I will ask. I know already this will be too wordy, too exhaustive, too analytical, but I am stumbling through very deep water.

---

1   Many years later I realized that Joel had given us a Zen experience. A Zen Master said, "Yes, Zen is the way *out*, but it is also the way back."

I have suffered in the past from many of what the world calls "neuroses," mostly of a pretty general type: fear of pain, fear of childbirth, fear of death, fear of men, fear of domination, fear of heights.

A new one I didn't know about before has been recently emerging to the surface, which I told Emma about the other day when she was chiding me about spending all my time in the kitchen at your house washing dishes – the day of the open house – I told her that as my onion skins have dissolved in the Infinite Way my *natural shyness* seems to be coming to the surface and I find I can't stand crowds, so that I had actually *fled* to the kitchen and she had done me a favor to *allow* me to stay in the kitchen.

Fear of pain and fear of childbirth were met together with the improved beliefs which had been going on over a long time, in actual "awake" experiences, about which I wrote you years ago.

I thought I had met fear of *death* and fear of *fear* in the death dream and the "Dracula" dream about which I told you in Los Angeles, and which you confirmed to me were valid spiritual experiences.[1]

After what happened to me night before last I know now that the illusions met in each case were partial, not total. Dissolving the fear of death was dissolving only the fear of life and death, of birth and rebirth. Since I have actually remembered previous lives and previous life deaths, it was fairly easy to meet – once I had been given some degree of spiritual understanding by you – by the recognition that I had *survived* all those deaths. I know now that one reason I met it with final equanimity was because I was equally sure that each

---

[1] Again, I misconstrued. Before the "Dracula" experience (recounted in full in my book *The Royal Road to Reality*) I lived with *terror*. Even as an adult I could not stay alone in the house at night. As I stated in that book, I have never experienced the emotion of fear since that time (1959). What I am describing here was really fear of annihilation, in the spiritual sense. That is, the "dying daily" that ultimately results in the loss of the sense of personal self.

death would be followed by rebirth. I wasn't aware of that consciously, but I now know I felt a subconscious assurance, that tho' I died, I would equally surely be born again, so what difference did it make.

Fear of heights and fear of crowds have both struck me rather forcibly here, as evidenced by my feelings at the open house; and by the fact that I have not been able to go near our balcony without a sinking feeling in my stomach and hanging on for dear life to the railing. Yet I haven't worried about either of them. I felt they were onion skins and didn't need anything from me but to be turned from, and for my mind to be fastened on God.

Till night before last – that is. Then I was given a dream – or more correctly a nightmare – which brought both those fears into focus and then revealed their symbolism. I will just tell it to you as it unfolded to me, hoping that you have not already lost patience.

I dreamed that my mother and I had gone to the beach. We couldn't get down to the water because of the high cliffs, but we decided to climb down onto the cliffs to get some sun. (I will skip all the long wandering that went on and just get to the point). Somehow there formed, at the edge of the sand, out over the water, a huge crowd in bleachers, or stands, row after row of them. They began laughing and jeering at us. They seemed so inimical that they began to frighten me and I decided to get away. When I tried to retreat I found that we had inched out on a terribly narrow ledge and all of a sudden I looked down and saw the sharp rocks below and my head began to swim and I became terrified of falling. I closed my eyes and pressed back into the face of the cliff. I couldn't move, I couldn't walk. I thought of getting down and crawling but my knees were trembling so that I felt if I even moved I would hurl myself off the cliff – and the noise of the crowd was getting louder and more hysterical.

Then, right through the dream, I said to myself, "Joel said in *Leave Your Nets* that every student would be brought one day to the cliff and be asked to jump and when he did, that broke the illusion. Now is your time, all you have to do is jump."

Joel, up until now, every spiritual challenge which I have been given to meet either "awake" or in "dreams," I have met – with its accompanying freedom. But honesty compels me to report that not only was I not able to meet this – but I was terrified, shaking with fear. I tried to dig into the face of the cliff with my fingernails, hysterically crying, "How did I ever let myself get out so far on this – why did I come here – – not me, not me, not me!"

I was so terrified that the dream couldn't go on. I woke up, in a sweat, with my heart pounding. Within about five minutes the human significance came to me – and then in about ten minutes the spiritual.

Humanly the fear of the crowds was because of a death as a Christian martyr, a death not of my own choosing. I had never before remembered that one – and I didn't know it was in my Karmic Bank.[1] The fear of the cliff was because of a previous life death falling from such a ledge on a horse. That one I already knew about. But these are both in the realm of illusion and unimportant.

In fact, it was questioning myself about just that which revealed the spiritual significance. For I quickly remembered the death dream I had had last year and said, "What were you afraid of? You are not afraid of death – you have already met the fear of birth and rebirth" – and then that word "rebirth" clarified it for me: I had been sure of rebirth, my lack of fear in facing death was based on the surety of a new life. "Then what are you afraid of?," I asked – and that opened up to me, which I am sure you have already recognized – I was being offered *true Christian martyrdom*, I was being offered the opportunity to be "broken to pieces" on "the rock."

---

[1] See Glossary, "Karmic Bank."

And I couldn't do it, Joel. The thought of eternal extinction of self in the Christ just reduced me to a blubbering idiot. And I have brought myself, in my mind, back onto that cliff many times in the last two days and the reaction has been the same. I don't see myself ever being able to do it.[1]

Intellectually, I can give myself all the obvious responses, such as, "Every time you have given up something hard, you have found that you really gave up nothing but erroneous belief. This, no matter how it looks, is just another erroneous belief. You already have no self apart from the Christ, so what would you be giving up?" – but it hasn't changed my reaction.

So I have tried to analyze my fears and they seem to take shape something like this: If I really died to all of my humanhood (as St. Paul says) I am afraid I would no longer love my children, I am afraid I would no longer love my husband – or whatever that emotion is that passes for love in the human picture – also, I am used to Barbara – I am even fond of her – even in her humanhood she has merits – she is a sincere, hard-working child – but above all I am *used* to her, I am *used* to birth and rebirth – in fact I have only recently got *comfortable* with Barbara and with birth and rebirth – I have even learned that Barbara is nothing, knows nothing; that, too, is comfortable – but above all I am *used* to her.

I used to have a passion for wearing my old clothes until my mother has been known to take them away and burn them. Likewise, if someone wants to take Barbara away and burn her, I am *willing*. But, Joel, must it be *suicide*? Do *I* have to do it?[2]

---

[1] Yet, one day, I did. As Joel said, "Spiritual death is not one crucifixion, but many." One day I "saw" that "the ridiculous is that I ever *thought* I had a life of my own."

[2] Life will do it. What we have to be is *willing* to lose the false, personal ('persona' means 'mask') sense of self.

Now I know that this is the $64,000 question. I know
that now that I have been presented with this one, there
is no more use in playing with the toys of improved
humanhood, of sex, or false appetite – they are nonsense
compared with this one. Yet, unless you have help for me
beyond anything I can imagine, I do not see how I can
ever do this.

Joel, I know you have met this. Perhaps even in the
same way – since you certainly wrote about jumping off
the cliff in *Leave Your Nets*. Will you tell me about your
own experience and how you were able to meet it? Or at
least give me your help and your advice for I, of myself,
can do nothing.

Rereading this it seems confused and childish – and I
am in grave doubt that I have, after all these words,
communicated the real point – which is simply that I am
afraid. I am afraid to find out what it is never to die and
never to be born. Like Peter, I believe I can walk on the
water, but I can't sustain it. Master you must help me. "I
believe, help thou mine unbelief."

                                        5:00 p.m.

Since writing this early afternoon, I have been to the
hairdresser where I read and read in *Leave Your Nets*. On
page 33 it says, "You will know right then that it is not
your will, and therefore you cannot succeed or fail...
because "I" have called you... in moments of temporary or
seeming failure...*that too may be part of the plan...to teach
you that you cannot fail and you cannot be successful*,
because the "I" that called you is the only success."

Could this have anything to do with what I have
been telling you?

Do you think you might have an hour, say on Monday, to straighten me out on this? I could come out then – or tomorrow – or Sunday?

I am in your hands,[1]

Dear Joel,   Friday afternoon

What a joy it is to have oneness, omnipresence proved in our experience. You will by now have received the letter I mailed to you yesterday afternoon in which I thanked you for my freedom. You will therefore know that the meat of last night's message was already given to me yesterday afternoon.

I use the word "meat" intentionally – for you certainly gave them meat, not milk, last night. All these years I have watched you giving principles, defining words, clarifying the meaning of prayer, God, man, error. Last night I heard you take away the principles, destroy the words, erase all the definitions. Last night you sank the "raft." I am very grateful that before you sank mine you had taught me to swim!

My freedom came to me at 3:32 p.m., July 5, 1962 in a paraphrase of the meditation I have been using literally without ceasing ever since the first day you gave it to us. I went to bed with it as the last conscious thought – it continued through my dreams – I awoke with it right there as the first thought, "Thou will keep him in Perfect Peace whose mind is stayed on Thee."

Yesterday at 3:32 p.m. the Voice gave it back to me as, "Thou will keep him in Perfect Freedom whose mind is

---

[1] Two days later I saw Joel. He was kindness itself. (Today, after 28 years of teaching and healing, I know he was also smiling to himself). He assured me that it was just a transitory experience and that I should just keep on marching. Which I did. He also said I had a tendency to dramatize. I said that two lifetimes as a writer no doubt developed that. He said, "It has to go." It did.

stayed on Thee – where the spirit of the Lord is *there* is liberty" – and the bonds burst.[1]

I know that I have been rebellious, Joel, and while I regret it – I also know that my rebellion has always been unavoidably linked with my passion for freedom. With my freedom the need for rebellion is gone. Now that I know you will not, can not, bind me, I yield – I bow to you. Now that I know it does not mean bondage for me I gladly bend my knee and bow my neck.

You have a pretty good "Zen stick" of your own when you want to use it. I accept it with the same meekness that I willingly have accepted the loving kindness you have also poured out on me when I sorely needed it.

What a master you are. What a master teacher. What a master spirit. I only hope everyone last night realized what he was getting.

I see that I am in no wise ready to be able to be the guiding light of a Study Center, and this morning I abandoned the idea of opening one in San Fernando Valley. So that must wait for what I hope will be my future unfoldment.[2]

I do not know what love means – and I do not know what gratitude means – so I cannot use those words any more, so I will sign myself with the only word I am sure of,

a student

---

[1] This was a steadfast experience. I really began to grow up; just in time! My teaching ministry was about to begin.

[2] The next day Joel *ordered* me to go home and teach, saying, "I have put everything I have into you for five years. You *have* the Consciousness, and if you will not go home and teach, I will not teach you any more." My demurrer, that I truly did not have the time nor the desire to teach, he dismissed with, "I do not care how busy you are humanly." I had to accept his ultimatum.

Dear Barbara: July 10, 1962

Your letter of Friday afternoon is, of course, the very finest you have ever written me, and this is just a brief line to express my deep and sincere gratitude.

Aloha greetings,

Joel

Saturday morning
Dear Joel,   EARLY!

Speaking of dramatizing – how's this one?

Last night I dreamed that I stood by while you were stabbed in the side and I did nothing to prevent it. Now I told you that my middle name is Mary – and I know that you know that I know that "Thou art the Christ." But even I can see that that's going a little far. It would sound to anyone else like I were on "the stuff" (whatever that is). Anyhow – I guess I'd better relax, because if the identification becomes complete there won't be anything left of me to go home.

Boy this trip has been a "gasser." I knew it was going to be "special" – but that is the understatement of the year.

Aloha from a student,

(I guess I can say "Aloha" because I never, at any time, even *thought* I knew what that meant).

P.S. In reference to your statement last night about your students "...liking you one day and getting mad at you the next," you know that is all in the human picture, and was based on my desire to be understood and accepted by you humanly – personally.[1]

---

[1] As Joel has said, "This is an activity of love and the beginning student does not know how impersonal the teacher is." The student *feels* the love and the hurt kid in us wants to

You'll have no more trouble from me, because I don't look at you humanly any more. All that nonsense is over, thanks to your having grown me up – considerably.

You are what you are, and I am obedient to it. And that's all there is to be considered.

In other words, the parent has to wean the child – and you did.

Saturday morning – later
7/7/62

To whomever you are, who is labeled Joel to our eyesight:

If I knew what honor were, I would offer it to you.

It is a very funny feeling not to know anything – not dismaying, not frightening, just funny. It is a little like being a giant and trying to walk on the clouds – the foot keeps going through – making locomotion ludicrous and difficult.

If I knew what respect were, I would offer it to you.

How kind you seemed in the class last night. But I don't fool myself that you have broken the zen stick – just temporarily parked it behind the door.

a student

---

be "special." A student of Joel's told me a story about *his* experience of wanting to be special. He fell on the floor in Joel's living room, "having a heart-attack." Joel looked at him and said, "Oh, W., get up!" This need to be noticed, need to be "accepted personally" is a common experience for a young student. A valid teacher recognizes it, smiles inside, and then says, as the Master Christ Jesus did, "What is hindering you? Get up and walk."

Dear Joel,   Saturday afternoon

I shall try to be very careful what I say so that you will not misunderstand me. I have spent six years, almost, writing to you about me. I have not held anything back, even though it was detrimental to me in the human sense. I have been perfectly willing for you to know all my human failings. I wanted you to know my motivations completely. I know full well that you have always seen me in my true identity – as well as all your students – or for that matter, anyone with whom you come into contact. Even as I, in a lesser way, can see into the human motivations of those with whom I come into contact, so I know you, too, can also see human motivation.

It is motivation I wish to talk about. Not only through your own insight, but also because I have willingly opened myself up to you, you know me better than any person in the world. Even as I know you, and your motivations. And when you may use a word carelessly, or sometimes in contradiction to the way you may have used it previously – for instance, when you have said at one time that we must not "reject" anything – and yet another time say that these "problems" or "appearances of discord" come to us for our "acceptance or rejection," I do not jump at a word from you – I consider everything you say in the light of what I feel you totally *are* – so that if one of your words sounds out of balance with what I know you totally to be, I ignore the word and search for your *true meaning*, which I know will not be different from what you are.

Even if I had used the word "psychiatrist," carelessly, you know me well enough to have known that I did not mean psychiatrist – and instead of jumping to criticize me, you might have asked if that was what I meant. If, that is, you trusted my basic motivation. That is what I would have done with you, because I do have this basic trust in you. This is the third or fourth time that I have felt rejected by you on the basis of my motivation. I feel you should also know my basic motivation regarding Edward, and not be so jumpy in that area, either.

If I have not reached a point where when I feel within me that a certain step is right – if I am not yet capable of judging that – and if you do not have sufficient confidence in my understanding of these principles that you can trust my saying that a thing is right, then you certainly cannot have enough confidence in me to allow me to teach these principles to others.

Yes, I said "psychiatrist" – true enough – but I often use that word to lump the whole field of psychotherapy. It is a careless use of the word, but one that is frequently encountered – and I repeat – if you trusted *me* I think you would have waited to find out just what I meant.

Of course, we were pressed for time – and for that I certainly owe you an apology. I should not have even brought up the subject when you were out there at the airport on a personal thing, to meet C. It was rather like the woman who encounters a doctor at a luncheon and asks him to take a few minutes to look at her tonsils. It was an unpardonable breach of good taste, and I do ask your forgiveness. I assure you I have learned that lesson and I will not make that mistake again.

I have also learned another lesson – that apparently I cannot communicate very well to you in words – for this is about the third or fourth time that I have said something to you which you have misunderstood on the basis of how I phrased it, instead of looking through to motivation.

I am tired of having my human feelings hurt and my motivation misunderstood and so I shall abandon that course with you. I am one with you, whether or not even you realize it. I can, and will, rest in that.

As always love and gratitude,[1]

Dear Joel,   July 17, 1962

It is hard to remember what the shouting was all about.

Thank you for your patience. And thank you for your impatience.

Aloha,

Dear Joel,   August 29, 1962

Well, haven't heard from you, so I prepared a small notice today which will be sent out announcing the class beginning October 1st.

Also, Sunday I begin my Bible Class for Adults at the church. Wow.

As you can well imagine (and I think it was kind of sneaky – joke – of you not to tell me that it would happen) there has been considerable warfare going on in me the last 2 weeks between Christ Consciousness and carnal mind. Carnal mind has been saying, "Stop somewhere short of dedication" and Christ Consciousness has been saying "your life is now dedicated to the souls of men."

---

[1] By now you can see that that was quite a week. Many of the students, including me, were weeping and going around mumbling to themselves about how mean Joel was. Years later, being in the same position, I knew why he was so sharp. We were all babies and he threw us out of the nest. Without that we would never have learned to fly. Also I learned that, when teaching, it was necessary for *me* to help students clean up the way they *said* things, because the way they *said* it was the way they *thought* it – even if they *meant* to think something else. Cleaning up the speech clarified the concept. Joel, as usual, was right. I die hard. It was a number of years before all of my "hurt kid" was grown up and integrated. Along the way I learned that God is *not* in a hurry. I also learned to be patient with obstreperous students.

I knew I couldn't do anything about it so I just have gone to bed for two days to *watch* the battle. The whole experience links in with my dream in Honolulu where I was offered the opportunity for Barbara to be broken to pieces on the "rock of the Christ." I knew after that dream that I had come to the end of my human resources; that I had gone as far as I was able to take myself; that any further progress had to come from Grace and be the work of the Christ.

So I just went to bed to watch the battle. It isn't finished yet – quite – so I don't know for sure which one will win. (Perhaps you would like to give a little hint?).

I know how busy you are – but when you have a minute let me know how the work is going. Mama has told us how wonderful the LA class in August was. I'm sorry we missed it – but we have ordered the tapes.[1] In fact we now have all the tapes from the 1st of June through the LA Aug. tapes and beginning Sept. 13th our tape group will start an intensive study of this work.

> I send obedience to you,

Dear Barbara –   September 4, 1962

Happy indeed to have your letter. Have purposely refrained from comment on your IW Center activity because I am sure you know your subject – and above all, love your subject – and you will do well with it.

Your inner battle also does not disturb me. No one ever said it was easy to "die daily" – *and you have a lot of "dying" to do.* It isn't going to be done easily or in a hurry. Nor will you be the one to decide how "dead" you will ultimately be. You will be surprised when you learn

---

[1] Edward and I were in New York.

how little we have had to do with the way our lives evolve.

Everywhere we go we find standing room only at our lectures. The increase is really astonishing. There is a something behind the Infinite Way which provides for its every need – and timely. We had 220 students in first London Class – 179 here in Manchester. Philip Unwin invited me to lunch and asked for two books for next year. This year he published *World is New* and *Spiritual Resources*. Also Fowler wants more – if we ever get settled with them![1]

So the work goes well – and it is a matter of whether our small staff can do all that is necessary.

Our united love to you & all the family,

Joel

Dear Barbara –   November 23, 1962

Did not write you because I had no word from you. When you hear the nature of the work across Europe & South Africa you will understand.

In order to get home soon am doubling the sizes of my Classes here – and 200 will not even get into Class! These are different times for the Infinite Way!

See you soon – & always my thanks to you,

Joel

Note: A number of the other I.W. teachers, who were also guest-teachers at the L.A. Center, had been asking me how my work had

---

[1] This was regarding his copyrights, a matter already mentioned.

been going. They were particularly interested in how my Bible class at the Presbyterian Church was being received. There were about 12 of them. The information was the same, so I wrote one report and sent it to all. I discovered later that it had met with a mixed response. Some thought I was being egotistical. Perhaps I was. Oh, well, live and learn.

Dear fellow-student friends, December 7, 1962

You have all been loving enough to send me your encouragement, notes, flowers, telegrams asking what was going on. I was deeply touched by all of this and this letter is by way of "thank you." Please excuse me for writing a general letter but the pressure of school, children, husband, parents and Presbyterians makes mandatory a single report to you all, or none at all.

First, the class for parents at the Study Center, about which there is still a question as to its fruitage. B. offered a thought, which was that many of the Infinite Way students were of an age group which was no longer particularly interested in studying how to be a parent – and I thought that (as I mentioned in the class the second night) since, by its very nature, a class dealing with the relationships between parents and children had to be largely concerned with that world of "seeming duality," it was quite likely that either Infinite Way students had no need of such a class (since it is the one principle in the world which offers a solution to the problem of human relationships) or that its dual nature was not a proper subject for an Infinite Way study group.[1]

In a meditation before the class, it came through so *strongly* – "The *world* needs this message." Out there, in the world, where problems in the home are the source of

---

[1] However, Joel had specifically asked me to teach a class for parents.

delinquency and misery for children, such an *intermediate message* is needed. A message bridging the gap between human ignorance and spiritual understanding. I still feel this way, but I don't know how it will unfold.

One Sunday, I had to miss church; apparently my Presbyterians missed me. One called my sister, said that in all her years of studying and teaching, herself, she now knew she hadn't learned anything, until now. Another wrote me a darling note saying they had missed me and that she wanted me to know how much joy it had given her that for the first time in her life she knew she was learning to know God aright, and that she was finding that the *Bible* was as exciting a book as I had said it was. Another called me last night and said his life had been changed and that of his wife, also, and that they were finding a joy in this new way of life that they had not known existed.

My idea is only to indicate the fruitage. Certainly every one of you to whom I write knows what has to be done to the self by the Self before spiritual fruitage can be manifested. My own blood, sweat, and tears along the way does not need elaboration to you who have come the same road. Except that I might say, as honest confession, that if ten or twenty years ago I had realized that suicide is the goal of the spiritual seeker I might have chosen just to stay a cheerful human (which I was). It still seems harsh to me that the individual has to lay his life down himself. It would be much easier if someone else would just take it away. However, the day comes when one no longer has a choice, so that's that.

First of all, this church group is not one I would have chosen for myself. The Board of Christian Education and the Session of Elders wrote me a letter and asked me to take the class for the month of September to see how we got along together. Previously there were only 5 who were meeting regularly, whereas we have 17 to 24 each Sunday, and some of those who have joined the group are notable exceptions to fundamentalism. Such as 90-year old Mr. J. who stopped Edward on the street outside the church a few weeks ago – not knowing he was my husband – and said to him, "I'm from Florida, retired, and I'm just kind of like an old dog who is looking around for a place to lie down, and roam no more. If this is the kind of teaching they're going to have here, I guess this is it." Two weeks later he joined the church, and he is a considerable spiritual light and a pleasure to have in the class.

The minister (the young one) had asked me to put the September classes on tape so that he could study them and use them with their men's group and other groups, and in re-hearing them I have been amazed at the amount of pure Infinite Way they have held still for.

I decided in September that if the Father wanted me there, He wanted me there disseminating the kind of Truth I have been taught by Joel, and I thought they might as well get a sample of it, so that they would have a real basis on which to decide whether or not they wanted to continue with me. So, the first lesson was on the difference between Hope, Belief, Faith and Knowledge – which I called the "4 milestones of Christian experience." The next four weeks were to be On the Nature of God, On the Nature of Man, On the Nature of Sin, and On the Nature of Prayer (in that order).

However, it didn't work out that way, because I had not let them open with the kind of mouthed prayer they had been using, on the theory that I couldn't very well let them do that for 4 weeks and then tell them they had been doing it all wrong. I just wanted to do without prayer until the lesson on prayer had been presented, and then begin from there. But some of the "hard-core" got so upset because "there wasn't any prayer," that I had to do the lesson on Prayer right after the lesson on God. By that time the decisions were split, either hard for me, or hard against me. Oh well, Rome was not built in a day – nor destroyed in a day, either.

In passing, I pointed out to them that it was not correct to say that the classes had been without prayer, because *I* had been putting in 30 to 40 hours each week in prayer in preparation for the Sunday Class. It was fun to see their reaction to this.

Of course, I had to explain to the class that when I talked about spending 30 to 40 hours a week in prayer and meditation, it did not mean that I was down on my knees for that length of time, nor even that I was sitting in silent meditation in my bedroom, rather was it that during the whole month of September I found that almost every waking moment (except for the 3 hours a day I spent in school) were spent with my mind preoccupied with God and the class. It was not so much a sense of praying as of "being prayed." I would often, for instance, be wakened at 4 o'clock in the morning, unable to sleep further (tho' I might have wanted to) and would be given instruction about the class.

This strange thing also happened to me each Monday of the classes at the Center. About 4 o'clock in the afternoon I would sense a kind of withdrawal, as if something were taking me over, and even though I continued with making dinner preparations and bathing the children, I wasn't quite "there."

After the month of September this intense preoccupation ceased with regard to the class at the Church, and I now find that from 6 to 9 of a Sunday morning seems to be enough.

Well, to try to bring this to a conclusion, I began to show them how to meditate – which we call "silent prayer." You can imagine my surprise when the following Sunday in our meditation we generated a level of Consciousness equal to any I have experienced. I was amazed – and humbled, too. Because I had to say, "Father, if they can release this kind of Presence they are a lot more ready than they know – they are a lot more ready than I knew, too, and please forgive me for having been a spiritual snob."

The following week it was mentioned that one of the regular members was not there because her sister was mortally ill in Arizona, having been given only a short time to live, and she had gone to be with her. I said to myself, "O.K. Father, you brought it up, here we go!" And we got into the subject of spiritual healing. By now they didn't even demur. Like good little kids, they just tried to do what I suggested to them.

I, frankly, didn't have the idea of healing anybody in mind. It just seemed an opportunity to open up the subject to them. So I shared in their surprise two weeks later when the woman's husband came to tell us that the sister was out of danger, would be sent home shortly, and that she, herself, knew it was our prayers which had healed her! You should have seen their eyes. That day we took up the subject of Mr. James' eyesight, and the following week he reported that his Oculist said his eyes were remarkably improved when they were tested.

All this is going on in the Church where the Minister (the old one) has said from the pulpit, "It is unfortunate that the ability to do spiritual healing is gone from the earth."

Wowie!

Of course you already know what my answer had to be to the young minister when he said, "Barbara, I have never seen such a change in people in so short a time – how have you been able to do it so fast?" I said, "J., I'm as amazed as you are – because I know that I haven't done anything at all except sit like a hole in a fence and allow Spirit to come through me – I'm just amazed at the way the Spirit can dissolve error."

And this truly is the case. Those who at first sat stony-faced, and silent, and critical, are now smiling at me and coming on Sundays not to criticize but to participate and share in the lessons. And, of course, as always, the big gainer is the one who tries to teach. How this solidifies my conviction of the reality of God and of His ability to do everything, when I can reach the point of doing nothing.

Well, that's about the size of it. Please know that I am so aware that all of you to whom I write could witness to healings and demonstrations which would make these I write about seem miniscule. I write them only because you expressed an interest and because the work is being done in an orthodox sect. It is proof to me that there is a place for the Infinite Way everywhere in the world. This is indeed a small garden we are cultivating, and an inexperienced gardener, but the green is showing – and if we all do it wherever we can, one day the Garden may be restored.

Love,

Dear Barbara –

Monday
December 10, 1962

Have just read your 9 pages. By my Talk yesterday, you know that *you are fulfilling exactly what I was asking.*

I am not too concerned about Inf. Way students – they will absorb from the writings, recordings and from each other. The task now is getting these principles in human consciousness at other levels. I could not say this publicly – but Dr. Fischer (former Arch Bishop of Canterbury) has a complete set of my writings presented to him by Dean Inge (The Red Dean) and uses these books for his daily morning meditations.

In Germany, the lady in charge of our Munich work was sent for by one of the three *Heads* of the Lutheran Church and he told her they were a Godless church in a Godless land – and invited her to give him a two hour weekly session on Inf. Way so he could pass it on to their people.

In South Africa I was called into the govt. – at top level, where our work will have a chance. In Egypt I was invited to the University of Egypt and the Am. Univ. at Cairo and was invited to meet Nasser (the second time) & missed out account of Cuba.

So you see, you are in the Church – & Hazel van Halonger is in the church in Chicago – several years now. And I will be the third when I enter St. Stephens Episcopal in Phila., and St Johns in Wash., DC, in May. The books are already in hundreds of churches in US – Canada, England & New Zealand. And the tapes are in one church in Chicago.

May stay on here a few days – so please phone me Wed. (I never have your number) – & the four of us can have some dinner here at this hotel.

Love to all the family,

Joel

Dear Barbara –   December 30, 1962

Heartfelt thanks for your beautiful letter and generous enclosure.

Of course, you will never be quite the same since something "clicked" in you that day. You are on a higher plateau. There will be further unfoldments – higher plateaus – and soon.

One united love to all of you –

Joel

CHAPTER 6

CORRESPONDENCE 1963

Note: 1963 was the year that God, and Joel, began to take me seriously. It was a year of turmoil, of the breaking up of old concepts, and uncovering and clearing out the wreckage of the past. Consequently, I was not so lighthearted nor so sure, like Candide, that life was "...the best possible thing in the best of possible worlds." However, going through the fire tempers, and by 1964 I had begun to develop some "spiritual steel."

Dear Barbara: February 1, 1963

Once again it is time to remind our practitioners and our tape group leaders that *our principal function is the building of new consciousness, spiritual consciousness*, for those who come to us, and everything that we do, everything that we say, is aimed at that direction in *helping to bring about the re-birth.*

Reading of our writings and of our *Monthly Letter* and hearing the tapes plays a part in building the new consciousness, but by far the greatest fruitage comes from actual study, meditation, pondering *on the part of the students themselves.*

Of course it is assumed that those who come to you are studying the *Monthly Letters* because you yourself know by now what goes into the activity of bringing forth these *Letters*, and the reason that this spontaneous material is made available to our students as the living Word each month.

Aloha greetings,

Joel

P.S.   Since I have given the Los Angeles, Princess Kaiulani, Chicago, Manchester, and London Classes in 1962, our students are not up-to-date on our work and on our ascended consciousness, until they, likewise, have been through those Classes and have been through them often enough, not only to grasp the meaning, but more especially to attain a higher elevation of consciousness. Therefore, while I am at home being spiritually renewed and refreshed, the students can catch up to me by the study of these Classes.

> *Note: Sometimes there can be "trouble in Paradise." The following correspondence is an indication. Rather than argue, I always thought it would be better to take the matter to Joel to be checked out for a spiritual solution. That would benefit everyone. I have always encouraged my students to do the same.*
>
> *Only the teacher should correct the students. They should never correct each other.*

Dear Joel,   February 12, 1963

Thank you so much for your letter.   Perhaps you didn't exactly intend it that way, but we construed that it means that you have taken us, as a group, under your wings for teaching and we are very happy about this.

It is a wonderful group Joel, small but wonderful. And it's growing a little bit at a time. In fact I attribute its slow growth to exactly the degree of dedication that we feel. We have been tried by quite a few, but they only come once, and apparently our "no nonsense" attitude is not altogether to their liking. But then, every now and then, along comes one who really responds to the consciousness in our group and says that this is what he has been looking for.

Joel, I received what I thought was a rather odd letter from B. I enclose her letter and my answer as being the briefest way to make you conversant with it. I would like you to please give me an expression of your attitude and desires on the issue involved.

Rest well – and love to you and Emma,

Note: Following is the letter sent from B. to me and to all of those who were attending the "25 Group" meetings.

Dear Friend,   February 3, 1963

This is a reminder that our "25" group world work meetings are held the first Thurs. of every month, at the Study Center, 10:30 AM

We must remember that this obligation is a personal one that we have all promised to fulfill and dedicate ourselves to. It is a great privilege to have been asked to participate in this group, *and your presence is expected.*[1] If you find that other matters interfere on these days please feel free to withdraw at any time.

Mrs. S. will be conducting the meetings until such time as the spirit indicates otherwise.

---

[1] Italics are mine.

This letter is not directed at any particular individual and has been sent to everyone in the group.

With love, B.

Note: Following is my response.

Dear B., February 12, 1963

I am sorry that I haven't had time until just now to answer your letter. It came as somewhat of a surprise to me because I thought all of us in the Infinite Way had a similar understanding of the fellowship of this group of people.

I became a disciple of Joel's on the first day, when I opened the book *The Infinite Way*, and read:

> "Illumination dissolves all material ties and binds men together with the golden chains of spiritual understanding. It acknowledges only the leadership of the Christ...This union is the free state of spiritual brotherhood. The only restraint is the discipline of Soul..."

I still hold to the white flame of this purity because any other kind of "joining" would be intolerable to one with my passion for freedom.

If, as you say in your letter, "my presence is expected," then this seems to me that you are looking to man and this would not be in accord with Joel's teachings.

Please know that while I always find it a great joy to come to your Center, and spiritually refreshing to be in the company of other dedicated students, I acknowledge no "obligation" except to the Christ, and I am under no bondage of discipline except to my husband in the material scene, and to Joel as my spiritual teacher.

Whatever association I have had with your Center (of any kind) has been the result of outgoing love and not from any sense of duty or obligation. From my standpoint it must continue to be so.

I do, however, feel that I would like to explain to you that I would very much like to come to all of the classes and meetings. I am well aware of the benefit I derive from these sessions. But my obligations at school do not permit this and it might explain it a little to you if I tell you that Joel, when he was here last, indicated to me that I was doing what he wanted me to be doing (with studying and my work at the church, etc.). I certainly checked this with him – as I never just trust myself to always know for sure that what seems to be unfolding interiorly for me is truly spiritual guidance.

I go to school because I seem to have (as I told Joel) an inner drive to be able to speak to other nationalities in their own tongues. (I have studied five languages so far). I feel sure that God doesn't intend to waste me – and that it will all be put to the service of the Infinite Way in some fashion. In the meantime, I must just continue to follow the line that continues to unfold for me.

Also let me reassure you that I do not neglect to do world work every day. That *spiritual* obligation I certainly do recognize. When my schedule changes so that I can join with the group at the center I will be more than pleased.

Until then you have my love and continuing support.

Sincerely,

Dear Barbara: February 15, 1963

Of course you are absolutely right, and B. is, without realizing it, thinking in terms of human attendance, and so forth. I am sure you can see that it is only a matter of spiritual immaturity, or she would definitely see that her attitude is one of organization. But that will come in time. Meanwhile, I will certainly let her know that the letter sent out to the "Twenty-five" group was not in order. I can see the value of two or more being gathered together for such a purpose when it is a free-flowing spiritual activity, but certainly it could never be that where attendance becomes compulsory.

I am truly happy with your activity, and surely you know now why I have no interest in numbers, whether numbers of dollars or numbers of students, or numbers of books sold. My interest is only in reaching those of my spiritual Household and sharing with them whatever Grace is given me of the Father.

I am benefiting greatly by my stay at home. I have about six or seven hours every day at the desk, and this leaves me free for more meditation periods and for raising the healing ministry to a higher level of consciousness.

It is always a joy to hear from you, Barbara. Emma joins me in love to you and to Ed, and all the family, and of course, all of the students with whom you come in contact.

Aloha,

Joel

Dear Joel,   March 8, 1963

Quite a passel of things. First, and most important – Very Happy Birthday – it was a wonderful day for the world "X" number of years ago – or maybe it would be more correct to say it was a very bad day for "the world" and a wonderful day for God!

Also, very good congratulations on having been smart enough to find Emma – and get married!

Also, thank you so much for your highly intelligent, mature, spiritual, and welcome letter. There's nothing like checking spiritual matters with headquarters.

In that connection – here is another one which arose just today. Like the other – I simply send you copies of the correspondence as the easiest way to make you conversant with the facts. Also like the other, I ask you to please let me have your evaluation and wishes in the matter.

Frankly, to me, it all seems like nonsense and much ado about nothing. Either it is childlike – or they've moved into the absolute – and in either case I wouldn't be able to understand it. Yet, I remember, a couple of years ago – after I had sent D. two or three checks I received a very sharp letter from her telling me that she didn't need checks from me – that the Christ maintained her – and I had to write her a calming letter telling her that in sending her money I wasn't trying to indicate that she needed me – but that it was just in recognition of the quality of the work which I knew was being done at her Center. That seemed to satisfy her – and thereafter she accepted the checks with thanks. Now – here we go again!

Love and kisses to you and Emma,

P.S. If you send back the birthday check I will assume your answer is negative! ! ! ! !

Note: Following is the letter to me from O.

Dear Barbara,   March 6, 1963

Thank you for your letter and enclosure, which I received while D. was away on Maui.

It was thoughtful of you to include the Center in your giving. However, I am returning the check primarily because I have a feeling that gifts from Christus Corporation would be tax-exempt, and the Center (or D.) cannot receive tax-exempt gifts. D. pays State gross income tax and Federal income tax on everything that comes into the Center. Therefore checks really should be made out to her.

All of the Center's income is to D. from her students in gratitude for healing or teaching or the tape recordings. The Center is run entirely on her own Consciousness, and any gifts of gratitude that you personally want to make to her should be addressed to her. Occasionally, when she gets over-loaded I do help her by responding to some of the correspondence, but this is only at her request. I am sure you understand my situation.

You must know or feel the tremendous work that is being done here, with Joel and Emma "on the field." We are very privileged to be a part of his consciousness now.

Wish you and Ed could be with us this weekend when we honor Joel and Emma on their 5th wedding anniversary.

Love and aloha,

O.

Note: Following is my response.

Dear O., 						March 8, 1963

I shall have to answer your letter one point at a time:

First, the check which you returned to me was made out in exactly the same way as all the checks which I have been sending to D. for over two years. The checks have always been made out to the Infinite Way Study

Center, Honolulu – just as the checks I send each month to L. and B. are made out to Infinite Way Study Center, Los Angeles or Chicago – as the case may be. It was also made out exactly the same as the check which you acknowledged to me for D. last month.

Second, I did not "send" the check to you – I "mailed" it to you. I did this because when you acknowledged the check for D. last month you told me that she was too busy with her practitioner mail to get to correspondence of this kind and that she had asked you to acknowledge it for her. It seemed, therefore, only sensible and kind for me to mail the check to you this month so that D. would not need to feel under any personal obligation to answer my letter.

Third, as to your "feeling that checks from Christus Corporation would be tax-exempt." You indicate a lack of familiarity with this subject. I suggest that you have B. explain the economics of the matter to you – or better yet – have Joel explain the matter from a spiritual basis.

To briefly explain it – no checks to D. would be tax-exempt – of which we are perfectly aware – and have been aware that no such check which we have sent to D., or Joel, or any other Infinite Way person would be tax-exempt – in itself. However, Christus Corporation is a tax exempt corporation and Edward would receive tax relief from any contributions which he or I make to Christus Corporation. Christus Corporation, in turn, is allowed to support any spiritual or educational activity. (For instance, Edward and I are now maintaining scholarships – which we have maintained privately for years without any tax benefit – through the Corporation).

When you say you are returning the check for the reason of this "feeling" you have, you give me the impression that you are criticizing the fact that we are doing this. Is then, our spirituality so much less than yours that you feel we can do something of which you would not approve?

Believe me, there is nothing unspiritual about business, nor taxes, when properly conducted. (Joel, for instance, is a supreme business man). Taxes are an expense, and anyone is as entitled to legitimately hold down this expense, as any other. Furthermore, the first person who ever gave me that idea that any of the money spent in connection with the Infinite Way might be deducted was D., herself. Until she talked to me about what her tax man had advised her we had just spent the money travelling, for lessons, etc., without a further thought.

However, after D. talked to me it seemed actually silly not to create a situation which would bring some of our "sharing" activities under a structure which would afford Edward perfectly equitable and legal tax relief.

I hope this helps clarify the matter for you a bit.

Now, as to the Center. Naturally I am aware of whose consciousness is maintaining it, and as I have told D. many times, these checks have just been a monthly "bow in her direction."

In the hope that the matter is now cleared up, I am enclosing the check again, which I ask you to pass on to D. for me. If it is not acceptable, return it – and be assured that it will not trouble you a third time.

Always love to all,

c c: D.
Joel

Dear Barbara, March 11, 1963

I am returning your check for your personal disposition.

B. joins me in Aloha greetings to both of you.

Love,

O.

Dear Barbara: March 12, 1963

I am returning herewith all of the correspondence included in your letter of March 8th, just so that you will have it in front of you when I say to you that I think that both D. and O. are functioning from some degree of spirituality that I myself have not yet attained. Seriously, it is not that at all, it is only that they want to bend backwards to do what they think is right. They know that I have refused large sums of money that were offered to me if I could accept them on a tax-free basis. Only last week I turned down a bequest that amounted to over $100,000, because I have no tax-free organization to receive it, and it would only be a bequest on those terms. So perhaps O. thought, at least, that because it came from a corporation, that that had something to do with tax-free on this end, and she knows, of course, that we do not have any tax-free organization. I really believe the whole thing was just due to her misunderstanding.

On the other hand, with D. it's quite different. Why D. should ever, for any reason, refuse a gift, I would not know. The only times in my professional life that I have refused money are when it is sent by those that I know, at the time, are not in a position to spare it. And certainly I do not want to take money from anybody at such a time, because it just doesn't seem right. But otherwise, I accept joyfully whatever is sent to me, small amount or large amount, and there is always some use in the Infinite Way for funds, and of course we make a practice of sharing also with other activities, such as Boy Scouts, Y.M.C.A., Community Fund, the local Symphony Orchestra, Art Museum, Bishop Museum of Polynesian activities, and so forth, and so I find no reason to refuse money. But I do believe that D. and O. just want to bend backwards in holding themselves to the activity of the Christ, and I believe that such efforts as they have made in this connection are mistaken efforts.

I believe that D. should accept anything that you or anyone else sends to her, and then either find some use for it, or keep it in the bank until some future time when there might be a use for it. Ann Darling Kuys has used several thousand dollars in sending out copies of my writings to the chaplains of the Army, Navy and Air Force, and still continues to send out large quantities of them. Just now another one of my books has to be published in French, and since there are no publishers who will publish books of this nature in France, I have to publish it myself, which I am happy to do. But this all indicates that there should be no reason for refusing money that is offered as a gift in a spiritual activity, so I am heart and Soul with you in your own conclusions.

I understand that you are going to have a night at the Study Center, and of course I am happy about it, because I know how much you have to contribute to those who have ears to hear and eyes to see.

And now my deep and sincere thanks to you for your thoughtfulness in remembering March 10th, and be assured I have accepted your check, and of course, with thanks. Above all, I am happy that I was brought to your attention at this time of the year and in this connection. I am perhaps one of those who rejoice at every birthday, because every year seems to me to be a gift that has been given to me, and believe me, it is one which I prize. Today an event took place that made me wish that I could look forward to another fifty or a hundred years, to be able to complete all of the opportunities that have been given to the Infinite Way, and I can assure you that there's enough work ahead to keep me busily occupied for the next fifty or a hundred years, if only I could find out how to stay here.

Can you imagine this, a Baptist minister whose ministry is television and radio, and who has the entire

Crossley chain as his outlet, and beginning in the next few weeks or months, he adds to this the A.B.C. chain for his daily ministry, and his wife also is on the air, and both the minister and his wife find occasion every week to quote from some Infinite Way writing and mention Joel Goldsmith of Hawaii? Isn't that a stunner for you? And this minister is here in Hawaii for just two days, and takes time out to spend an afternoon with me, and has made an arrangement to return here in April to spend a week studying with me. Doesn't that make us feel humble?

And he told me that a psychiatrist who is one of the fifteen doctors on President Kennedy's Health Panel has come to him for instruction in spiritual healing, saying that they have no way, in psychology or psychiatry, of healing people, and that this is the outlet they must seek and find, and of course you know what instruction will be given to him after the minister's return from this trip.

I only wish every Infinite Way student could have been just behind a tree as we sat in the lobby of the Royal Hawaiian Hotel and overheard the things about the Infinite Way that this minister had to share with me.

I guess you can see why birthdays are happy events to me, and I don't care how many of them pile up, as long as I am permitted a clear mind and a healthy body with which to work.

My love to you and Ed and to all of the family, and in this Emma joins me also,

Joel

Dear Barbara: April 17, 1963

Thank you for your letter, and of course I recognize that you were just reaching out and touching Consciousness.

We have been having a hectic time here, since so many students have been coming from Australia, New Zealand, Canada, the U.S. and England, since I haven't been going out to them. On top of this, I have just received my advance copy of *The Contemplative Life*, and this really is going to become one of a trio: *The Contemplative Life*, and right next to it, *The Thunder of Silence*, and right next to it, *A Parenthesis in Eternity*, and I am sure that these three books have a tremendous destiny.

Parenthesis has just gone off to the publishers in New York and London, so we might possibly have it by the end of the year.

Then, a Protestant minister with a very large non-denominational ministry has been over here studying with me for a week, since he has quoted some of my writings on his TV and radio programs, and now wants to go further in meditation and actual spiritual healing work, and so, after a two-day visit and then a solid week, he has gone home, and when he can arrange it, will return for another session. He is really carrying a great deal of the message of the Infinite Way into the orthodox ministry.

We have already started editing the 1962 *Letters* for publication, and then I do an enlarged and revised version of *Leave Your Nets*, and so there is still some busyness ahead of me.

Plans for enlarging this home at 22 Kailua Road have been okayed, and the estimate has been made, and now we are waiting for contractors to arrange a contract for us to sign. Then we will undoubtedly have to move out and establish headquarters somewhere else until the new home is built. All of which means we will be at home here for quite a long while to come, so do not hesitate to write at any time, and if you ever have the opportunity of flying over for a brief visit, or even a longer one, just remember the welcome mat is always at the door for you and for yours.

Emma joins me in sending heartfelt greetings to you and Ed, and to all of the family,

Joel

Dear Joel,   April 22, 1963

Well, here comes the "book." There has been so much going on – and I am so anxious to bring you up to date on me – particularly because I want to ask you to help me in working on the matter of the Church (the Presbyterian) which I will tell you about a little later.

First of all – I do want to thank you again for the beautiful maturity and spirituality of your letters to me in the matters of B. and D., O., et al. I must say that when both things first occurred I had a momentary wonder as to why I was being involved in such matters which I had not engendered myself, but which seemed to have been brought in from "left field" as it were.

It quickly became evident that I was simply being used by the Spirit as a channel for their increasing spiritual understanding -- and that since I could see in both cases that the matters arose out of spiritual immaturity, a lesson needed to be forthcoming to them. But I am not their teacher and I felt that I should not be the one to point out to them their errors. This is the reason why I sent you all the correspondence and did not hesitate to involve you in what otherwise might look like a private matter – because you are their teacher and if a lesson was indicated it should have come from you. Obviously this was the right thing to do – because the matters have evolved spiritually and correctly.

First of all B. and I have had a meeting of the minds on our matter – she expressed herself as understanding my feelings perfectly – and agreed with them. Her attitude was entirely loving and generous and has actually resulted, I believe, in an increased closeness between us. At least, I feel that way.

Likewise I have received a beautiful letter from D. in which her attitude certainly confirms what I know her to be. And she, too, expresses herself as having learned a "lesson" from you in the matter. So those two matters are now water under the bridge, and the error has been dissolved by Spirit. Thanks to you.

Had I written this letter to you two weeks ago I am afraid it would have sounded like a funeral dirge. I had been going through such a wringing out process, such an "emptying," that I actually felt almost physically like someone were wringing me out, and wringing me out, until I was tempted to say with Lady MacBeth, "Who would have thought there would be so much blood in him?"

But it was apparently the precursor of the $64,000 one for me. This is the one that began just before I last saw you here in Los Angeles when I told you the Voice had said to me, "Your salvation lies in silence." Well, that just germinated for a long time. I made beautiful progress in listening for a while after my lesson with you, but gradually the pressures of the world cut in on it, and I seemed to slip backward.[1]

Then came this wringing out – and last week I had a tremendous revelation – it came first as a recognition of what had actually been the motivating drive of my life. It was apparently so very much a part of me that I had failed to ever look at it objectively. That was a drive to "communicate." I think it may have been this which you felt and interpreted as a drive to "teach." I truly have never felt a drive to teach – but it has certainly, I now see, been the paramount compulsion of my life – to "understand" and to "be understood."

---

[1] What happened was that, after hearing this, I immediately began to try to stop talking. It ended in a social fiasco. When I took the problem to Joel, he said that I had *misunderstood* the Voice. He said, "Your salvation lies in silence did not mean stop talking. It meant start to *listen!*" A tremendous lesson.

Well – along with the revelation of its existence, came the release – with the phrase from the Voice, "*I* do not have to communicate with anyone." That was all the Voice said – but immediately followed the recognition that if *I* is all there is – there is no one *to whom* to communicate. "I already *am* that which I seek."

20 times a day, since then, in situations where I previously would have pressed forward in an effort to communicate – the Voice has said, "I do not have to communicate." And immediately a great breath floods through me and I am released from drive – from action – and a great peace descends. I really feel, Joel, that of all the insights I have ever been given – this is the greatest one – so far. Because it seems to me now that this need to communicate was holding me in the world. I was really loving people more than God. And it was holding me in the world.

Which brings me to another point I wanted to check with you (I told you it would be a book!).

I was reading a play of Aeschylus the other day – *Promethius Bound.* And some of the dialogue was very interesting (for having been written 500 years before Jesus) – such as "pierce his feet with these nails" – "it is for loving man too much – for giving him the gifts of the gods that I am here crucified."

These words started me on a train of thought – and all of a sudden it seemed to me that that was the mistake Jesus made – he actually loved men more than God – and that was the reason he was crucified.

What do you think about this?[1]

By the way – before I forget – I have had – as you can imagine – a terrible longing to touch base for at least a couple of weeks – and I think I could make it sometime in

---

[1]   In 1987 I was given a revelation on this. The Voice brought through in a class, "It was Jesus' *humanhood* that was hanging on the cross, and it was his Christ that put it there."

July – probably the 2nd and 3rd weeks of July. By your last letter it seems that you will be out of the Kailua house by then – do you know where you will be?

I have been going Wednesdays to the Study Center and continuing the classes on Children. The attendance is very small – 3 to be exact – but they come regularly – and express themselves as being very grateful for the information. I, myself, still have a feeling that this kind of class is not really a proper Infinite Way activity – having to deal so very much with human footsteps – as it does – but I shall go along until it is finished – as long as anyone wants it. In fact – it would be such a joy to me to be able to teach a class to Infinite Way students in the history of Christianity – or the *Bible* – or anything that I could present as a pure Infinite Way activity – but I seem to be held in this position of bridge – or transition teaching – and "it's not mine to reason why."[1]

But this brings me to the Church. Now, Joel, this class that I have been teaching there for 7 months had been a pleasure. The Curriculum has been open enough for me to be able to teach with complete spiritual integrity – although, of course, I have only been able to give them milk. But they have been coming along – Consciousness has been developing – and they have been aware of it. In fact, just last week one of my students actually had her first experience of enlightenment – a real flooding of the Presence – and she was so stirred and joyful that she called me up in tears to share the wondrous excitement of it.

So – it is evident that as a "hole in the fence" the Spirit has been able to work through me to some extent. Also, many others have expressed their gratitude – in ways that I have already told you in my previous 8-page "book" that I wrote about this class.

---

[1]   I did not know, then, that God was preparing me to bring forth the "How to" which would complement Joel's "What."

However, there is a young man around – a man getting his Ph.D. in brain surgery this June, who has questioned me closely from time to time – and about a year ago he said to me, "You sound heretical to me" – well – I just grinned – not taking it too seriously – and said, "That word would put me into some pretty good company including Jesus and the Father of Protestantism, himself, Luther" – and so the moment passed.

Now, Joel, I am perfectly aware – having been down there for as long as I have – that the greatest single error – the thing that bogs the Church down – is its erroneous concept of the "uniqueness" (as they label it) of Jesus. Their idea is – as you know only too well – that God entered the world only one time in an historical event – in the person of one man – this Jesus – and that He has never done so again. And I would not have rushed this at them – but they have been drawing it out in class – and the other day from within one of the students it was revealed – and she said out loud – in a tone of great astonishment, "Why then the Christ is Spirit" – and the others took it up.

I was gratified – you may be sure.

But, to get to the point, this Doctor has been coming the last four Sundays and two weeks ago said out in class that he considered my concepts "unorthodox and dangerous."

Of course, this brought up no reaction in me – any more than if he had said I was yellow with green spots – so I just grinned at him and said, "I don't see anything dangerous about them" (of course, later I realized that he was perfectly right – without knowing why – because Truth is certainly dangerous to any long-held cherished – but erroneous concepts – and he is full of them).

Anyway, I was going to let the whole matter pass – but all week in my meditations the Voice kept saying, "You cannot let it pass." And I would say, "But Father, why me? I don't want to fight – why can't I just skip it?" But again, "You can't let it pass."

Now – perhaps I should also tell you that some time ago I was attending a teachers' meeting at which this young man was presiding and he was putting forth his principles quite strongly – and to my surprise, the Voice said to me "get to work – this is anti-Christ." I was, frankly, astonished – because, as I have said, I have not tended to take this young man too seriously – I have just considered him young and unawakened – but I have been learning that for some time he has constituted himself the "gad-fly" around the Church – criticizing the Session, criticizing the Worship service – etc. In fact, finally, I think they elected him to the Session 2 months ago – just to stop his criticism.

Well, in any event – last Sunday I brought the thing out in the open. Asking him first, if he knew why I came there on Sunday mornings (the class knew very well that it was because I was *witnessing* to the redemptive power of the presence of the Christ in my life, which I was willing to share with anyone who wanted it). He hemmed and hawed and finally said, "I suppose it is because you want to share something that *you think* is important (with emphasis on the "you"). I said, "Yes, that comes pretty close to it." I then asked him if he knew that I had been invited to teach, in writing, by the Session and the Minister – he said no – he did not.

I then asked him, "Do you believe that the Spirit of God indwells every man?" Again he hemmed and hawed and said, "Well, that depends on what you mean by God and what you mean by Man – and I have no evidence to support this."

I said, "I did not ask you *if* God indwelt man – because it is very evident to me that you do not have any evidence of this – I merely asked if you *believed* that He did – and for the purposes of answering – I will accept your concept of God and Man. Any way you see it. Well – finally – he did say, "No."

I then pointed out to him that he could not possibly agree with other things that I said – because we were in fundamental disagreement on this basic principle. That I recognized his right to disagree with me – but that I found him over-fond of labels – and I did not think he should carelessly bruit about such terms as "dangerous" and "heretical" in a church situation where these terms, in times past, have been sufficient to cause persons to be burned at the stake.

I then said that I thought he should be free to express his disagreement and disapproval of me to the class without the determent of my presence – and that I would absent myself and let the class then decide whether or not they wanted me to come back. I am informed that after I left he said to them, "You are not thinking at all – you are just being led around by the nose by that domineering woman who comes in here every Sunday and tells you what to think and what to believe." I am also informed that the 15 people who were regular members of the class rose up in one voice and clobbered him! "She is not that way at all!"

And, of course, I have not been. Countless times I have said to them, "Don't take what I say as Truth. Don't believe it just because I say it. Truth is a synonym for God. And God is not anyone's statement about Him – not even in the *Bible*. God is an *experience* and all we can do with our words is to go *around* Him – describing aspects, faculties – but it will never be Truth for you until you take these statements and throw them up against the "personal radar for Truth" which each one of you has within him – and when it announces itself *to* you it may be Truth *for* you – not before.

In other words – you can see that you have taught me well! And I will not betray that.

Well, one of the members of the Session heard that he had labelled me a heretic – and they have got all excited about it (although, frankly, I am not at all sure that they have not welcomed this as an opportunity to censure him who has been censuring them unremittingly – human nature being what it is) and I understand that they are sending three members of the Session to visit my class next Sunday (to decide whether or not I am heretical, I suppose).

Now – you can imagine how this affects me. First of all it makes me laugh hysterically – me – the rebel – the non-joiner – who wouldn't have anything to do with an organized religion just because of these ridiculous factions – and all this kind of nonsense – now find myself caught up in the middle of being brought before the "Sanhedrin" on the charge of heresy! It is really hysterical!

It would be very easy for me to simply walk away from an unpleasant situation and say, "Look – I do not need an audience on Sunday mornings – particularly an audience of only 15 people – good-bye and God bless you." But – for some reason – my "inner" is not allowing this. It is saying, "Be still and behold the salvation of the Lord." "The battle is not yours – but mine."

And again – I am wondering if I am being an instrument for something?

(This may go on all night!).

Oh, I forgot to tell you – that for some time the lines have been forming in this little church with the "advanced" thinkers – and the "fundamental" thinkers. And schism has been developing. The young minister has left – and the old one will be gone in 2 weeks – and the task is before the church to select a new minister.

Now, whether or not I am a part of this, I couldn't know. If I am a Christian Soldier – I guess I just have to stay in the line. Certainly the next couple of weeks will tell the tale. My class is behind me 100%. They, and like thinkers – may prevail. On the other hand, there are some in the church who would only line up behind William Jennings Bryan (who put the cause of

240

Christianity back 100 years, in his argument with
Clarence Darrow).

But , really, Joel – what should I do in this situation?
I couldn't care less about this kind of orthodox, sectarian
nonsense! I do feel a kind of obligation to this class which
has come regularly, devotedly, and expressed itself as
more than grateful for what they have received. But
what about all this churchgoing nonsense? Do we have
to hold still for this? And if so, will you please help me
this week – to just let it unfold for the glory of the Father?
I really want you to tell me what to do, because as far as I,
personally, feel, I could just shake the dust off my feet for
the whole thing. But I don't want to react personally –
and I don't want to do anything that will not be
spiritually productive – so please give me the benefit of
your advice.

Also, let me know where you and Emma will be in
July.

Love to you both,

Give up?

P.S. It is funny how over the years this life I live with
you has become the real one – and the other one seems like
a role in a stage play. Particularly since having been freed
from a need to communicate – [1]

Now the length of this letter – I realize – may belie that
I have been freed from a need to communicate – but
somehow – my relationship with you is slightly
different. With you, I have the feeling rather like that I
am a marigold in the ground – and as I grow – I seem to
have the desire to turn to the sun and say, "Is this the
direction you want me to go in?" – and that's it – more
than a need to communicate.

---

[1] Oh? I hadn't noticed!

In any event, if you can make any sense out of all this, write me all the answers, and I will go on working in my Father's garden.

B.

April 23, 1963

P.P.S. Well, I thought I had it all said and then this morning I woke up and realized that I had failed to ask you about two very, very important things.

I was so full of the peace brought by my healing on my communication drive – that I forgot to tell you that right along side of that there is a most painful thing going on at all times in me. I seem to be just overwhelmed with a sense of my own inadequacy, the fact that I am a sinner – and a realization of my own dreadful unworthiness.

But now I realize that the Father cannot wait for an instrument to be perfected before using it. If He had to wait for that, especially in me, it could be a whole lifetime – or more.

I am aware that He has used me, and I have been of service to some. But this sense of unworthiness is just devastating. I also realize that the fact that He can use an unworthy instrument makes His perfection evident in my imperfection – but it is painful. Now, my question is, does one ever get over this sense of sinning? Or must I look forward to having to live with this thorn in the flesh for the rest of my life? It is not a sense of guilt – I long ago forgave my guilt – but it is a sense of being so ignorant of, "Father, I cannot *live* without you." In fact, in times past when I was without contact I did not have that sense of starving – but I do, now. Sometimes I have the feeling of a fish that has been thrown out of the water. It has also had a funny reaction in connection with my classes. Particularly the Infinite Way class.

In the theater I never knew what it was to have stage fright – and now I am so terrified every Wednesday that I just have to whip myself to go down and give the classes. Once I am there – and started – it seems all right – but to go is just like walking over hot coals. I really wonder if I should be doing it when it is so painful and when I am so conscious of my own inadequacy? In fact, I now look wistfully upon a life where I might just live in a little hole, surrounded by my books, just being able to study – quiet and alone – as a peace beyond price.

Now, there is another problem, Joel, which I need your help on and, it, too, is very complicated.

As I have told you, a year ago last Christmas Eve I was awakened in the middle of the night with the Voice reading a piece of scripture out loud which clarified the verse about "Nothing can go in the mouth of a man which defileth him" – and that I have never been able to smoke since then. In fact, it is so *gone* – that it is difficult for me to remember that I ever did. But it has not been the same with drinking. Now, I don't want to exaggerate this. I cannot say I have a "drinking problem." I actually drink very seldom. But I am perfectly aware that, as you have said, "This has no place in our way of life." I am also aware – as you told me about smoking, "Giving it up will not make you more spiritual." Yet the smoking did fall off of me.

Now occasionally, when I am tired, or social, or, particularly, with Edward, I do take a cocktail. I have determined not to fight it – as I had finally determined not to fight cigarettes. I am also aware that it simply represents a dark area in me where the light has not yet penetrated. I know that it is an ignorance – yet, I am also fully aware that it is out of place in one who is at the same time being used as an instrument for guiding the spiritual growth of other people. In fact – it remains the single unresolved piece of human stupidity in my life. In all other areas I am able to let the Spirit guide me completely, without bogging down into humanhood.

My reaction to the world has become almost nil – yet a couple of drinks can pull me right into the human.

I just don't quite know how to meet it. This is the reason I am asking you to help me. If this were an illness or a growth or some other kind of organic disturbance which I was failing to meet, I would certainly yell for help, and I am yelling for help for this one. Certainly it is something which I am quite – more than quite – ready to be healed of, but it has not dropped off me. I don't know why – except that, of course, it represents spiritual immaturity. But I don't seem to be able to get sufficient light to dissolve it.

I ask for your help in achieving my release from this nonsense. It gets in my way and interferes with my clean operation as a wife, mother, student, and teacher, and I should like to see the end of it. But, at the same time, I cannot fool myself but that it represents an as yet unresolved ignorance in me that I do not seem to be meeting.[1]

Well, I really must stop or you will just have to give me up for fatigue.

By the way, in connection with the church matter, after I finished the first part of my letter last night I talked to a friend of the young doctor who said to me, "I think you have begun to crack him, if you will just stick to your guns." Of course I have no alternative than to stick to my guns, because to do otherwise would mean giving up my spiritual integrity, and that's all I have.

But, it may be resolving already.

---

[1] I continued to have long periods where I did not use alcohol at all, followed by periods where I did. I attained total freedom from this in 1979. I don't know how long St. Paul struggled with his last "thorn in the flesh." My lesson was a long one. It *did* ensure my humility.

In any event – please help me in this matter.

Good-bye again,

Dear Barbara: April 26, 1963

Of course you now have one of the top secrets of the mystical Path, and you will understand why I frequently refer to Emerson's statement, "What you are shrieks so loudly I cannot hear what you say." We are always communicating, and what is very sad for most people, we are communicating *ourselves*. We certainly are communicating our state or level of consciousness, and that is the very thing that most people try to hide behind a mask of personality, and so forth. But we are always communicating, and we do our best communicating in the Silence, when we are *letting* Consciousness express Itself.

And now, regarding your comment on the passages from *Promethius Bound*. In some of my Classes, probably not transferred to books, but still left in the tapes, you will find that I have said exactly this, that Jesus broke the laws of the Essenes movement by attempting to give ultimate Truth to the masses, and of course, for this he was crucified. Naturally, it was *his false sense of love for man* that compelled him to go out into the highways and the byways, giving a message *that can never be understood through the mind*. It was with this revelation that I received my instructions in how to proceed, and how to actually accomplish the result that they failed in, those who went out into the highways and byways, and of course, today I am witnessing it come true in so many different ways. The very ones we had hoped to reach, like those of the church, we are reaching, and if we had ever gone out to preach to them, we too would have been crucified in one way or another.

Be assured we will be here throughout the month of July. As a matter of fact, our plans have changed, and the plans for re-doing this house have been scrapped, and last

Sunday we bought a beautiful home, Japanese style, in a very beautiful section of Kailua; in fact, the most beautiful, I believe; where we will have ample room for our little family, and a large swimming pool as well; that is, large for out here; it is 38 by 18. The house was built only seven years ago, and only one family has occupied it, and so it really comes to us in fine condition, and with the landscaping all completed. We move into it June 16th, and certainly by the middle of July we should be well settled, with new furniture, and so forth.

The very experience that you are having with even a few students on this 'children work' is preparing your consciousness for an unfoldment that will enable you to really do as you know it should be done for an Infinite Way activity.

No, I do not want any classes taught in the Infinite Way on the history of Christianity. If anything, I will do everything in my power to discourage students from undertaking such a study, which is in line with what I have done for the past thirty years. At every opportunity that I have had of discouraging someone from taking up such a study, I have exercised it, and never with any regrets. Studying the history of ignorant superstition, mythology, paganism, will not get anyone anywhere on the spiritual Path, and all it can lead to is a million questions as to whether Moses really crossed the Red Sea, or whether Jesus Christ actually walked across the ocean, and of course, the history of its churchianity is a disgrace that could well be forgotten.

Your work in the Presbyterian Church has been of an entirely different nature, and this I can readily go along with. If you have read the paperback *Honest to God*, by the Bishop of Woolwich, you will realize, of course, that your experience is, in a lesser degree, what he is experiencing now in the Church of England.

Regarding this matter of inadequacy, of course, *without this you would be worth nothing on the spiritual Path. The moment that you begin to feel adequate, resign from whatever it is that you are doing, because you will have outlived your usefulness.*

And regarding this matter of the social drink, I can only say that there are no sins, but when our consciousness reaches a certain point, things of that nature will fall away.[1]

Well, I think that this about covers the entire situation.

Yes, I think you will find *The Contemplative Life* is a tremendous book, and certainly one that will sit on my bookshelf alongside of *The Thunder of Silence* and *A Parenthesis in Eternity.*

Happy indeed to have heard from you, and I do hope that I have shared a little of the bread, meat, wine and water that is so available to us.

Aloha greetings to you and to all of the family,

Joel

Dear Joel,   May 1, 1963

Thank you, again, for your so quick response by letter, and for your immediate response with your Presence.

I found myself actually *worrying* about the church situation. About Friday afternoon I began to feel your Presence – Saturday quite strongly – and Sunday morning I woke up with complete peace and the quiet assurance of just what to do.

As far as I am concerned it was a complete triumph of Spirit. I simply reminded them of what I had told them many times – that I was not there as a teacher, but as a

---

[1] Joel was right, as usual. This sank in, and I have used it many times in my own ministry to bring peace to my students. We all suffer in the same way. We are all healed in the same way.

student, just like them. That to me God was the only teacher, and the entire objective of the class had always been, as far as I was concerned, to make ourselves available for the Holy Spirit to work in us and do the teaching each Sunday. I said that it was not a class in theology, because I was not a theologian and would not be equipped to teach theology since I didn't know any. That, furthermore, I considered the study of theology, as such, to be almost a complete waste of time – because theologians down through the centuries have never agreed with each other; that theologies have changed with the wind. I pointed out, however, that there is a body of Christian literature which has been left to us down through the ages, written often by men and women thousands of miles apart, and hundreds of years apart, but that there has never been any disagreement among them. That the men and women who have written about the *experience* of God have always agreed and therefore, to me, that was a far more important body of literature than all the theological arguments.

Two men from the Session attended and brought their wives: a Mr. W. and a Mr. O. Nothing but material vibrations came off of the first one – but the other was very loving. *Mrs.* O. came up to me after the class and took my hand and looked very, very deep into my eyes and said, "I cannot tell you how wonderful I found this. I thoroughly enjoyed every minute of it. I got a great deal out of it and I thank you very much." So – I said to myself, "Thank you, Father, I hope this is the handwriting on the wall."

Now, today, I talked to the Minister who tells me that the result of their meeting last night was that it seems that "You are an inspiring teacher, but you don't know very much about the Presbyterian way. The Class has been very helpful to those who have responded to it. No definite decisions have been made. A Member of Session will from time to time visit your class – not to *spy* – but just to see how it is being taught, (now there's a non sequitur for you). Also, we will replace Mr. B. (the doctor), who will return to teaching the High School class, with M.T., who will be the representative of the Session in the Class."

Now M.T. is a convert from Judaism. A very, very close friend of the doctor's – but he has split with him theologically over this issue of the universality of the Christ – and I feel that this may be partly the basis for the doctor's undoubted personal resentment of me as well as his disagreement with my principles – that he feels I have estranged him from his friend. But of course that's all human – and I simply impersonalize it. Since it really is only that D. is allowing himself to be used by carnal mind. With M.T. in the Class, the Class would really, I feel, return to being of one mind and could again be the joy which it has been for me in the past.

However, Joel, and I want you to tell me how you think I should be reacting to all this –

I had a talk with a Mr. S., who is no longer on the Session but who was a member when the Session invited me to teach for the first time. He tells me, "Of course you do have Mr. K. and Mr. A. very strongly against you – and since all this has come up maybe you should quit." It is quite true that Mrs. K. came a few times at the beginning – didn't like the Curriculum (provided by the Church), and I was very much not her cup of tea – so she just didn't come back.

Now, Mr. K. and four others started this little church 25 years ago – and while in the interim it has become Presbyterian and even joined with the United P. it was not at first – and I kind of wonder if I have the right to be there presenting a viewpoint in such contradiction to their long-held, cherished (but, of course, erroneous) traditional views?

The Session decided to let the class continue, kind of on a temporary basis. They agreed to go along with me for a while – but nothing permanent. Of course, that aspect is perfectly all right with me, because I have never considered myself "permanent," since I don't know from one week to the next what you or the Father may ask of me.

Naturally, I feel no attachment whatever to the Church. I do feel some sense of responsibility to the members of my class who have been devoted, regular in attendance, and who have expressed continuing appreciation for the class. But they are only a very, very small part of the total membership of that Church. And the "leaven" has already been established. Many of them are leaders of men's and women's groups in the Church and they may be able to take the "message" to the others in a much more palatable, or acceptable, way than I could.

Of course, you are right that the history of the Church is a disgrace. But in my classes at UCLA I have been forced to study church history, as well as Italian Civilization, and it has been interesting to me to see the pattern of cycles – the almost universal mysticism of the Middle Ages which resulted in the bursting of the Renaissance (which others mistakenly attribute to the rediscovery of the Greek and Roman Classics); with the Renaissance "devotion to humanism" resulting, in its turn, in the "barren period," the frightened period of the Baroque – then the recognition that man was "sinking" and the desperate effort to shore up his world with "reason," which he mistakenly labelled "enlightenment;" which, in turn, resulted in the greatest holocaust of blood and tyranny we have ever seen (including Hitler); namely, the French Revolution. I think the history of men's failures (which are many) and their spiritual successes (which are few) is interesting. But, again, to know about it is certainly in no way necessary for spiritual growth and, as such, as you point out – not a proper activity for the Infinite Way. It was just a thought and I didn't put it forward too seriously. Of course, I accept your viewpoint completely.

I will get the paperback *Honest to God* – thanks for letting me know about it.

Much love, and much gratitude. It is wonderful to have a teacher,

Dear Barbara: May 6, 1963

Thank you for your letter of May 1st, and you have, of course, come to an inevitable part of your church experience. You see, as long as you had a minister partial to your approach, or willing to be convinced, you could work in a completely harmonious atmosphere. But since churches have a way of changing ministers it is inevitable that those Infinite Way students who would work in Protestant churches must inevitably come across a minister or a president of the board, or someone in authority in the church dedicated to ancient orthodoxy, and this, of course, is where the friction comes in, and this actually is where your service probably will come to an end.

Personally I believe that this is inevitable, and it is for this reason that I am skeptical at all times about an activity such as you have been engaged in. Not that I oppose it or object to it, and certainly not that I do not believe that a magnificent work has been done, but I do not believe it is the way to present the message of the Infinite Way.

To begin with, I believe that for an individual to benefit by the Infinite Way they must first of all desire it, and then secondly, they must devote themselves to it, and thirdly, they must *sooner or later abandon all other teachings and set themselves wholeheartedly to adopting the specific principles that comprise the message of the Infinite Way.* Now, you can see that this has not been done in the case of those to whom you have gone in the Church. To them you have merely added something to that which they already had, and of course this cannot be done.[1]

---

[1]   Italics are mine. In my teaching ministry I have found, absolutely, that those who continue to "Message hop" (try to mix other things with the I.W.) end up making *no* progress.

It is a recognition of this that caused the Bishop of Woolwich to write his book, *Honest to God,* even though he must have known when he wrote it that he was going to bring down upon his head the thundering hoofs of three-quarters of the ministers and higher-ups of the Church of England. Yet he had the courage to say to them in his book that they must stop presenting the "Father Christmas" or what we call "Santa Claus God," and that they must stop presenting this super-human Jesus, and that *they must give up all concepts of God, because no concept of God can be correct,* and he told them that *prayer is not talking to God, but listening to God,* and several other principles of the Infinite Way.

Now, he did not tell them that they could add spiritual wisdom alongside of their present teaching, but he told them that they would have to *abandon* the present teaching in order to receive the truth. But you see, you were not telling your people that they had to abandon the Presbyterian teachings, or the Protestant teachings; you were merely giving them something to add to what they already had, whether or not that was your intention. Of course it wasn't, but that is actually what was taking place.[1] In the same way, the Pope, in his Easter message, has given the principle of impersonalization and says that you must never attach the error to the person who errs, because the person who errs always remains the full human being; of course he meant by that the man of integrity; and that because of this innate quality, that eventually he would break through these sinful thoughts or deeds and realize his complete pure nature. And the Pope continued that he felt that the time has come to re-state this ancient philosophy. Now, this, of course, is in contradiction to all of his church teaching, which condemns the sinner and excommunicates him, and relegates him to hell to burn forever and forever, and here he is, not saying that you must accept this

---

[1] Joel was, as usual, entirely correct in his analysis. The whole thing was just a preparation experience.

impersonalization *alongside of,* but that the time has come to renounce that and accept this ancient philosophy.[1]

What I am saying in this letter concerns a specific principle upon which the Infinite Way has functioned since its beginning, and which carrying the message into the Protestant Church violates. Of course, since I do not make rules, I do not forbid it, and as a matter of fact, I have enough curiosity that I would be glad to watch experiences like yours, or experiments like yours, to see if they do not confirm the principle upon which the Infinite Way operates, and up to now your experience has seemed to be the only exception to the general rule, and of course I have naturally been interested to see how long the experiment could continue until you hit up against a situation such as you are meeting. Now, I cannot, within the confines of even a long letter, explain to you the principle upon which the Infinite Way is functioning on a worldwide basis, but the next time that we meet anywhere and have an hour or two, I will explain this principle to you and show you the fruitage of it.[2]

Not that I haven't explained it to you before, but you did not catch it, and it is for this reason that you went ahead with this work. But now I would ask you to sit down in a corner all by yourself and ask yourself how many people in that Church, in the course of all of this time that you have spent there, have abandoned their false theology and orthodoxy and received spiritual enlightenment. And remember, this is the spiritual teacher's main function; not merely making people comfortable in their bodies or in their orthodoxy, but rather to fulfill the mission of the Master, "I am not come to bring peace, but a sword."[3]

---

[1] "Neither do I condemn you."

[2] "I, if I be *lifted up* shall draw all men unto me," i.e., *no* prosyletizing, no advertising, is *ever* needed.

[3] I did catch it at this time, and that was the end of my "Church career." It was all rather odd, anyway, since I had left my own church at age nine and had always been a non-joiner. Still, it did serve as an educational experience which confirmed to me my scepticism about Church.

We cannot accomplish our mission by carrying the message of the Infinite Way out into the world. We can only fulfill our true function by sitting at home, or in an office, and "letting my own come to me," as Burroughs would phrase it, *and then, when the receptive and responsive consciousness comes and is willing to lay down all of his preconceived ideas, beliefs, superstitions, ignorances*, and reach out, even if painfully, even if by abandoning all others, then can we fulfill our function and lift all men up to our level of consciousness. If we go to them, they try to make it fit into their present state of consciousness, and of course we cannot blame them, because we failed in our function as spiritual teachers.[1]

Of course you know I will be interested in every step that you take along the spiritual Path.

Aloha greetings,

Joel

Dear Joel,   May 15, 1963

Thank you so much for your letter. I fully realize now how privileged I am that you would take the time to write me a three page letter. You have expressed yourself very clearly and it goes without saying that I will study it very carefully.

The classes for parents at the Study Center are about drawing to a close. I think two more sessions will complete it. And, quite frankly, I have been having very strong feelings to withdraw from every commitment and concentrate on increasing my own level of Consciousness. I just have the feeling that I can't be of any more value to anybody until I rise higher in Consciousness myself. In fact it is revealing itself as a kind of "passion for anonymity."

---

[1] Every year that passes shows me over and over the supreme wisdom of this counsel.

Edward says we can't get away in July but could the last week in August. Do you still expect to be around then?

Thank you again for your letter.

Love to all,

Dear Barbara: May 18,1963

Evidently our letters crossed in the mail.

At the present writing it certainly appears that I will be here throughout August, because so far I haven't the faintest idea of traveling. Actually I have come to a decision today that will make it possible for me to do my work without getting as far behind as I have been. Even with a nineteen-hour day and seven days a week, I have not been able to catch up, but I think that I will be able to from now on in.

I had lunch today, by invitation, with the minister of the largest Protestant congregation here in Hawaii, and have been invited to give a series of talks on *The Contemplative Life* next fall. Well, they will soon be lessening their activities owing to the summer season, and as we get closer to the fall we can come to a decision on that.

And so my answer is, I certainly look forward to being here for a long time to come, and it will be a pleasure to greet you and Ed over here.

Aloha greetings to both of you and to all of the family,

Joel

Note: Following is my Letter of Resignation to the Presbyterian Church.

The Session   June 4, 1963
Westminster United Presbyterian Church
Los Angeles, California

Gentlemen:

In the past few weeks, the curriculum which we have been using in the Adult Class has made me increasingly aware of the importance of the "church invisible" in the world.

Together with many hours of meditation, this has resulted in the strengthening of my long-held conviction that there is a universal brotherhood of all men in Christ, even of those who have not yet become aware that we are brothers and all members of the one "church invisible;" that the Christ includes all men. It only remains for them to be made *aware* that we are all children of the one Father, all brothers in the one Christ.

I now believe that this sense of universal brotherhood can be better served by dedicating myself to world work on a non-sectarian basis. It is, therefore, my intention to withdraw from membership in Westminster Church. Naturally, it is also indicated that I withdraw as teacher of the Adult Class, which I will do at your convenience if you will kindly let me know which Sunday you would like me to terminate.

For my part, I am willing to serve until you can find a replacement, although I could not serve after July 28th as we will be out of the city after that date. In the five years' association which I have had with Westminster I have learned a great deal from all of the people I have met there. These relationships I will always remember with gratitude and affection.

I sincerely hope that you all understand that this decision is the result of a great deal of serious thought and is not undertaken lightly.   Equally, I am sure you understand, every person must serve his own inner spiritual integrity – a concept which is so clearly outlined in your "Confession of Faith" – and this is the basis of my decision.

I am not familiar with protocol in these matters, but if it is necessary, would you please send me a letter of release of membership?[1]

Kindest regards, and I await your further instructions.

Sincerely yours,

Dear Joel,   June 20, 1963

Thank you so much for the "talks."[2]   I really can hardly wait to get there, because what is coming through in these talks is the greatest, and the clearest, and the most direct teaching that I have ever experienced from you, with the single exception of the "teaching beyond words" of our private sessions and the P.K.[3] class last summer.

It is proof of the infinity of the Christ that you can continue to "top" yourself in an unfolding upward spiral – it's endless, isn't it?

There is so much going on here – and so fast – that there seems almost no point in writing you about it because the unfoldments are coming daily. Yesterday's manna is "old hat" before I could get it on paper. Except for one big one. One of my Wednesday night students presented me with a card containing her expression of

---

[1]   They told me there was no such thing in their church as a "Release from Membership." I said, "In other words, you could excommunicate me, but I cannot resign from you?" They answered, "We have no provision for that." So I presume I am still in their Little Black Book.

[2]   These were the wonderful "Honolulu Talks" of 1962 and 1963. Joel had stopped recording his sessions, but they were taken down stenographically, xeroxed, and sent to the Teachers and Tape Group Leaders.

[3]   Princess Kaiulani Hotel, Waikiki.

gratitude for healing – and a $100 bill! I had 2 reactions – first was shock – then surprise – then the feeling, "My consciousness can't be worth a hundred dollars to anybody." Then immediately the Voice came through with the statement, "Certainly not – but *Mine* is."

The second reaction was a feeling that the Father had, with this, put the seal of professional responsibility on me. I have ducked this all along – and thought I was getting away with it – that I could just stay a "happy amateur" – but this seems the evidence that I am already past the point of no return – and my private life is over.

Did this make you sad when it happened to you? I find a sense of sadness in me.

It looks like I will, for sure, be bringing three students – and maybe five – in August. Oh, my lord, there are so many things I need to talk over with you. You'd better lay up some strength and get ready for me to bend your ear!

I can't remember whether or not I told you that one of the most valuable fruitages from the hard serious work that was done on the Presbyterian Class has resulted in that Edward and I meditate together every night.

Love till later, when we can deliver some in person.

Dear Barbara: June 24, 1963

Happy indeed to have your letter of June 20th, and I know that when you receive the July and August *Letters*, that you will know beyond all doubt that something of a tremendous nature is unfolding. What a wonderful experience to have such a fine healing as to bring forth gratitude and its visible expression.

My entrance into the healing practice was such an unusual one that there were no feelings possible of any nature. One day I was asked to pray for someone, and I was astonished that such a thing could happen to me, but a healing took place, and the next day I was asked by another person, and again a healing took place, and two or three days later, another experience, and this just kept happening for the next eighteen or twenty months until I found myself with more patients than customers, and so just opened an office. I never dreamed, throughout all of these months, that anything of that nature was happening to me, and just seemed to be taking each day as it came along, without even knowing that I was doing that, and then all of a sudden, there I was in an office, so I really had no opportunity to indulge in introspection, which is the thing that we ordinarily would do.

> *Note: The above paragraph is a condensation of a really wonderful story: Joel's business (importing) had been going down and down. He asked for help from a practitioner. It didn't help. So he asked for help from an additional practitioner. As he said to me, "I finally had five practitioners working on it and every time I added a practitioner it just got worse. Finally, one day I returned to my office and the man I shared it with said, 'You have had twenty calls and none of them for business. They are all calls for help. When are you going to wake up and see that you are in the wrong business?' I figured I couldn't do any worse at being a practitioner than I was at business so I closed my office." Well, we all know the end of that story.*

We have a wonderful program worked out here for the students who are coming every week, and there are always several, of course. I have four teaching sessions during the week, and D. takes three to teach meditation, her particular way of conducting a ministry, and showing those who are interested how she conducts her activities at the Center. Altogether, it makes a full week, a ripe and a rich week, and those who have been here all feel that they have been mightily blessed. In fact, they are sending others as soon as they get home.

Of course this is a tremendous joy that has come to you with Edward, and actually this should be the fruitage of spiritual work. If it doesn't unite us more closely in our family life, we are really missing part of our spiritual fruitage. As you know, it has re-united me with Charles[1] and with my sister, and since they are the only two living relatives that I have, that is, close relatives, I can say that my spiritual activities have fulfilled themselves in uniting me with my family in a closer bond than we ever had when it was just a blood relationship.

Our heartfelt greetings to all of you,

Joel

P.S. We will be in our new home about July 1st, so the meetings will be in the new home, and I am sure you will like that.

Dear Joel,   July 17, 1963

As you can see by the date on the attached there has been a stir of activity at the Church. But I did not want to bother sending you the information until it had resolved, since I certainly didn't know how it would work out.

A few weeks ago they accepted my resignation. Some of the students wept when I read my letter to them and said how could I abandon them and what were they going to do, etc. But I told them my decision was at the dictates of the Father and that it could not, therefore, possibly rebound to hurt anyone. That they should be patient and perhaps a blessing would unfold for them.

---

[1] His nephew.

Three weeks ago I was given the signal to introduce the class to you, your writings, and to the Infinite Way. I told them that they didn't need me, that they could go to the same source where I went for my inspiration, and that since I had learned everything I knew from you they could use your books to continue their study of scripture; that is any of those who had responded to my kind of teaching.

Well, last Sunday, I also had the go-ahead to tell them about the class at the Center, which I did. It's funny, I thought perhaps the Father would not give me this signal and I was certainly prepared to say nothing. But two Sundays ago, one of the class students stopped me outside and said there was something she wanted to tell me. She said that her husband was 62 and had suffered from a skin disease all of his life; that he had been to doctors, and to Christian Science practitioners, and had spent thousands of dollars but had never been free of it, and that now it was just gone – disappeared – and that they knew it was due to my Consciousness. She also said that she had had an unusual experience during our meditation that morning. The Voice had said to me during the meditation, "Tell them they must not work for this, that any effort they make will only defeat them" – which, of course, I did, when the meditation was over. This lady said that during the meditation something inside of her had said, "You're working too hard." She wanted to know if this was "thought transference," or something. I told her of course it was not; that there was no such thing as thought transference; but that she had had her first experience of omnipresence and of the fact that Consciousness is one.

I also told her how she could now see, then, in relation to her husband's healing, the illustration of the principle I had been relating to them in connection with healing work, that we did not need to know the name of the person nor the condition, because as I said to her, "Mrs. M., I didn't even know that your husband *had* a skin disease." I said that the spirit works like a broom of light, sweeping out any dark corners, as long as we are generating Consciousness, and we don't even have to know where the dark corners are.

Well, to continue, some of them reached for pencils and wrote down the address of the Center. But, of course, whether or not they will really stir themselves to come down remains to be seen.[1]

Tonight we are completing the class on "Family Relationships," with one which I have called "Hierarchy in the Home." I am taking the theme for this from I Cor. 7: 12-16, Eph. 5: 21-31, and Eph. 6: 1-4. It will probably come as a surprise to them, as it did to me, when I realized that I had been practicing this for a long, long time before it became a theory! It has become very clear to me that insofar *as the human picture is concerned* "it is a man's world;" that there is a very sure role the man must play; and an equally sure role that the woman must play, if the marriage relationship is to be a successful one. These roles are not one better than the other – only different – and mutually complementary. But in this country of ours, which for so long has dwelt on the "equality of the sexes" (which really becomes the "battle of the sexes"), I feel sure that this will come as a surprise when I tell them that the man absolutely must be the head of the house. As I say, I have practiced this for a long time before I finally arrived at the realization of the theory.[2]

Well, I have to get ready for the class – and Edward is bugging me – so I will close for now.

Love,

P.S. If you want to see me in August – find me a housekeeper!

---

[1] One did, and has been in our classes ever since.

[2] Many years later, when the Relationship classes came through, this was clarified and expanded by Paul's statement in the New Testament that the *husband's* responsibility is to *cherish* his wife, and "...never to anger his children." Some challenge.

Dear Barbara: July 20, 1963

Happy indeed to have your letter of July 17th and to read all of the news of the working out of this church situation. Perhaps when you study the four teachers' tapes that I have made, and with particular attention to the minister's counseling tape, you will realize what you are really up against, which I know you have no way of knowing in advance. As you hear this tape and remember that I am talking to a Baptist minister, incidentally, a classmate of Billy Graham, and try to imagine the shocks being administered to his system, you will then know what you were doing without knowing you were doing it. And for me it was easier, because at least this man had already come to the realization that there was something wrong about the church ministry, whereas those to whom you were talking were still under the belief that everything they were thinking was gospel truth, and they possibly were further believing that you were confirming that truth. *Certainly they had no idea that you were contradicting them.*

Some day you will agree that out of the entire experience you are the one who benefited the most, and of course that was the real purpose of the experience. It had nothing to do with the church or its members. *They were just instruments for bringing experience to you.*

Well, I have just had an experience with a new-born baby born paralyzed, deaf, dumb and blind, and within two months, completely restored to normalcy; and a drug baby, that is, one of those born without arms or hands, and with deformed feet owing to that German drug that was used here for awhile,[1] and both arms and both hands have been restored, and the feet have become normal, and so I am sure if the activity of the Christ could bring about such transformations, there is no reason to doubt that it can bring a housekeeper out of the Invisible to you.

---

[1] Thalidomide.

Harpers are spending $5,000 to publicize *A Parenthesis in Eternity* before its release, and they are going to start also a campaign on *The Thunder of Silence*, so we will probably be finding ourselves with a still wider field of activity.

No other news at present, so our united love to all of you!

Joel

Dear Joel,   July 25, 1963

Thank you for the thrilling information about the healings with the babies. This is really a break-through of incredible proportions. It makes one look at the headlines of a newspaper with a sense of, "My God, don't you people know what is really going on in the world, of importance?" And, God willing, the world's sense of values may be lifted. I read that portion of your letter to my Wednesday night class and they were, of course, struck speechless. We are all deeply humble in the recognition of, and gratitude for, the level of your Consciousness. You have lighted the Path and I told them that this is the goal we must all be shooting for – and never be satisfied to stop short of it.

As to the Presbyterians – it isn't a matter that I will "one day" agree that this experience was for me. I have known, Joel, that I was being groomed and that even the experience in teaching their junior high school was training ground for me. (Groomed for what, I certainly don't know). But following a policy of not outlining, and of just being a beholder – I have simply gone along for the ride and allowed the entire thing to unfold as it would. Certainly the experience was not to teach me about the very humanness, politics, and hypocrisy in the church. Those were the very things that sent me out of the church and onto the search for God – who, I had decided when I was nine, was not *there*. I never went to a church again until my Infinite Way activity moved me in that direction. I was amazed that it did so – but, as I said, I just went along for the ride. I still don't know exactly what I have learned of any importance – because it only seems to have confirmed what I already knew instinctively; but of course, they did accept me a long time ago in a teaching capacity, and I have learned a lot from just the doing. This was long before I should have been doing any teaching for the Infinite Way – so maybe that's it. In any event it is over – and so much for that.

As I have said to you many times – I am willing to serve in this way and have gone along and done so when asked, in the conscious awareness that I was being taught and groomed, but I have always been reluctant about this, and I am still reluctant, mostly because I am so aware of what an imperfect instrument I am. But, of course, Paul's quote where God says, "My perfection is made known by thy imperfection," is the rebuttal to that, and I am aware of it. So I just go along – slipping and falling – but mostly doing my best – and sometimes there seem to be some students who receive benefit from my Consciousness. (I just received another check yesterday and a most gracious expression of gratitude for what this student called "the transformation of my life through your consciousness"). They attribute to me a virtue I do not possess, and yet the very fact that they are getting help is evidence that the Father is using me, so I have no choice. I guess I just have to plod along and do as I am asked.

We finished the parents' class last night. I frankly told them I was glad to see the last of it and that I felt a strong desire to wash the human off of me and off of the class and to steep myself in your teaching instead of my own, and for that reason the rest of the Wednesday nights until we leave for Honolulu will simply be conducted as a tape group.

I don't know whether or not I have told you, but I stopped my Thursday night tape group in my home. V. set up a Thursday night tape group in the valley which was more public in its nature, and I closed mine and asked all my people to go and support that one. But we will be having a tape activity at the Center on Wednesday nights until August 23rd.

R. asked to borrow some of my tapes and I would have been perfectly willing for him to do so because I think they should all be in constant use, but B. says Emma told her tapes should not be loaned. Is this still in effect? Or would it be all right for me to do so?

One thing more – of course my remark about the housekeeper was a joke – and for a moment I considered so labelling it – but then decided that with a person of your intelligence and sense of humor such obviousness would be out of place.[1]

It really is fascinating how the wheels grind out. All the hard meditating over the Presby. class resulted in Edward's and my meditating together and has completely transformed our relationship and it was, I am sure, entirely due to the fact that I asked you to be with me that week. *He* works in mysterious ways – and in so multi-level a way – that we couldn't possibly understand it anyway. And so to try is ridiculous. To just *be* is enough.

Well, papa is bugging me to go – again – so will close for now.

We are both looking forward to basking in your and Emma's consciousness more than I can say.

Love,

---

[1] Oh, dumb Barbara. It is very evident, now, that his remark was a joke, too. I took everything *so* seriously in those days. But then it is *hard* to be a human being, and *impossible* to be a perfect one. Nonetheless, experience has taught me that some of it is funny, not deadly. I especially love Joel's tapes that start out, "Now relax."

Dear Papa,   July 30, 1963

Well, I have come to more conclusions this week! Among them that one should never write tortured letters – they are only evidence that we are in the midst of the struggle – and the struggle inevitably results in a lesson learned. So it is better, I think, to wait and write only the results, not the struggle.

As I am sure you realized when you received my last woebegone letter, I was really in the midst of one. However, I had hardly got it into the mail before I began to get a little light on the subject, and then along came the August *Letter*, which threw more light exactly where I needed it.

To be as brief as possible. It is now very clear that it doesn't matter how imperfect Barbara is so long as she is *out of the way*. The devil is so, so insidious! As long as he can keep me worrying about how imperfect Barbara is, so long does she stay alive. To *ignore* her and her sins is death – which she, apparently, mightily doesn't want. I don't know exactly how to work on this except to keep the mind on God – and to endeavor to keep *her* out of the way. I would appreciate any wisdom you have on the subject. [1]

However, if you do not receive any more letters acknowledging my imperfection and inadequacy, do not construe that it is because I am beginning to feel adequate! It will only mean that I do not consider my sins worth recounting.

In other words, I have understood that Barbara can get in the way – even prevent anything from coming through – but if anything does come through from Spirit, Barbara cannot defile it, because it is undefilable. So we will work from there.

---

[1]   Oh dear! He had been writing me his wisdom on the subject for five years.

I guess you know by now that V. has left the Center. I don't know what all this nonsense is about, but I do wish to report a very good sense of rapport with B. which *I* feel.

Be patient with me. I am trying to be patient with me, too.

Love,

Dear Barbara: July 30, 1963

It is so good to have your letter of July 25th, and I know, of course, that a whole new area of consciousness has been opened to you, and that, of course, means a new experience.

Certainly B. has misunderstood Emma, because of all the people in the world to make such a remark, Emma would never be one of them; that is, that you should not lend your tapes to R., or to anyone else who you feel to be a serious student. As a matter of fact, practically everybody who buys tapes lends them, either to groups or to individuals. Without that, we would just be running a great big money-making institution, and I am sure you know that never has been our intention. We feel that the wider the circulation of these tapes, the greater opportunity the message has of reaching human consciousness. We have not only approved of the lending of tapes, we have even approved of lending them where there is some small fee involved; that is, some of our students lend their tapes to others, or groups lend them to individuals, and charge them one, or two, or three dollars, as the case may be, so as to help replace tapes and secure new tapes.

Without the tape lending activity, I can assure you that there never would be as many people hearing tapes as there are now. To begin with, you know we have no control over the tapes once they are in your hands, they are yours, but under no circumstances do we ever wish to restrict the circulation of tapes. We do object to the duplicating of tapes, whether for resale or to give away, because in this way we lose all control over the quality of the tapes, and this eventually could ruin our tape activity. There are some tapes right now being made in Los Angeles, and sold for $10, and some of the quality is so poor that the excuse is being made that our masters are poor, which is really not the case at all.

Of course I hope you do know that I understood your housekeeper remark was a joke. What else?

Be assured we are looking forward with great joy to greeting you.

Aloha greetings, meaning love to all of you!

Joel

Dear Barbara: August 3, 1963

Thank you for your letter of the 30th, and by a strange coincidence, in the same mail that brought your letter today I received the enclosure from Sig Paulson,[1] and it certainly answers the first part of your letter, and therefore I have an idea you will enjoy this.

The desk is heavy with mail today, so Aloha for now,

Joel

CO-OPERATING WITH GOD

It is difficult for us to believe that our minds and hearts are acceptable to God right now, just as they are! We would prefer to clean them up before we enter the Divine Presence;

---

[1] See Joel's letter of August 20, 1963, p. 269.

but the disconcerting truth is this: the human sense of good is so closely related to the human sense of evil that neither has any permanent standing in the light of Truth. Both have to go in order that a greater may take their place.

The only really notable change in our living takes place when we let God accept our minds and hearts, regardless of their condition. Once we have permitted God to accept our minds and hearts, they can't remain in their present condition because His love, life and joy start to flow through them, and the words of our mouth, the thoughts of our minds, the meditation of our hearts, the functions of our bodies and all the activities of our lives become charged with Truth. We become co-operators with God. His Spirit operates us, and we give individual expression to infinite love, life and joy.

When this happens, we finally stop trying to operate God. We realize that Truth is not a special "gimmick" working for our benefit. We are restored to our rightful place in the divine scheme of good; we know that we are co-operators with God, expressing infinity in a unique way for the benefit of all.

In joyous service

Sig Paulson

Dear Joel,   August 15, 1963

Of course Mr. Paulson expressed so very well what I was expressing badly, but we did come to the same conclusion and that's what counts, I guess.

I have often noted in the past that sometimes when I wrote you about a thing on which I apparently did not have sufficient light as to operate from a spiritual standpoint, you simply did not answer me on that subject, waiting, I presume, for more light to penetrate me about whatever subject it might be.

And, of course, over the years, I have seen increased understanding so that, in looking back, I can see that I have often made statements out of spiritual immaturity which at the later point I would not make.

I do not need to write you about human-picture things.

See you soon.

Love,

P.S. Who is Sig Paulson?

Dear Barbara: August 20, 1963

When I do not answer you on a subject, one of two things can be taken for granted; one is, there is no comment that I could make that would serve any particular purpose, and the other is that I have overlooked that point in your letter and forgotten it, and if there is anything that should have an answer, you should write me the second time and remind me. You would be surprised how many times I overlook questions in letters, unintentionally, but only because I am sitting here always anywhere from one hundred to two hundred letters behind in my dictation, and perhaps I do not pay attention to every sentence or every line in the letter, and thereby am apt to overlook it.

Sig Paulson was the Unity minister in New York City, and is now the head of Unity field work, with headquarters at Lee's Summit, Missouri, but actually traveling the entire world as chief executive of all field work, that is, all work pertaining to all of the centers, practitioners, teachers, ministers, etcetera. This makes him about number one in Unity.

Besides that, Sig Paulson and his wife, Janie, are two of our very, very close friends who are in touch with us just about every week of the year, regardless of where they may be traveling, regardless of where he may be traveling, Africa, the United States, Europe, or at home; a letter comes about once a week, and a letter goes off from me to him about once a week, because that is the close bond that has been established between us for many, many, many years.

Of course we are all looking forward to greeting you and those who are coming with you over here.

Aloha greetings to you and to all of your dear family!

Joel

Dear Barbara: September 24, 1963

Our activity here increased, with one student arriving from Paris, France, and others arriving from the Mainland, so that we were twenty-four here in the study this morning, Monday.

The tapes of both Series, that is the Sunday Series and the Private Class out here, continue to intensify, and I am sure that this is going to be an important work for you and your students.

My sincere thanks to you for your very thoughtful enclosure, and Aloha greetings to all!

Joel

Dear Joel,   October 3, 1963

Of course the increase of activity which you mention is not surprising. When the lotus is in full bloom the bees must come buzzing around.

I have ordered all of the 1963 tapes, though whether or not any of my students is ready for such a message is a matter for some speculation. However, since it is the spiral road, and since we have infinity, and since there is nowhere to go but up – we must just get at it, and not worry about the inadequacies.

The new class began last night, urging the loosing of old concepts and pointing out the large difference between hope, belief, faith, and knowledge, with knowledge of God the goal to be achieved. B. tells me that several of them stopped at her desk and said they enjoyed it very much or that they got a lot out of it. I ran into one at the Brown Derby afterwards and she told me I had so enthused her that she had bought *Practicing the Presence* and *Art of Meditation* and was going to get to work immediately. There were 12 students besides B. and R. and my family.

Although it pains me to write you things like this about myself, you said you wanted me to write you about any fruitage of my teaching or healing activity so I will tell you that while I was in Honolulu the husband of one of D.'s students asked to see me and after he had briefly outlined his problem I talked to him about 20 minutes explaining principles and afterward he said, "That is one of the finest Infinite Way talks I have ever heard." I have since heard from him that his problem is dissolving.

I have seen definite fruitage in two of the people I brought with me to Honolulu – in raised consciousness and new understanding (of course, that certainly is not entirely due to my activity with them). It is very embarrassing to me to write things like this; particularly since I know perfectly well that I of myself can do nothing and I only feel a sense of gratitude that the Father is willing to work through me. I hope some day you will decide you know me well enough to take my activity on faith and my spiritual integrity for granted. Until you do I will do my best to keep you acquainted with everything as it occurs.

Of course we can't look for fruitage from the new class for several weeks, since they are mostly new students – new to me and some even new to the I.W. The next four weeks' classes will be the Nature of God, followed by the Nature of Man, then the Nature of Error and lastly the Nature of Prayer, since those are the four basics. What will follow that has not yet been made clear to me.

By the way, Joel, I wanted to ask you if you have heard from any of my friends who came with me, either with checks or letters of gratitude. Would you let me know, please.

I also wanted to ask you if my name is on your list of teachers and practitioners for the Los Angeles area? I think it might be important to B. to have it here, since V. told her that the only people authorized to teach in the I.W. were those whose names were on that list – and I know that B. is anxious to keep her center (as she says) "pure."

Thank you for bringing me up to date on your plans.

Something that might interest you – there is a young man who was part of my Presbyterian Sunday class. I discussed *Honest to God* two Sundays there and it apparently bore some fruit. He is also the same young man to whom Virginia (my sister) and I gave your books about two years ago.

He is now up at San Anselmo (the Presbyterian Seminary) headed for the Ministry – and he writes me that *Honest to God* is the text book for one of his classes and will be the subject of a Seminar in October. He also states that his room-mate has three of your books on his shelves.[1]

So it seems the young man isn't able to get away from the right influences.

Love to you and Emma,

Dear Barbara: October 7, 1963

I think you left here just before the tremendous increase of activity began, because it seems to me that nothing like the past two weeks has ever happened before. There are more papers and more tapes than I have ever known in a comparable time. I presume that you have been receiving all of the papers since you left, and that you know that there has been a fifth tape added to the Teachers' Series, and that there are now twelve tapes in the Sunday Series and the Kailua Private Class, and of course you probably know that the group that came out here on Fridays and Mondays finally had to sit outside on the patio, as there was no more room inside.

I will just summarize this message in the following paragraph:

This new work has its basis in the revelation that there are two levels of consciousness, one, "the man of earth," and the other, "the man who has his being in Christ;" or "the natural man," "the creature," who knoweth not the things of God and receiveth not the things of God; and the child of God, which is, of course, heir of God. In the first instance you have, of course, the human race, "the natural man," "the man of earth" completely cut off from God, definitely not supported, sustained or maintained by God, <u>surely not protected by God</u>, and in no way serving God. Then you have that which you will of course recognize as our spiritual

---

[1] This young man was the M.T. spoken of previously. For many years he has had a fruitful ministry in San Diego, and the last time I talked to him he still referred to himself as an "Infinite Way student."

identity, or our true Selfhood, or the Christ of our being, or our divine Sonship, that which is one with the Father and which hath all that the Father hath. Knowing that there are these two levels of consciousness, and knowing that we ourselves, as humans, represent the first, the lower level of consciousness, the next step deals with the attaining of the higher Consciousness, that is, our divine Selfhood.

You can readily understand that this is an exciting message, a challenging one, and of course, not a simple one.

You need never be pained to write me the fruitage of your work, since I think more than anyone else in the world I know the impersonal Source of fruitage, and therefore I know you are never talking about yourself or your spiritual capacities, but are always referring to the Source of our spiritual fruitage.

And of course, regarding your classwork, I do not possibly see how you are going to gauge this subject, of fruitage. I have been giving classes since 1947, and I still would have no way of knowing how to gauge the fruitage, since I have witnessed miraculous healings only to discover later that they were nothing more nor less than physical healings, or financial healings, with no opening of the Soul whatsoever; and on the other hand, I have witnessed the opening of the soul where there seemed to be no immediate physical or financial fruitage. And sometimes I have witnessed students going through four, five, six, ten classes, with not much to show more than their faith, and then all of a sudden begin to blossom, and I have witnessed some who seemed to blossom like the rose, only to fade away the first time a strong sunlight hit them. I really can tell you, out of my experience, that *you should not look for any fruitage from your classwork,* but that you should give it from the Center of your being, and disregard what may seem to be fruitage, *because it could really fool you!*

I have a standard of judging the spiritual progress of students that has nothing whatsoever to do with any *apparent fruitage, but has to do with what I behold within, and the secret of this lies in the fact that <u>with the attainment of the transcendental Consciousness a vision is given to us which has nothing to do with eyesight, and it is this vision that enables us to see the heart and Soul of the individual in a far different way than they can ever see themselves, or ever know themselves.</u>*[1] At the moment I can only answer your question about the students who were here with you by saying that I have never heard from R. since he left here, nor even when he left here, and last week I did receive a letter from Mrs. H. with an enclosure of thanks, although nothing from her children, even in the way of a message. If I were to judge of the fruitage of your having brought students over here, I would say that it was about as complete a failure as can be imagined, both from your standpoint and from mine.

If we were to judge from appearances, neither R. nor the H. family received anything from their association with us, not even the recognition of the tremendous experience that took place, nor the privilege that was granted them in permitting them to even be in such an activity as took place here, because you must remember, no such activity has ever taken place on this earth in the last two thousand years, and very few have ever been invited to such a feast, and these four never even recognized that a feast was being given to them. This is, of course, judging from appearances, because I have no way of knowing but what all four of these may awaken ten or twenty years from now, and realize what took place, and then, of course, we would say the fruitage was tremendous, and it may well be. It is for this reason that I caution you, do not judge fruitage from appearances, or you will be discouraged with students of this kind, and you will be encouraged by students who will react emotionally and seem to gain something, and later you will discover that Judas has again been in your midst.[2] If

---

[1] This Consciousness was given to me about six months after I began teaching. It has greatly increased my ability to help the students.
[2] How right he was. I had my Judas experience. It strengthened me, and we changed the end of that story.

I have any way of imploring you to do your teaching work without looking for appearances of fruitage, then let this be my prayer.

And now, regarding your name being on the list of teachers and practitioners, surely you know that there is only one way in which that could get on there, and that is by your requesting it of me and my feeling your readiness for it. It will go on at once, but not because of the reason that you have written, because again, it cannot be true that the only people authorized to teach in the Infinite Way are those whose names are on that list, because there are thousands of students all over the world whom I have never met, and do you think for a minute that if they began healing work, that I would in any wise stop them? And if they do healing work, how can they help doing teaching work, because *in healing it is certainly necessary to impart the principles of the Infinite Way, and this is teaching.* Perhaps you do not recognize the fact; in fact, I know you don't recognize it, because you really haven't listened to me hard enough to hear what I have to say, or else you would know that *I personally do not expect to be on earth forever, and I expect the Infinite Way to go on unto eternity, and therefore, <u>authorization for healing and teaching will come by virtue of the consciousness of the individual, and not by any personal permission of any "man whose breath is in his nostrils," nor do I ever expect to leave anyone with the divine authority to authorize healing and teaching.</u> The Infinite Way is the activity of God in individual consciousness, and when that consciousness becomes a healing activity, it cannot be authorized, nor can it be stopped in its operation, and <u>when that consciousness becomes a teaching consciousness, not even God could stop that teaching on earth, much more Joel,</u>* or anyone who may hereafter be active in leading roles in the message of the Infinite Way.[1] When your hearing ability increases, or perhaps your listening ability, I am sure you will

---

[1] For this one paragraph, alone, this book is worth having been published.

discover many of the secrets that I have imparted to you that you have not yet heard.[1]

We will be at the Picadilly Hotel in London October 10th through November, and I certainly shall be pleased to hear further from you.

Aloha greetings to you and to all of the family!

Joel

Dear Joel, October 11, 1963

Well, to answer your letter gives me quite a lot to cover. First of all my first strong reaction to the letter in its entirety was, "Oh, how I respect you." It is a magnificent letter, Joel, strong in wisdom – and I shall keep it immediately by me for a long time for constant reference and study.

But I do want to give you my reactions blow-by-blow, too, as well as bring you up to date on my classwork.

October 21, 1963

Well, what has happened to the last 10 days. It is very difficult for me to find a quiet time at home to do correspondence and I usually have to wait until I can get a morning at Ed's office to catch up. But in this case, I think it is for the best – because so much has happened since the 11th that another letter would have been indicated in any event.

I had made up my mind to try to hold down my letters to you to one page – but to do that and still fulfill

---

[1] What sympathy I have for him. I have experienced that sometimes students not only do not hear – sometimes for years – but also, sometimes by the time what has been said is passed through their "filters," it gets turned around 180 degrees! In many of my prayers I am still moved to acknowledge, "Joel, I'm *sorry* I was so hard-headed."

your request to keep you abreast of the class work I find very difficult.

First of all – to your letter – I have been seeing the continual clarification of these two principles all year in the Sunday talks and that is exactly what seems so exciting to me about this year's work. The issues are being reduced to the basic simplicity of "keep the mind on God." Not that it hasn't always been that – but it seems to be a dwelling, a hammering on this single issue – so that there will no longer be an excuse for a single student to miss the point.

Now as to your remarks about gauging fruitage. What ever gave you the idea that I *look* for fruitage? I would never do that, because that would be outlining and outlining is one of the elementary pitfalls not to fall into. Furthermore, the only result that I would *consider* fruitage would be a "change in Consciousness."

I do not consider healing, whether of health or supply, fruitage, but the "added things." I would not even consider the opening of a soul "fruitage" – for the obvious reason that we do not know whether anything more will develop. But a change in Consciousness we can see. And since it is very, very unlikely (not impossible – but very unlikely) that anyone would ever drop back from an achieved state of Consciousness – this would be, to me, fruitage.

Your admonition, however, to "give it from the center of your being" is another matter – spiritual wisdom – and your remarks have already born fruit in me (change of Consciousness fruits I mean). But that has to do with my class work and more of that later.

I am perfectly aware that your developed spiritual discernment enables you to see within a student and often beyond what they can discern (even spiritually) about themselves. This is the entire basis for my obedience to you – even when I have not been able to see the reasons behind some teaching of the moment. Furthermore, I, too,

at my level, can see into the withinness of my students –
beyond what they are able to know of themselves. So I
am well acquainted with this faculty, and know that it
has nothing at all to do with intellectual measurements.

Now, you tell me that while you received a letter and
check from Mrs. H. you have not heard from her
children. But it must be that you have not related a name
to the people, because her daughter told me last week of her
husband having received a letter of thanks from you for
her letter and check sent to you, and, furthermore, that
you had told her husband, that you would help him
with a physical problem with his leg.

Now, as to the matter of my name being on the
teacher list – you can see how differently we view this.
You say the only way my name would have been put
there was for me to ask for it, and for you to have felt my
readiness. Whereas, from my standpoint, I would have
considered it a boldness unbecoming to a person of any
real humility to *ever* ask to be put on such a list (and I
never would have mentioned it if the subject had not
been brought up by B.). Going back to my complete
understanding of the very point you brought up of your
being able to see into a person – knowing this full well – I
would have expected that whenever you found that I had
developed to the point where I should be put on such a list
– you would simply have so informed me – saying that
you were putting my name on such a list and that I must
fulfill the responsibility indicated.

As I say, except for the fact that I was teaching at B.'s
center, and that it was important to her, I would never
have mentioned it, nor asked to be put on such a list, even
if I had waited for another 10 years. I would have waited
for *you* to tell *me* when I was ready.

Now, I will confess. Certainly I know that
authorization for healing and teaching must ultimately
come to every man from the Father – even as it so came to
you. But for the very reason that you state – that you do
not intend to be around forever – and because I have

already seen evidence that there will be grave danger of the "all too human" erupting in the Infinite Way the moment you are not around to stop it and, above all, because, like you, I am dedicated to maintaining the purity of this message – it is helpful, even necessary, to have your statement to this effect in writing.

In fact, I take an especial joy in the totality of your statement on this matter; further evidence of the validity and truth of your own consciousness – which must always be a beacon light for us all.

As to the secrets you have imparted which I have not yet heard. You know very, very well that I have *always* listened as hard as I was able. And when I did not *hear* – it simply meant that my state of consciousness was not sufficiently developed. But you are the one who taught me that it is useless to ask any individual to be more spiritual than he is – and the continuing development of my stages of consciousness are ample proof that I have listened – if not completely. But you must be patient with me, even as the Father is.

Now, to my class. First of all, my way of conducting a class must arise out of my own experience on the spiritual pathway. I cannot teach anyone else's road, because I have not travelled it, and that would be imitation and fakery. The only conviction I have about what will work are the methods I have used to bring myself along this path to the point of reaching the state of Grace – of having the "hidden manna."

In the beginning of my study of the Infinite Way, and also with others to whom I have given your books for the first time, I have found that one of the stumbling blocks is simply a lack of clean semantics (actually knowing what words mean – not just taking it for granted that we know what they mean, when perhaps our conditioning through the years has been planted in us by ignorant parents); and of understanding the special vocabulary of the Infinite Way, and above all the special way in which *you* use words – which is sometimes different – even from the usual sense in which they are used in the field of metaphysics. Your definition, for instance, of the word Christ. This definition is unique to the I.W., as is your definition of the word Consciousness, and spiritual healing (vs. mental healing) etc. There are many others.

Persons, for instance, to whom I have given your books, many months later will still be asking me, "But what does he *mean* when he says Consciousness?" And I can well remember what it felt like not to know this – because it took a long while for me to understand what you meant by that.

Anyhow, based on this, on the first night of my class I gave everybody little 10¢ notebooks – vocabulary books – and told them that as we went along we would acquire a list of I.W. words and their spiritual meanings, so that in reading the writings, if something were obscure, they could refer to their vocabulary books. And we began with the meaning of "hope, belief, faith and knowledge."

Well, two weeks ago, there were some criticisms of my work which B. reported to me, saying that one woman had said to her, "I got all that note taking in Unity – that's not for advanced students."[1] B. also said that she thought my work was elementary, and dealt too much with the letter of truth.[2]

There was also another technique which I started them on. What I call the "flashcard." It is practiced, as I told them, as a *mental* exercise for accomplishing two things: 1) imbuing the mind with truth, and 2) forming the habit of dropping an appearance of discord out of the

---

[1]   An amusing sidelight to this is that this very student was, nonetheless, moved to come back two weeks later – and has been with me ever since. She remained "hard to teach" but I love her dearly and I had to be as patient (sometimes impatient) with her as Joel had been with me.

[2]   On tape after tape Joel cautions, "You must have the Letter of Truth (the *metaphysics*) "down cold" before you can *hope* to understand the *mysticism* of the Infinite Way. Many students who have come to my classes, even after reading Joel for years, have tried to leap to the mysticism. They have not made progress in their lives; and do *not* make progress until they go back and fill in that lack.

mind *instantaneously,* so as not to feed it with the substance of the mind.

I have been using this practice with my tape group and with my other class for over two years, and the results have been simply wonderful. The way we do it is this: we agree right there, in the class, that during the next week we will all take the same statement from scripture (that week it was "My Kingdom is not of this world") and that at any time an appearance from the human picture would appear to our minds, we agreed to drop it out instantly and bring up the flashcard, and to hold the flashcard to the front of the mind until we achieved that sense of release, or the dissolving of the picture.

Then, the following week, we take some time at the beginning to share with each other how we have been able to use it in the past week – or how we have failed – and how we might have done it better.

B. said the criticism of that was that (and I'm not sure this one was not just B.'s – since she told me she felt that way about it) some felt that if they had had a spiritual experience during the week, as a result of using the flashcard, it would be secret and sacred and they would not want to talk about it. Or B. said she would feel she had to make something up.

Two weeks ago Wednesday – during the day – I had a terribly tight feeling at the pit of my stomach (this was a different feeling from the simple one I always felt before a class of just being inadequate). During the class it went away, but by the time I got home it was back, full, and didn't go away until Friday. In the meantime B. had told me about the criticisms and I was doing some meditating on that. I told B. that these two methods had been very successful for me, so that I couldn't accept the criticisms of them as such – but that it simply meant that they had missed the points involved.

However, after about 5 hours of meditating I had begun to see the lesson in the whole thing for me.

You see, with the Presbyterians, as I have told you in the past, God never taught the lesson *alone* except for two times (both of them when you were working very closely with me). I understood that this was forgivable because it would be very difficult to do this and teach from a prepared curriculum, which I had to do there.

Also, God shared the billing with my class for parents – for the reason that I have already told you: the very nature of the subject means you are dealing with the consciousness of two persons – which holds it to the human picture to some extent.

But, while I could see that the nature of this new class should be different – I started out the best I knew how. I put the first two weeks on tape with the idea of sending them to you in London to see if they were what you wanted. But after talking to B. I listened to them myself and threw them in the wastebasket with the remark, "There's no use sending these to Joel. I can see, myself, that they're too intellectual – and while I do not think the criticisms of my methods were valid criticisms – and if I had it to do over I would still do it this way – nonetheless, I can clearly see that I have been afraid to go on just Consciousness, whereas that is exactly what the Father wants me to do – to get out of the way."

So I called B. and told her that I could see I had been scared to go on just Consciousness, but that I could equally see that it had eventually to be that or nothing. There was no use in putting it off any longer, so that the following Wednesday I would do just that.

Well, last Wednesday, about 5 people didn't show up (there were 12 remaining, besides me, 13 has always been my lucky number!). But by then I had had a week of meditation, almost all day and all night, and I was ready for it. I told the class, "Well, I see we have lost the "advanced" students. Now perhaps the rest of us can get down to the business of a change in Consciousness."

I went on to tell them that one measurement of our spiritual maturity is the way in which we deal with criticism; and that, therefore, I was going to let them peek behind the scenes to see how I handled it. I said the first thing to do with criticism is to admit it – just let it in – with some statement such as, "Well, they're probably right." I pointed out that by so doing we are not resisting evil, which throws the devil off-guard; and we are not allowing to rise in us that instinctive human reaction of trying to justify ourselves. So I told them to just accept and meditate on it for a few hours, and then quietly begin to evaluate the criticisms for their validity. "Sometimes," I said, "you will find that they are valid. If not, you can quietly re-affirm your own convictions. But then begin to look for the *lesson* in the experience, for if it is not to be found in the criticisms themselves, it will surely be found somewhere behind them. And the lesson is what we're after."

Then I took the two criticisms and dealt with them. I told them that these methods of mine were not just games devised for their amusement, but the results of 30 years of search and effort on my part – the last 6 of them in the Infinite Way – and that they had brought me to a state of Grace (in combination with the indispensable practice of meditation).

I pointed out that I do not label myself a teacher, that their teacher is within them, but that I was a student like themselves. That I had reached the point of being able to contact the 4th dimensional Consciousness, the "hidden manna" – and that the only value I could be to anyone would simply be to share my experiences on the road, in the hope that they might prove useful to them – plus, through my own developed Consciousness – lifting them during our meditations.

I further pointed out that if there were anyone in the room who considered himself an "advanced" student, my

class was not for him, because I was a beginner and
would still be a beginner 50 or 60 years from now when I
made my transition.

I pointed out that on the "spiral road to infinity" there
can be no such thing as an advanced student. Advanced
in relation to what? Only ego could cause us to even
think we were advanced students, let alone say it. I
cautioned them not to fall into this trap – and above all
not to say it to a person who has even opened the door to
the 4th dimension, because we would simply be giving
ourselves away as not having reached it ourselves – since
anyone who *had* would not be caught dead making such
a statement about himself.

I then took up the other issue, that of not sharing our
spiritual experiences. I pointed out that by all means,
while we are in the midst of any experience, any lesson,
we must hold it to us secret and sacred because our Christ
is then still a babe. But that once the demonstration has
been made, or a point achieved, due to the intervention of
the Christ, we are honor bound to *share* with others on
the Path, because in so doing we strengthen each other in
faith. I said that anyone who felt he might have to
"make something up" had missed the point entirely. I
pointed out that the serious work I intended to be done
with one of these statements from scripture would raise
such a fright in the devil (who also is interested in going
after the strays) that he would immediately open
anyone's Pandora's Box and we would be attacked with
all manner of temptations – some we might even have
thought long gone from us (at least that has been the
experience of those who have been using this for the past 2
years).

I said, "You can't take within you a statement of the
power potential of 'My Kingdom is not of this world' and
really be trying to put it to practice, without *your* world
starting to crack up." I pointed out, that the previous week
– when the sharing had all been sweetness and light – I
had realized that no one was yet really *realizing* that
statement, because no one reported any failures. Whereas,

in my previous class and tape group, for many weeks we had only been able to share our failures.

Well, of course, the outcome was a great sense of relief that the Father finally took me through a class with no preparation on my part – and that there never has to be any again – except the hours and hours of meditation. Of course, this is also going to force me within in a way I have not yet gone, in order to assure that the Consciousness is there.

So another lesson, and another lift in Consciousness. At my tape group last night, M. had her first spiritual experience of the Presence.

Well, that's more than enough. Please, if you can find the time, let me have your reactions to this.

Love to you and Emma,

Dear Barbara –   October 29, 1963

I use the idea of taking a specific quotation for a day or a week as you may note in the Portland Oregon experience which is now elaborated on. At that time we shared experiences first as you asked – but it is the only time I can remember except when working individually with students.

However D. has students share experiences but I believe has them write them and with no signatures. Sometimes she asks them to share experiences but only in the groups that already have placed their confidence in her.

Regarding Practitioner List – you are wrong. I cannot possibly know when students are free enough of home ties to accept a practice. Remember – a wide practice involves phone calls all hours of the night and answering mail by the dozens etc., etc. [1]

You are quite right – I have heard from H. & now from M. My original evaluation still stands. They missed the boat.[2]

Am enjoying a rest about three days a week except for the mail.

A Parenthesis in Eternity has arrived – and it is beautiful. Harpers have done mighty well by it & turned out a 366 page book with 6 additional lines on each page – for $4.50. Unheard of!

Our love to all of you,

Joel

Dear Joel,   October 31, 1963

Oddly enough, anent the sharing – that next week I explained to the class that this was the way I taught privately, and that while the class was small they should all take advantage of that kind of teaching, because if the class grew much larger we could not continue the sharing on the flashcard (both because of numbers, time, and a lack of intimacy) and that I would have, then, to take that activity back to my tape group – which was a small, intimate group.[3]

We have been working the past two weeks on Love Thy Neighbor (which I interpreted to them as meaning "unconditional acceptance" of our neighbor) – and then last week we took "unconditional acceptance" of *ourselves*.

---

[1] There is some inconsistency, here, because in 1962 he *ordered* me to teach, and said he did not "care" how busy I was, humanly.

[2] And, of course, he was entirely right. I have not seen them since.

[3] I was wrong about this. It was a very effective method, one which I have continued to use. The progress in my students is sufficient proof.

As I suspected, they found the week of accepting their neighbor much easier than to try to accept themselves. But it fitted in nicely with the lesson which came through last night on the nature of sin.

I pointed out that the word sin which we read in our English *Bible* is translated from 4 Hebrew words (in the Old Testament) and 1 Greek word (in the New) – all of which simply mean, in the original languages, "to miss the mark" or "to make a mistake." The only sin they can commit – or *the only mistake they can make* – is the "belief in a life separate and apart from God."[1]

Just as I thought I was finished a very nice meditation came through on the "temple not made with hands."

I am now satisfied with the quality of the work being done, from the standpoint of its having spiritual integrity, I mean. I don't know how it will unfold, but then that's not my concern since "He will perform that which is given me to do."

I understand *Parenthesis* will be in Los Angeles within the week. We are looking forward.

Love to you and Emma,

Dear Barbara –   November 5, 1963

Thank you for your fine letter today. So glad the adjustment has come to please you. This makes the work more simple.

My job has been a very difficult one.

The unfoldment (Papers since Aug. 16, & 12 Tapes since Aug. 18) changes the entire nature of our work.

---

[1] Years later this came to me as a *Realization*, with the words: "The *ridiculous* is, that I ever *thought* I had a life of my own." That put the nail in the coffin, but it still needs a knock every now and then.

Working steadily with our top students over here in England, Sweden, Holland, Germany, Switzerland, So. Africa – has brought to light a whole new approach which pleases me mightily. It remains now to gather together our USA workers and explain it all.

I think Harpers recognized *Parenthesis* as *my spiritual autobiography* & decided to publish with no comments.

They have used no comments on the cover at all. There is no doubt that there exists no other book of mysticism of the nature or character of this one. It probably cannot be evaluated except by one who has witnessed the fruitage of these principles or those who have come into contact with those of 4th dimensional consciousness. This is a new discovery for the western world.

Am sure this is a book for Edward. Will certainly be interested in your comments & Edward's!

Love to all of you,

Joel

Dear Joel,   November 7, 1963

First I want to tell you that I think that – had I thought about it – if I had waited with my flashcard work until the confidence was established (as you mentioned D. did) it would have been better – and I shall remember it for the future. However, it turns out that I only lost 3, and by the looks on their faces I am sure I would have lost them anyway. I feel sure they not only didn't like my work, which they said was elementary – but my face nor the way I wore my hair, either. But one thing I have learned is that not anybody is everybody's cup of tea – and I am not in the least concerned about that – nor about numbers. As I told them, "I am here because Joel asked me to be – and because I am obedient to what he is – and as long as there is one person who wants to hear what I have to say I will continue to be here. When there is not even one – I shall retire with gratitude back to my family and children." As far as I am concerned, this whole thing is in the hands of "you know who" (not me).

Most of the class is showing forth upheaval and changing. I pointed out that they can't change without changing – and that often means the cracking of old forms. Also, while it shouldn't be so – it unfortunately seems that as human beings we cannot grow without friction. I told them not to judge by appearances but to learn to listen within, and they will find that each of these seeming disturbances will result in increased freedom – and that is what they should judge by. They are all reaching out to my Consciousness now – via telephone calls – and getting relief from depression, pain of wrenched knee, children's temperature – or sometimes the call is just "tuning in."

Last night rolled along well. It was on the nature of prayer. It begins to feel like next week will be on the working of the Holy Spirit, how it works in us, and why.

I want to ask you about this Joel, and check it with you as to validity.

It seems to me that during the week the Father will in bits and pieces be teaching me – ideas will come – statements, etc., and then that is what seems to unfold on the Wednesday night.

Now what I want to know is this – does it happen this way with you, too – or do you just never have any idea of what you are going to teach until you are actually in front of the class? If you don't – then I am afraid that it may be that this is still intellectual teaching that I am doing – and yet – the thoughts are given to me from within, during the week.

Or sometimes – an idea will be sparked from a question that I get from a student in a telephone call during the week, and they draw forth a lesson which I think will be useful to all, or of general interest – and then I speak on that for a bit.

I am so inwardly taught – and have been for so long – that, frankly, it is difficult to always tell where the Father ends and Barbara might begin. I would appreciate your sharing your experience on this with me.[1]

I have a strong desire to be in London with you, but I guess it's just desire and not instruction from the Father, because nothing seems to be unfolding in that direction.

Love to you and Emma,

Dear Joel,   November 11, 1963

It was wonderful to hear your voice. Sometimes – even though I am very conscious of oneness – it seems necessary to contact the physical presence.

I received a letter in the mail last week from a Mrs. S., which said that you had recommended me to her. I was deeply touched at this vote of confidence, Joel and I will do my best to be worthy of it.

Quote from L.: "I was happier than you will ever know to be able to attend your class. In you I see a real gift for teaching, a capacity to put things clearly, a really special gift for lucidity." Quote from E. (with whom I correspond quite frequently): "Welcome to the practitioner list – you will be a shining light to those who call upon you." If you think I'm not basking in these pats on the head! I am!

---

[1] Not any more, it isn't! One is "intuition" (being inwardly taught), and the other is "thinking." They can be measured by "what they say." There are some things that God *never* talks about – for instance, anything "human."

Only those like you, Joel, who have actually done this, can possibly have any idea how tough it is – not tough any more from the standpoint of content – because I have no concern about this. The Father has never failed me and I know He never will. Even if I sit there in silence – once I have felt the Presence some good will result.

No, that's not the problem. For me the problem is the need for continually increasing dedication, discipline, and meditation. And on the other hand there is the pull, constantly, into the world from a marriage, house, and 6 children. Boy, if I can prove it under these circumstances, then *anyone* can.[1]

Still, it all resolves itself to the fact that there is just no alternative. I do not have a choice. Freedom and free-will are nonsense. We simply exchange bondage to carnal mind for bondage to the Christ and we have to grow up and face that fact.

We are burning candles in the hope that you and Emma will see your way to coming by here on your way home.

Ignorantly, but obediently yours,

London
Dear Barbara,   November 14, 1963

Thank you. See you soon in L.A.

Joel

---

[1] During one of my "dark nights" I was complaining to God, asking why He had put me to this work – telling Him that, in my opinion, I was the least likely to succeed; that I thought the computer had "thrown out the wrong card." I said that I had never heard of a spiritual teacher who also had as many human responsibilities as I had, etc. His answer came, "You have taken away their excuses. No one can ever say to you that they don't have time." It's true. I had had to learn to meditate while bathing babies, washing diapers, cooking meals. Some of my best meditations were in the car going to market. But I still think the computer threw out the wrong card.

Dear Joel,   November 26, 1963

Well, here is the story of my ultimate conversion.

You may remember years ago that you said to me, "How much more spiritual do you think you would be if you didn't smoke?" – and that was the end of my struggling with that. I just determined not to ever fight it again – that it would go off me spiritually or not at all. As you may also remember, it did leave me two years ago – without any desire, without any of the withdrawal symptoms such as I had experienced previously when I had quit with "will power."

For almost 2 years I have had, from time to time, a very strong ooch to have a Center in the Valley – but every time I thought I had found a place something shut the door in my face. I always accepted this with complete detachment – simply thinking that if it were of the Father it would unfold with harmony and that, therefore, this was not yet it.

I discussed this with D. while she was here just to check out my evaluation on this whole thing. She, too, said that she felt within her that I should and would have a Center. It probably just meant that the right one had not yet emerged. I told her that this was not a matter of concern to me – that I realized perfectly well that, if and when the Father wanted it, it would come up and slap me in the face. Yet, there did exist within me this strong ooch from time to time. Ed said, almost in passing, "Well, *when you're ready* it will unfold." This startled me so that I went into his bathroom to be alone awhile and think about it.

I realized that I had considered that I *was* ready – not from the standpoint of my having demonstrated perfection, goodness knows – but only from the standpoint of desire and willingness. So I asked the Father, "Am *I* the stumbling block to the Center? Is it really that I am not ready which keeps shutting the door?

I don't understand -- you have me healing and teaching -- and I have been doing this for a long time -- what is the difference? I haven't felt ready nor adequate to do this healing nor teaching -- but you have me doing it -- please explain this to me." The answer came very quickly, "Ah, yes -- and you must go on healing and teaching, and I am pleased with what you are doing -- but you may not be my ambassador to the world with anything less than 100% commitment."

Again -- no more words -- but a definite feeling, "I'm not telling you to give up anything now, and I am saying I am pleased with what you have done so far, but also, you may not be my ambassador in the world with less than 100% commitment." That was all.[1]

Of course, it is still too soon to say, but we will see by what evolves if this were a valid spiritual experience or not. I believe it to be valid.

As to the classwork, we are going on with studying -- some healing -- mostly minor, sprains, pains, flu, children's temperatures. But they are being lifted out of these and meanwhile being exhorted to learn and practice the principles until they can stand on their own feet, and then help others. The need for world work of a serious nature has been explained to them. We shall see what happens.

Now, in connection with my invitation, I just, once again, would like you to understand that I realized in Honolulu that you had reached a new dimension -- total disassociation from the "social" -- and my invitation was just the form of politeness in the human picture so that you would not think that you had not been asked. Now, however, since you have clearly stated your own needs and desires in this field -- be assured that we understand completely, and accept this -- and no further invitations

---

[1] 100% commitment must have been attained, bacause in February, 1964, Joel dedicated my San Fernando Valley Center. We maintained this for about a year and a half, after which we began to make the move to the Ranch in Saugus, where we have been ever since.

will be forthcoming from us – not because we would not want to see you socially – but because we wish to save you the burden of refusals.

You have always been first a spiritual light and my teacher, and only secondarily a pleasant dinner companion. I do not need the second – and I shall never get over needing the first. However, my spiritual oneness is established with you for all time and I do not need your physical presence for this to be so.[1]

Kisses to Emma, love to you both, obedience to you,

Dear Joel,   December 6, 1963

One of the things I wanted to check with you was this communication I had from Mrs. S., who is the woman who I assume had written to you and to whom you gave my name. I don't think it is necessary for you to wade all through her letter which is simply a recounting of the average human ailments, sickness, an unsympathetic husband, fear of breaking away from her Catholicism, etc. But I would greatly appreciate your reading my answer and telling me if you think I said anything wrong.

I have never heard another word from her, which I realize could happen under any circumstances, but I just wanted to have you check me to be sure that it was not something which I did wrong. I had Ed's secretary call her to make sure she had received my letter, and she had.

There were 5 new people at the class Wednesday night, and if you don't think I was scared realizing I had to follow you! But actually it was the most "taken over" class I've had. Something seemed to take me over and speak with such authority that it almost unnerved me, because my own, personal way seems to be more placatory. It was rather like going riding and then

---

[1] Joel, too, could change his mind. As soon as they arrived he called me and said, "How about dinner?"

finding once you were in the saddle that the horse had twice as much power as you had thought. Have you had this experience? Or do you think it's just a crazy notion of mine?

Are you going to answer my last three letters?

I haven't had a call for help from one of my students for 2 weeks, yet they are still coming to class and seem interested. So maybe it means they are beginning to learn something.

Happy Holiday greetings to you and Emma,

Dear Barbara: December 12, 1963

I am enclosing herewith your letter and Mrs. S.'s letter. First of all, regarding Mrs. S.'s letter, I would have answered exactly as you did, with one addition, and that is that I would have said, "You may be assured that it is my pleasure to be consciously with you in meditation today for the upliftment of your consciousness, and to give you help in this regard as you may desire it." Otherwise your letter covered everything as it should be.

It will be interesting to watch your work at the new Center, because I know that when you undertake anything, your whole heart, Soul, mind and body goes right into it, and therefore nothing less than an unusual experience can be expected.

You do realize that the direct fruitage will be your own consciousness made manifest, and therefore you must expect it to be of a changing nature, because *while Consciousness Itself is always at the standpoint of infinity and completeness and perfection, our awareness and demonstration of that perfect Consciousness is always unfolding.* To make this clear, I could point out to you that every principle of the Infinite Way that I have taught in 1963 is to be found in *The Infinite Way* and *Spiritual Interpretation of Scripture,* which were the first two books.

The principles do not change. But my state of awareness does change, because it is an unfolding consciousness, and therefore, with the years my consciousness has deepened, has become enriched, and has become more experienced. My first classes consisted of two hours each night for twelve nights. Eventually this became two hours each night for six nights, and then eventually one hour each night for six nights, and now I find it difficult to give a class of more than two to four hours.

Truth has not changed. The divine Consciousness has not changed. The healing Consciousness has not changed. But my individual expression of Consciousness has changed, and that change can be traced through the writings.

So with you it is to be expected that regardless of how fine your work may be in 1964, you should be able to look back upon it in 1974 and smile. And if you can't smile, you just don't have a sense of humor![1]

I would like to call to your attention the fact that our 1964 *Letters* will consist of twelve issues containing specific instructions in spiritual healing in accordance with the principles of the Infinite Way, and will constitute a whole year of healing instruction. Also, that *The Contemplative Life* should be looked upon by our students as a virtual Bible of the Infinite Way, and it should be their constant companion. And, of course, it is my hope that our students will see to it that the world outside of the metaphysical world receives copies of *A Parenthesis in Eternity* to help us open this vast subject to the world at large.

Emma joins me in heartfelt greetings to you and all of

---

[1] He was right. But the smile was always about Barbara and her struggles on the Path. My *conviction* has grown, and my "awareness" has grown. But I would not have to change a word that has been *taught*. That was always "through" not "from" me – and pure. As to the sense of humor, new students who hear our tapes have often been astounded at how much laughter there is in my class.

the family, and of course, Holiday greetings to all of you and to the students,

Joel

Dear Joel, December 23, 1963

Thank you for your wonderful letter. It is really a mine of wisdom for me and you can be sure I will take it all to heart.

I am fully aware that you came in with this message full blown – and that *it* hasn't changed, but it also seemed to me that you underwent unfoldment – and now it is very interesting to me for you to tell me that that is exactly what happens.

I continue to be awed and amazed by *Parenthesis*. It is hard to imagine what the world could need besides this. It is so clear, so straightforward, that it really seems to me that the dedicated study of this should do the trick. Of course, I am far from finished with even a first time through.

I think you can count on my sense of humor.

Christus wants to make some kind of contribution to the distribution of some copies of *Parenthesis* right after the first of the year. Do we send this to Ann Darling, or whom?

Joel, I want to tell you how spiritually correct and mature B.'s attitude has been about the new Center. I have detected absolutely no trace of person, nor envy, nor any other piece of human nonsense. Her attitude seems to be a full awareness that what is good for one is good for all and does not want me to stop the class at her Center so I guess I shall move the current one to the new Center – since it has taken on the nature of a private class, anyway, with me using the Socratic way of teaching (questions and discussions). And I would like, anyway, to have a class in Meditation, which I will do Wednesday nights at the the Wilshire Center; having my class in Principles of the Infinite Way on Mondays, at the Valley Center, and my tape group meeting on Thursdays, at the Valley Center.

I have seen fruitage from my class this week – what I really call fruitage, e.g. the announcement within of the Spirit, followed by change in the level of Consciousness.

One student has been having classes with a metaphysical teacher named N. for about a year – and since October has also been coming to me. Two days ago she called and said, "I'm not calling for help – I just had a strong urge to call you to say how much I thank you for your class. The meditation we had last Wednesday was really something and I felt it within me for the first time. Also, I find that after your class I just can't listen to my other class any more – it's just nothing. I don't know why, nor how, but somehow today I'm different – and I know it is a result of your class – and I just wanted to say thank you."

I have told them that I will be in meditation every hour on the hour and that they can tune in any of those times if they wish (actually I am in meditation more than that – and know that I actually must never come out of it – but I presented this to them as a first step, as an indication of what kind of discipline they could have if they wanted to). Another one told me, "At 11:00 o'clock yesterday when I tuned in something took hold of me like light inside and wow!" She has been a long time reader of the Infinite Way, but hadn't, apparently, ever learned how to put the principles to practice and I have been working closely with her on the practical side of this. Now I think we will get somewhere. (Although, I am not concerned about this – not looking for fruitage – as you warned me about).[1]

---

[1]   I have had many calls from students who have been reading Joel for many years but they seem not to be "self-starters" when it comes to *practicing* the principles, nor, in fact,

A third one had the Voice announce itself in a word of caution from scripture, "Judge Not." This is the first time it has welled up from within. She has been very good about practicing the "pump-priming" which I label the Flashcard – and this week the living water came back. She was really thrilled, because she is a very intellectual type and I have finally brought her to the point where she realized she had to go beyond that. But she had thought it never would happen to her – and here it is.

I am very grateful for this Christmas Week. We listened to your 1962-63 Christmas message last night and it is also covered in the December *Letter* – so we study it again tonight. I think the class as a whole is beginning to feel something happening, now, and they are beginning to realize that this is no pink-tea metaphysical lecture, but a serious job of work on a most difficult subject. One thing that pleases me is that I have as many men in the class as women. I don't know why that pleases me, except that I think it is important for men to get this, since the human picture rests so much on their shoulders and I like to see it get into the business consciousness.

I am enclosing a copy of Presbyterian Life, their monthly magazine. I felt that the article "You can't explain Christmas" would interest you. It's wonderful to see It coming up – not like flowers – but like weeds.

Ed, my two boys, and I are working hard at painting and fixing up the new Center. Hope to have it in operation around the middle of January or the 1st of Feb.

I know what Christmas is. I have witnessed the birth of the Christ in three students this week – and I am overflowing with humble joy.

Love and greetings to you and Emma,

---

really understanding them. I was so blessed in having him in person to teach and correct me.

Dear Barbara: December 28, 1963

Thank you for your letter and for this magazine article. Yes indeed, it is easy to see that Dr. Shoemaker is reading Infinite Way literature, and that he has caught its major premise of the nature of God, which of course ultimately leads to the realization of *the incorporeal spiritual nature of man.*

I am returning the magazine herewith, because I believe that you will want to keep this article, because it will serve a great purpose in speaking to many whom you meet who probably would be impressed by the fact that a Protestant magazine would publish an article of this nature.

Parenthesis continues to gain recognition. *The Saturday Review of Literature* listed it as one of four books on religion for the holidays and *Christian Century* made some very nice comments, very favorable and to the point. I probably told you that we are now supplying the Episcopal Church with Infinite Way books for nine hundred lay ministers at their request. Yes indeed, if you would like to make a contribution for the gift of *Parenthesis*, do send it to Ann Darling Kuys, 55 Coveland Drive, Avon Lake, Ohio, and you can be assured that within a matter of days or weeks, the books will be on their way out into circulation. I am so very happy to read in your letter of your own activity, because for nearly a week now you have been so much in my mind every day, and my thought has been with you and with your Center.

You will notice one thing about teaching the message of the Infinite Way, and that is, the effects of it are cumulative. *It is hardly to be expected that teaching a message like this will make very much of an impression the first day, week, month or year,* because even though you are addressing it in and through Consciousness, to a great extent *it is being received by the intellect,* and it is only as students hear the message day in and day out, week in and week out, year in and year out, that onionskin after onionskin is peeled off of the intellect, and the message eventually reaches to where they say, "Whereas before I was blind, now I see."

Believe me, I rejoice with you in your activities.

Emma joins me in heartfelt greetings to you and the family, and a joyous New Year to all of your household!

Joel

Dear Joel,   December 30, 1963

Just a quick note to say Happy Holidays (meaning My Peace; by which you will know that I heard the 1963 N.Y. tape last night). In fact the tape group was just left speechless by it.

The new little Center comes along. We are finished with the painting. Carpets and drapes come next and I look to be open for business about the 15th. I am very pleased that Edward has involved himself so with this – both in time and money. It has proved to be a lot more expensive to do than we had anticipated – but, what the heck! It's only money, and I certainly hope that it proves to be a blessing for the community as a whole and for the students, in particular.

As for us – Hawaii calls and calls – but right now I must cultivate my own garden.

I do have a question, though, Joel. B. tells me that she thinks there might be some possibility that you will come to LA some time next summer to give a class. Do you think there is any hope of this at all? I don't mean for you to commit yourself – but I do have a reason for asking.

I have been thinking of taking those of my class who want to go to Wawona in Yosemite for a week's retreat, and real digging in, some time next summer – and I wouldn't want to schedule it badly in relationship to a possible class with you. Before your class would be the best – because I am sure a week of the kind of concentration I have in mind would go a long way toward preparing their consciousnesses for your class.

The reason I bother you now is that it (the Wawona Lodge) is a rather small place, with limited accommodations, and we have to reserve far, far in advance to be sure of getting what we want. Eddie and I have gone there every summer for the past 14 years and we usually make our reservations in January. Naturally, if you cannot tell me anything about it, I shall just go ahead and make the reservations and cancel them if they prove to conflict with any class of yours here.

Love to all,

CHAPTER 7

CORRESPONDENCE 1964

Dear Barbara: January 3, 1964

Happy indeed to have your letter of December 30th, and I note with a great deal of interest that your Center is coming along nicely and will probably be open by the 15th. I am sure that it is going to be beautiful, and I shall look forward to seeing it on my next trip to Los Angeles.

Of course I do not believe that any of our students really knows *The Thunder of Silence*, *The Contemplative Life*, or *Parenthesis*, and when you stop to think of the 1963 message, which hardly any student has even seen or heard, you know what a tremendous work is ahead of them, because all of this was a preparation for London and *the astounding revelation that came forth in London. 1963 was undoubtedly the most tremendous year*, insofar as the message itself is concerned, but now we have got to look forward to fruitage, and certainly we are entitled to the tremendous fruitage from the work of 1956, '59, and '63.

So far as the message is concerned, we are witnessing the fruitage, because when you stop to think of *The Saturday Review of Literature* naming *Parenthesis* as one of four religious books, and *The Christian Century* reviewing *Parenthesis* and Joel, and Michigan State University recommending *The Contemplative Life* to Chevrolet sales managers, and the University of Colorado including *Parenthesis* and Joel in a chapter in a new book on mysticism, and the Episcopal Church ordering Infinite Way books for nine hundred lay members; well, I would say that fruitage is taking place in the message of the Infinite Way, *but the experience of our individual members does not show forth fruitage in proportion to this*, and until we see more fruitage with the students, we will have to keep plugging along as we are doing, instead of being ready for a tremendous advance.

Happy indeed to keep you posted up-to-date, and I am sure you will do the same with me.

Aloha greetings and a joyous new year to you and to all of your household!

Joel

> *Note: This was the beginning of Joel's expressed disappointment in the lack of progress in the students. It culminated in his saying to Edward and me, in April 1964, "I can't understand it, they have the books, and the tapes, and classes, but they are just not getting it." I couldn't understand it at the time, either. But I came to see, in my own teaching ministry, that there is a difference between the "what" and the "how to." They were getting the "what." But, as I learned, the "how to" cannot be taught with a class here and a class there once or twice a year. A group has to sit down together on a regular basis – and dig into the principles until they are understood; and then "woodshed" them until they sink from an intellectual acceptance and understanding, to being part of one's flesh and bones, permeating the soul, and the mind, and the body. That is why I do not lecture. I have held only workshop classes. That method has borne real fruitage.*

Dear Joel,   January 21, 1964

Golly, Golly, Golly – where does the time go?!

The thing I like to do the most is write to you, because it gives me the feeling of contact – but here is the first minute available.

First, it was so nice to hear your voice the other day, and to know that the Valley Center was an object worthy of your talking about it. Secondly, and thirdly, it is certainly an unexpected joy to know that you will be here so soon and will get the Center off to the right start. As I told you, we are just operating secretly, now – with my tape group moved down from the house – but I have sent out no notices – although I am having invitations mailed out for your opening of the Center. I will send you a copy as soon as it comes from the printer.[1]

There seems to be an increase of activity in general about my classes and I, too, seem to be undergoing growth in regard to them. My own Consciousness keeps expanding and as I get more light I pass it on. Those who have been with me for some time now express themselves as very grateful to have found me. But as we know, when the teacher appears, it means the student is ready. It is amusing me to see myself in them – they are all a lot like me – which is, I guess, the way this thing works. It seems that those of "my household" have come through similar experiences – and that is probably the reason I can be of value to them. It also makes it clear why we then need thousands and thousands of teachers, ultimately, to light each area until the whole world is alight.

I could have a bite to eat and pick you and Emma up at the hotel at 2 o'clock, which would give plenty of time for a leisurely trip to the Center and I could then bring you back afterward. If this meets your approval, would you let me know?

---

[1] Joel's dedication of my center in the San Fernando Valley, in February, 1964, was recorded and can be purchased from The Infinite Way, P.O. Box 2089, Peoria, Arizona, 85380..

I am enclosing a tentative schedule for the Valley Center. Please let me know if it sounds all right to you. It seems rather ambitious, as I look at it, but these are the *needs*, as they presented themselves to me – and ultimately, I guess, I shall be pressed into doing a class on the *Bible* as well as on *Parenthesis* – because the students are beginning to bug me about it. But I just can't give another night at present.

I particularly would like you to review my statement about the Monday night class. I have found some "curiosity seekers" to have attended this class when it was at the LA Center – and, quite frankly, unless you tell me I am wrong – I feel too much respect for my own blood, sweat, and tears, trying over many years to reach the state of consciousness which I have attained – and too much respect for the Infinite Way Message, itself, to want any longer to put these principles before the casual drop-in, who may still have one foot in Religious Science, Christian Science, or what-have-you; and who have not yet made the choice for the Infinite Way, as *their* way.

The Wednesday night class at the LA Center is now a class in instruction and practice of meditation. I feel this can be open to the public, because I just sit there and let the Presence be felt and do the work. But in the other class I "Zen stick" them a little – and indicate that I expect them to be serious and to actually put these principles to practice in their lives – and I check up on them from time to time to see that they are doing it. My students hold still for this, in fact, they love being urged to action – but not all would – and I feel the class in meditation to be more impersonal and therefore more suitable for the general public. Also, I am not then involved with any sense of responsibility that the message be fully understood. Whereas, with the other class, I do feel some sense of teaching responsibility (as long as they remain serious and put forth their efforts) and try every way I can to come up with a concept, or word picture, that will make each principle so clear that it finally penetrates.

Correct me if I am wrong in all of this.

Love to you and Emma,

Dear Joel,   January 23, 1964

Your last letter, which, incidentally, was written on
my birthday – certainly makes it clear that you have
done your work very well, and that, as you say, the
Infinite Way, itself, is well established. You are certainly
correct also, in the remarks about the students not
showing forth the same unfoldment. I don't know about
the rest of the world, but if they are all like my students –
there is a great "slip 'twixt the cup and the lip."

Since I do find a great deal of sincerity and
willingness on the part of these students, it must be two
things that are holding them back: they have not yet
come to the recognition that this is actually a "life and
death" matter – and therefore are lacking in *devilish
earnestness*; or they have not figured out for themselves
that these writings contain *principles for living*, and that
they must be practiced. Goodness knows you have said it
often enough. I heard it just the other day again in the
1959 tapes where you draw the parallel between reading
the I.W. and reading a book on piano playing. I guess
that's the ultimate use for guides or teachers, simply to say
to them as I do to mine, "If you are not satisfied with the
results in your life there can only be one of two things the
matter – either the message is not true – or you are not
practicing the principles in your daily life. We have seen
enough students hit the mark with the practice of these
principles to be sure that the trouble does not lie with the
message. So, you just have to make a decision," etc., etc.
You know all too well how often it has to be said.

Yet I have patience with them, remembering myself.
And also it was very helpful to have your last letter to
remind me that this is not, after all, a chemical formula –

but a matter of a gradually developing faculty – and that it is a flowering process – not an explosion.[1]

Let me hear from you about all my questions, both in this letter and last night's, please.

And my kindest wishes to you and Emma, as always,

Dear Barbara: January 27, 1964

Just returned from Maui, where we had a beautiful few days of rest and visits with our students, and now back at the desk to answer your letter of January 21st.

You have, of course, arranged a very ambitious schedule for the Center, and it would be an impossibility to comment on it, because it is only as you work with it and work with the students that you will eventually discover what has to be eliminated, what has to be added, or what changes might be necessary. No one can gauge at the start just how the work is going to develop, or on what particular day, etc.

I have repeatedly warned students going into an active spiritual ministry that *there are three major temptations, and that one or more of these temptations will come to them, forcibly requiring a very definite and specific and firm stand.* A few of our students have heeded me, but many have not, probably not so much because they do not think that I have sufficient experience to know, but probably because they feel that they are superior to any possibility of temptation. To begin with, *whatever of humanness is left in them is definitely not beyond temptation, and every one of us has some measure of humanness left in us,* otherwise we would be transcending the demonstration of Christ Jesus and Gautama the Buddha, and I doubt very much that any of

---

[1] In 1989 I learned that *God* is not in a hurry, so there is little point in losing patience with ourselves, or anyone else.

us has yet accomplished this. But I must confess that too many students have refused to heed me, have met up with these temptations, and have not overcome them. *Had they   been willing to agree that there is sufficient humanness left for one or more of these temptations to at least be offered them they would then have been prepared and recognized the temptation when it came, and of course that is all it takes, the recognition of it as a temptation, to meet it.*

First of all there is the temptation that concerns *money.* In this work there are two possibilities; the first is that at first there may be a definite scarcity of money, a definite *lack*, and this can bring such discouragement and frustration that it may cause a student to give up. This lack may also appear as a lack of patients or a lack of students, or at least a lack of sufficient patients or a lack of sufficient students, as well as a lack of finances. This is a grave temptation. On the other hand, *with some, money comes thick and fast, and when it does, this is even a deeper temptation than the first, because here the ego becomes inflated, and one really begins to think that they are good, or spiritual, or have God on their side, and this is fatal!* So, either *lack or abundance* can come in the form of temptation, and how the beginner in this ministry meets these temptations determines, in part, what the final outcome is going to be.

The second temptation comes in the form of *fame, reputation, success*, and just as you have seen what this does to young actors and actresses, more especially in movies, where name, fame and fortune can come quickly, be assured that even though we are operating, not on a national or international scale, but within the circumference of our own particular frog ponds, *we can become big frogs in little ponds, and this is just as bad as being a big frog in a big pond. How we handle the praise, the flattery, the gratitude, the recognition*, also plays a big part in determining the nature of our own spiritual unfoldment.

The third temptation is, of course, *sex*, although it never comes to us in this work as sex, *it always comes as love. There is such an element of love in a spiritual work that it is not difficult to get snagged,* and many have fallen for this belief that now they have met their Soul-mate. *Experience has shown me, however, that there can be a Soul-mate discovered every year.*

And probably this is the worst temptation of all, because it is so very evident that *I* could never be a victim of it, and *you* could never be a victim of it, or whoever the particular individual is. Of all things, that is the one temptation that could never come to them or make them yield. *The spiritual world is strewn with the skeletons of those who have fallen for sex under the guise of love, and strange as it may seem, no one ever seems to grow so old that they are not susceptible.*

Well, I'll be seeing you soon and will save the rest for then.

Aloha greeting,

Joel

Dear Barbara: January 29, 1964

Since I am to be with you on Saturday afternoon at the Study Center, would it not be possible for you and Ed to have Saturday night dinner with Emma and me at the hotel, since you will be driving us back there to the hotel and could just as well remain for a bite of dinner, and we could talk over any remaining questions, since that will undoubtedly be the only opportunity we will have for such a meeting. You know, of course, with so few days in Los Angeles, that my time will be more than filled, and so, if it is possible for you to keep Saturday evening free, it will be a good solution.

Aloha,

Joel

Dear Joel,   January 30, 1964

I am still awaiting your answers to my many questions contained in my last letters – but not impatiently – since I know how very hard it is for even *me* to answer *you* right away – and there are far more demands on your time than on mine.

But I have been sitting here at the Center by myself, this morning, and listening to the last of the Teacher Tapes. I have just been crying, and crying, and having the best time. And in my earlier meditation this morning I just felt pressed to thank the Father for His infinite graciousness in having found me worthy to be made one of his servants – handmaiden to the Lord – and was really counting that blessing. Then started the tape – and I am so full of the sense of being blessed in having ever been drawn into your Consciousness – that I just had to sit down and write you this fan letter. How real is your wisdom – how deep the understanding that flows out. How marvelous that we all have these tapes for all time – how warm and how close it makes one feel to actually be able to hear your voice.

Well, I think you know what I mean.

I think I can now tell you that our work here is flowering – there are quite a few new students (but also some who come and try me once and apparently don't like me very much).[1]

There seems to be very, very little illness to deal with, and if so it is quickly and easily handled. Lots of human relationship problems which are bit by bit working out as they come into the understanding of "unconditional acceptance of my neighbor."

---

[1]   There have been quite a few times when I have had to say, "I am not a 'cloud 9' teacher; there are some who are, try them."

One of these might interest you. It is M. (one who came to Honolulu with me last year and who, I think, mentioned to you his problems with his wife being so resistant to the I.W.). He told me that you had told him divorce was a waste of time, in effect, – which advice I had also given him long before – stating that once one was on the spiritual path there was simply nothing to do but learn to handle every problem spiritually – and that even if he did get a divorce he would marry the same woman again, with only a name change – that he would one day see that she was his great blessing, that "needle" which constantly forces us to put up or shut up.

Well, last week she finally gave him an ultimatum. Either quit coming to classes or she would leave him. He called me and I told him that there comes a time in the life of each one of us when we are given the opportunity to choose man or God – and that this was one such opportunity for him. Now I knew that this girl was a very strong physical attraction for him, among other things – and so I do give him credit for deciding for God. I then said, "All right, if you really mean this then don't do anything at all to prevent her walking out – just sit still and behold the salvation of the Lord."

She walked – and I must admit that even I was surprised at how quickly it resolved. Within 24 hours she just walked right back in and said, "Now I know I have to let you go to God." It was another subtle lesson for me in not outlining – because when it happened so fast I realized that, whereas I had been absolutely sure it would resolve, I had actually had some period like a week in mind. So I learned a lesson, too.

This same man is in real estate, a broker, and he came to see me about 3 weeks ago and asked for help on supply, saying that whereas he had been very successful for years, since returning from Honolulu he had not made one sale. I told him that in that case his previous demonstration of supply had been in the mental realm, because once supply had been spiritually demonstrated it could never be shut off – unless, of course, the person were so foolish as to deliberately shut himself off from his Source – and that I felt this was merely an opportunity to rise higher in his understanding of the nature of Supply. So we have been working on this for 3 weeks. Today he called me and said the opportunity for a million and a half deal was dropped into his lap yesterday. He said he thought that would cure his "poverty complex," which he had had ingrained in him since childhood. I said, "Yup – I reckon a million and a half is just about the right amount to cure anybody's poverty complex!"

Well, those are the most interesting developments. But there is actually detachment developing in all of my students to a degree that is amazing them, if not me, and an increasing devotion to the search for God.

All in all – I think it's constructive.

Those who are regular with me – and who express themselves as very grateful for what they have learned – I must say put themselves completely in my hands as to their instruction – and then they do go away and work, and try to put it to practice. To such an extent, in fact, that the flashcard we have had the last 2 weeks, "Take no thought for your life," has really rocked everybody's boat to a terrible degree.

But last week I told them, "Don't mess with the Christ unless you are very, very sure it is what you want – unless you don't have a choice. Because one of the ways you will know that this is a valid message, and that the Christ is really operating here and not just another pleasant metaphysical teaching that "God is All" – is that when you come up against the living Christ it will never leave you where it found you. If you think you can just add God to your humanhood, go home and don't come back, because you are in for a shock. The Christ will change you – and if you aren't ready for a change – you'd better look out." But they keep coming back – and getting changed.[1]

Well, I sure have a hard time holding my letters down to one page.

One more thing – and then I'll let you go. As I told you, part of the reason for raising up the Center was the need to get my tape meeting out of my house. It was very hard on six children to have to be quiet as mice for an hour and a half – although they did it pretty well most of the time. And then, too, I was unable to get private time for quiet study at home, since that factory was always humming – even the helpers kept interrupting me – so Edward and I thought we could also use this little place to stay on Friday nights (I think I have already told you it is a little house) and with this in mind we bought a couch that makes out into a bed.

Well, the Father never said a word – except that I have never been pushed and driven so to get a thing done. I had had the idea of getting it ready in a leisurely manner (before, of course, I knew that you would be in Los Angeles in February) – but people kept calling me up and offering to help *tomorrow*, and so I was kept working, too.

Just in passing – unless I have already told you – I laughed one day looking at Edward down on his hands and knees scraping paint off the floor and said, "Boy, I'm glad I don't have to pay *you* by the hour!"

For some unknown reason the couch seemed unsatisfactory – and I sent it back with the idea that I wouldn't get another until after the dedication because I really need the room empty, anyway.

Well, Friday night the Father quietly said, "That is not your place – it is My place – and you and Edward may not stay there." So I told this to Edward and he said, "You

---

[1] A sample of "not a 'cloud 9' teacher."

know, I've kind of been getting that feeling, too – it is a sacred place – and shouldn't be mixed up with any kind of human living – so I guess it's the ranch for us." I thought it was kind of sneaky of the Father to let me get it all done first – don't you?

Also – I was finding myself feeling an anxiety that you, perhaps, might not like it – but now I'm off the hook on that one – because I didn't do it – so if you shouldn't like it you'll have to "take your complaint to headquarters."

Well, I *was* going to quit – but the phone just rang and I'll quickly tell you about it. It was the 21 year old son of M., who has begun coming to my class. He was calling to say that his problem seemed to be that he felt so "useless." I said, "You know why we have those feelings of being useless? Because we *are*. You know why we feel inferior and inadequate? Because we *are*. As human beings there isn't one of us who is worth a nickel – but you wait until you are making your God contact and then when you find out what God has in mind for you to do, and let Him govern your life – you will discover that you are very, very useful – not only to yourself but to the world – so don't worry about feeling 'useless' – you are – but not for long." He saw the point.[1]

Love and gratitude,

Dear Joel,   January 31, 1964

Thank you – it was a very tough lesson – but it finally sunk in, after talking to you on the phone. I didn't get it out of the letter.

---

[1] In 1989 he began his own ministry and is a blessing to others. Many of my students now have healing and "serving" activities of their own. So we have achieved what has never before happened. This message has now passed to the third generation without adulteration, and we have the fourth generation of children now being brought up living the Infinite Way and making their own contact with God, whom they refer to as, "The Big G in H" (Big God in Heaven).

Also, I realize that this is one you have tried to teach me before but I was incapable of receiving it. Several years ago you wrote me that I was to remember that when you wrote me you were never writing personally, but I misconstrued your meaning (communication by means of words is really very difficult isn't it, since one has a tendency to hear only what he wants to). I thought you meant that you would always be writing from the standpoint of principle (which I understood) but I still thought you would be writing to me, personally, to Barbara.

Then in Honolulu you tried again, when you told me "I don't care anything about you personally." I heard it – but I now realize I didn't really believe it.

But yesterday it sunk in. And, of course, I now know it has been that way from the beginning. I now realize that you are too pure to even "behold" me. You don't even *see* Barbara. And I do understand it – because to some extent that is exactly how I view my students – impersonally – I just had failed to equate the same relationship between us. But the lesson has been learned. Thank you.

Impersonally, then, your letter about the temptations couldn't be more true. I have watched this in operation – not only in the I.W. – but in other areas. In fact, like with Ron Hubbard, all three of those temptations are what adulterated his integrity. Ed and I were both very aware of what was happening to him, while it was happening, and we fully realize that in the human picture this is such a general pattern as to be almost "classic."[1]

---

[1]   As I mentioned previously, right after the book *Dianetics* came out, Edward and I went to Elizabeth, New Jersey, and were in the Group of five who constituted the first class Ron taught. I went to find out if he knew any more than he had put in the book, "pre-existence," for instance. He didn't, but began to investigate it at our suggestion. Later he lived in our house when he gave the first Los Angeles class. It was then that we discovered that his goals were ambitious and personal. I, personally, decided that he had a closet full of "the Emperor's new clothes."

Equally objectively, I have already had too many opportunities to be felled by lack-abundance or fame-rejection, without slipping, to be really worried about being vulnerable in those areas. Although I naturally realize that any tomorrow could be another day and that it is certainly, as you say, necessary to be alert and to continually heed the warning. In fact, I take this so seriously that I have put your letter in my calendar file for the 1st of next month, and shall make it a point to read that letter on the first of every month for as long as I am doing this work.

My "Achilles Heel" might be the third one. But the Father has been gracious enough in the past 5 years to show me on three different occasions that while the devil may not be able to get at me through pride, nor greed, nor ambition, he might still get at me through sex, particularly if he can get me to take a cocktail. Alcohol seems to be an aphrodisiac for me. Nothing destructive has ever happened, they have just been lessons learned, and I am fully aware that I was being shown this weakness out of Grace and Love. In fact, I realize that I may carry this "thorn in the flesh" – this "desire to be loved" – right up to death (I can certainly sympathize with Paul). Still, I can only do the best I can do because I can't save myself – only God can do that. "Thou will keep him in perfect peace whose mind is stayed on Thee."[1]

Further about the Dedication. You realize, I know, that I am very inexperienced at arranging a place for you to speak and I would appreciate it very much if you or Emma have any thoughts in the matter of just how you would like it done. For instance, I was hoping that you would be intending to put it on tape – and if so, would Emma like me to get the tape and have my Wollensack

---

[1] I was of course speaking of the past. I don't know whether it was Grace, or a specific healing from Joel, but I have always been held free from any temptation of this nature. I realized early on in my work, that when a sincere student comes to you he is putting his soul in your hands. If one were to violate that, it would seem to me to be a mistake that probably could not be recovered from in this lifetime, and one would be *removed* as an instrument of the Father.

ready? If so, what brand does she prefer to use? Anything else you may think of I would be glad to hear.

Oh yes – I find, after bothering you about it – that I do not feel right about taking the discount on the books, so will not. I simply want to have them here as a service to the students and, anyway, Christus is not a profit-making corporation. And as I told you over the phone, I would maintain this out of my own pocket even if there were no income at all from classes or healing work. So that decision is met and made.

I am enclosing check for January "first fruits" of the Center.

Love and gratitude,

Dear Barbara: February 3, 1964

Thank you for your letter of January 30th, and this time I really mean thank you. Thank you because the entire letter is right on the beam of spiritual unfoldment! You are quite right in your statement that your work there is now flowering, and that is exactly what it is doing.

Regarding the physical appearance of the Center, I am sure you know that all that I will notice is its vibration. I can be just as content doing my work in a stable, and be assured, some of the places that I have worked in in this message have been just a little bit better than stables, and of course I have been in stables far better than some of the places I have worked in. But it is the vibration that counts, if I may use that word, the atmosphere. And of course I don't have to wait to get there to feel that, I know now that all is well at your Center.

No other news now – the desk is piled too high with mail.

Aloha greetings,

Joel

Dear Joel,   February 6, 1964

I am enclosing a sample of the invitation to the dedication of the Valley Center for your approval. Please let me know right away if you think it is all right because, if so, I would like to get them in the mail as soon as possible, or if there is some correction, to get it done right away.[1]

Also, one further word about the proposed schedule here at the Center. It really isn't quite so ambitious as it looks at first glance. Because first of all, I find it necessary to hear a tape every day, myself, and would play it for myself in any event – and it would, in a way, be a blessing for me to be held to a regular schedule on it for my own sake. And as to the 3 night activities, these 3 nights I have been devoting to the I.W. for a long time anyway – so that represents no additional obligations.

As always,

Dear Barbara: February 7, 1964

First of all, my sincere thanks to you for the "first fruits" enclosed in your letter, and please be assured I am thankful.

You are not going to carry any problem with you right up to death, so get that idea out of your mind. You are merely creating this picture in your mind and

---

[1]   Joel answered, "Beautiful."

perpetuating it. Since we live in the *now*, nothing can be perpetuated tomorrow except what we ourselves carry over into tomorrow, so why carry that any further than this very minute, when you can drop it?

It may be a very good idea to tape the message at the dedication and so, if I were you, I would have the Wollensack handy. As you know I prefer to speak sitting in a chair with a table in front of me, and for this reason it is necessary that I be elevated at least ten or twelve inches above the floor, and this requires a platform. If it is not convenient for you to have this, I can just as readily stand and talk, but it has always been my preference to sit, if possible.

The Minnesota Mining professional tape is the one that we use for our masters.

Well, we'll be seeing you soon, so Aloha greetings to all of you!

Joel

Dear Joel,   February 17, 1964

Just a short note to let you know what is going on with the class work. Mostly, they are all being shaken up. There are really some big changes taking place. Some of them are accompanied with physical distress, but I point out to them that their minds are the substance of their bodies (until they become spiritually governed, that is) and that when they are cleaning out old conditioned "cob-webs" in their minds, and letting go old concepts, it is very likely also going to show in their bodies – that they must just relax and let this housecleaning go on and be glad that their Augean stable of old humanhood is getting washed out. They have all accepted this, and I think for the first time in their lives are looking at their bodies differently, as *belonging* to them, instead of *being* them.

One amusing thing – I had a call for help on supply the other week, a person I have never yet met, but B. gave him my name when he called her Center. I spent over an hour on the phone with him (he had been doing some reading in your books) explaining how we view supply in the Infinite Way and that he must first demonstrate the presence of God. Well, I thought some of it stuck. But he called me again and said, "Well, I haven't got a job yet!" After my first gasp, I realized that this is all for my training, and that there are lots like him – so I said, "I think you must have the wrong number – this isn't an employment agency." "No," he said, "don't you remember me? I called the other day and told you I needed a job." I said, "I remember you very well, and I remember also that I told you that in the Infinite Way we don't work for 'things'. Now, if you want someone to work to demonstrate a job for you, you had better call someone in one of the other metaphysical teachings. You will be able to find someone who will try to demonstrate a job, or money for you, but no ethical practitioner in the Infinite Way would do that for you. In the first place, even if I could demonstrate a job for you I wouldn't – because that would just be mental manipulation and I would be right out of the Infinite Way. No – our business is God – and only God. Now if it is the presence of God you want, I will give you immediate help but you have to make a decision right now as to which you think you need, God or a job – and if you decide for God, remember that you may have to be willing to go hungry until you get it."

"Well," he said, "I realize now you told me all that last week – but it didn't sink in. You mean that if I can get God all these things will follow?" "Something like that," I said. "Well," he said, "let's go for God." "O.K.," I said. And we did. Of course, how many times this may have to be gone through with him, I don't know. I can hold out as long as he can!

We inch closer and closer to the day. I'm excited – and kind of scared, too. In fact, I'm showing anxiety symptoms and heart thumpings – but I said to the devil this morning, "If you think you can frighten me with that heart-attack business, you're kidding yourself, because I could put this body down this minute and just look forward to a good rest. You can't even scare me about my kids, because even they, now, are far enough along that they'll be all right even if I'm not around – so go ahead and flutter, but you're wasting your time." And that's the case.

As always,

Dear Joel,   February 19, 1964

Last December I asked my class to make a little "Inventory" of the work we had been having since October 2nd, on the 5 basic principles of the I.W.

In subsequent classes we began going over these (I was startled, in most cases, at how *little* had stuck) but what with trying to cover the *Monthly Letter* and some of the *Honolulu Talks*, and answering questions – time elapsed and we didn't get finished. So the other night I asked that they turn in their papers to me and said I would go over each, individually, and have a private session where it might be necessary to straighten out some of the points.

I intended to send you a copy of this Inventory together with *my* answers – but I received a paper Monday night from one of my students which was so nearly correct that I thought I would send it along to you. It is by far the best paper I have received – all of the others dribbling down to as low as 50%. But it has the value of showing me what needs to be done with the students. (This is my Monday night class – which is a very intimate, hard-driving, "expectation of results" class. They want to be examined and kept on the beam.

Naturally, this could not, and should not be done with the open, casual drop-in class.)[1]

Will appreciate any comments you have. I hope you don't find the handwriting too hard to read, but even if you do, hope you will feel it's worth your time.

As always,

Dear Barbara: February 20, 1964

Just answering your letter of February 17th to let you know that we are really getting ready now, and in just three more days will be on board the Lurline, set for a five and one-half day period of complete relaxation, so you might just as well make up your mind to relax in the same consciousness.

Aloha greetings,

Joel

Dear Barbara: February 22, 1964

Thank you for your letter of February 19th and the practically perfect paper enclosed. I am returning it, in the event that you may have some further use for it.

Indeed I am sure that you must be startled at the number of students who have been reading this message for years and haven't even begun to understand the correct letter of Truth, and yet they are so surprised when they discover that they do not have the necessary spirit of Truth or consciousness of Truth to produce harmonious experiences.

---

[1]   I have discovered that it was exactly this kind of hard work that has produced the results in, and changed the lives of my students. I have found the Socratic method to be the best way of helping the student make progress.

I do not know whether L. and D. use written questions and answers, but I do know that they use this method of teaching orally, and evidently they feel that the students do have fruitage through it. I do not know of any others that use this method, and of course I never have, but that isn't saying that it cannot be fruitful, because I know that D. feels it is a tremendous help to her.

Together with the five teacher's tapes, we have now added four new tapes, all of a practical teaching and practice nature, which, together with the weekly papers that have been sent out this year, would follow right along the line of the way you are teaching.

Well, we are packing now and going on board ship tomorrow, so Aloha greetings!

Joel

Dear Joel,   March 4, 1964

I am still walking around on Cloud 9 from the impact of your presence and of the Sunday night class.

Everything conspired all week to help me take a giant step forward – especially the evening spent at dinner with you and Emma. The silent teaching that I was getting behind your words was the most tremendous experience of my life and has resulted in – I don't really know how to say it – a sense of ordination? – and the feeling that I have accepted the responsibility of this.

I am enclosing check for February "first fruits."

Our gratitude for the dedication will be forthcoming. (Whatever it is, it will be inadequate for what you gave us).

Love to you and Emma,

Dear Joel,   March 11, 1964

Well, it is getting close to class time, so I may do no more than get started with this – but there is so much going on that I think I had better start.

Really, just to keep you posted with my work. A lady from Michigan – who had come to town for your class – visited my class in meditation last week and afterward came up and said, "Oh, I wish I were going to be around here – this is the first time in all of these years that meditation has ever been made clear to me."

Had a call this morning from a 2-year student who has been going to another I.W. teacher for a year – she is in a very mixed-up state about smoking – she has the illusion that she is constantly being fired for smoking. She said this other teacher had told her she "just had to see it for the nothingness it was" – but she said the "voice" told her to stop. I said, "What voice?" She said, "The voice of God." "Oh," I said, "do you think God cares whether or not you smoke – or whether He knows anything about it?" Well, it didn't seem likely to her. "But still, the voice..." So I said, "Well you may have heard a voice – but I doubt it was the Voice of God – and if it were not – whose voice was it?" She didn't know and I said, "The devil." "Why," she said, "there isn't any devil." "Carnal mind –" I said, "just another synonym." "Why, carnal mind is nothingness," she said, and I said, "That seems a foolish thing for you to say at this point when you are so obviously in its grip."

"I know it is nothingness," says I, "because I can demonstrate that – but as Joel says, 'Don't tell me my headache isn't real unless you can heal it.' Carnal Mind is all the power there is in your world until you can *demonstrate* its non-power." Well, she went on and on talking about how she "had the presence." – "How do you know?," says I. "Because of the feeling of living waters, and because of the ecstasy." I said I had never felt that so I couldn't comment on it – but that I had felt the Presence – and that I had a simple way of checking on whether it was the Presence of God – or self-hypnosis – and that was, "When He uttered His Voice, the earth melted" – and a healing, either for me or someone else, showed forth.

Well, she said that she had had a healing from smoking for 3 weeks – but that it had come back. I said then it wasn't spiritual healing, but mental – because spiritual healing was permanent – and that I knew this from personal experience, having been spiritually healed of smoking.[1]

Well, she quoted your writings – where she said you said that some healings took a long time – and one just had to be patient and stick with it until it was dissolved.

I pointed out that she had totally misunderstood your meaning – that certainly, some healings took time – that, for instance – if someone had a claim of cancer, it might take months – and one should just stick with it until freedom was attained – but that the cancer wouldn't come and go for 6 months.

Gadfrey – I am having my eyes opened in this teaching work.

Well – I am seeing her tonight – and I can see that she must just begin with the understanding of basic principles. It is very evident that she does not understand carnal mind nor its operation. So I shall try to give her the healthy respect for the "devil" that I give all my students.

I just must express my thanks again for the grace in having been lifted into a correct understanding of these things.

---

[1]   Over the years I really began to see the value to my students in *my* having had to overcome so *many* human problems.

Oh, there's tons and tons more to say – but I will spare you and close.

Love to you and Emma,

Dear Joel,   March 21, 1964

H. said to me the other night, with some degree of surprise in his voice, "You know, Barbara, I have the feeling that your Center may become very, very important to Los Angeles." I answered him, "Well, I hide my dedication under a breezy attitude, but it's there." I thought later, "Perhaps Joel doesn't know that, either, and perhaps I had better tell him." So if you didn't know it – now I have said it.

Also, Joel, so much has happened this last week which puts an entirely new light on my activity – that I feel I want to bring you up to date on it.

By the way – did you get my letter of March 4th in which I enclosed the check for February "first fruits" – and in which I mentioned to you a sense of ordination which I had?

Also, did you get my letter of March 11th in which I outlined some work I had done with a student? I mentioned this to you in order for you to comment on whether or not I was following a correct line, and I would appreciate your reassurance or correction.

This "kookie" keeps calling me, and asking me to perform "magic" for her (a cheap lawyer) and for terrible pains in her uterus (she had been diagnosed for a tumor a long time ago), etc., etc., and while I know I don't have to tell you that I do not work for these things – she must at least be receptive – because in each instance a few days after calling for help I get word from her that everything has worked out – including being entirely freed from pain. Well, she has also been useful to me by giving me kind of a text-book of cases to deal with. But a week ago Saturday she handed me a lulu.

I was at the ranch and she called me there to say that she had just had a call from Cleveland (her home) that her mother, who had been suffering from cancer for years, had had a heart attack and was in the hospital not expected to live. She said, "I know you have powerful prayers, and I cannot get there for 2 weeks, and I know you can keep her alive until I get there."

I told her I would help her. She called me the next morning and said that she had had another call from her sister that at 10 o'clock the night before her Mother had suddenly got up out of bed and begun walking around and there was great hope for her recovery. Four days later I received word from her that her mother had been sent home from the hospital. (I don't know what happened to the cancer – but I'm not going to pull up the carrot to see if it is growing, either).

Now – other than gratitude for having been channel to show forth the glory of the Father – this experience showed me something else – that my consciousness is becoming one that can be of service.

There is another experience I want to tell you about. Last January when the flashcard "Take No Thought" was given to me for use by my class I determined to ride that one out spiritually until I actually would be given some light as to its real meaning (much as I determined to ride out "There is nothing that goes in the mouth of a man that can defile him" – which resulted in my healing two years ago from smoking – and also the understanding that the "him" that statement refers to is the spiritual man, the undefilable – and that the "body" can be defiled. You may remember that I told you about this and you told me this was correct understanding).

So I literally "took no thought" with the result that I lived on candy and coffee, practically, for two months – I abrogated all I had learned about diet as an intelligent human being – I took no vitamins, I took no food supplements I just took no thought, period. I took no thought about rest, either – all of this I had previously done as a human from the standpoint of what seemed humanly intelligent.

The result was (as you probably have already divined) that I got good and sick. And I got sick in the worst possible way considering my work – it hit me in the throat, and I was so hoarse I couldn't even get a whisper out. This meant that I couldn't teach my class. Well, I knew I had 24 hours to get a voice back – and boy, I really went in and asked the Father to straighten me out, and show me the real lesson in this for me. And, as always, when I ask Him, He tells me.

Statement after statement from your classes began rolling through my mind: "The body is under physical law, the mind is under mental law, and always will be. It is only when they are spiritually governed that they show forth spiritual harmony," etc., etc. And then I saw it was exactly like the Law of the Ten Commandments – that, as you say, *you are not under the law when you are under Grace – but being under Grace you would never break the law.*

That paraphrased itself exactly in this other situation. "When you are spiritually governed, under Grace, it will follow as night the day that you will not – can not – break mental law nor physical law – you will be inwardly guided to live harmoniously under them."

But – and this is a big but – it also follows then, that until you *are* under Grace it is highly desirable to live in accord with good physical law and good mental law. Or, in other words – unless you are totally under Grace you had better *not* break physical law (e.g. the laws of good nutrition, exercise, and rest) nor mental law (e.g. a mind imbued with Truth instead of error) – and, *under Grace –* you *will* not.

Also, the Father said to me, "When you were singing you took perfect care of that instrument, just for a human reason – why won't you do it for Me?"

And then, "Your body is not your body – it is My body – and you are to keep it in perfect order as an instrument of My will."

Well, the upshot of the matter has been – that I have gone back to all the intelligent things I did before, humanly, only this time it is because the spirit within me tells me to. Actually, if I forget to take my vitamins, the Voice reminds me. If I forget to take my brewer's yeast and other protein supplements – the Voice reminds me. If I am staying up too late – the Voice sends me to bed.

Now, as always, Joel – I am telling you this in order to check it out with you as to whether or not you think this is a valid spiritual experience. As you know by now, I have never been one to kid myself and I'm not about to begin now. So please don't ignore all this – but do tell me your reaction to it.

Well, class night rolled around – and Ed said to me, "You're not going down there like that, are you?" And (voiceless) I said, "I certainly am. First of all, I have had a corker of a good lesson which will be of value to them and I want to share it – and anyhow – somehow I will have enough voice to get by."

And that was the case – a soft, gentle voice – hardly like mine – but afterward some of my old students came up and said it was the most wonderful class we have ever had. It was the class in meditation – and one new student said that she had gone deeper into herself than she had ever been able to before.

I, of course, have learned a very big lesson as far as public work is concerned. And I hope I shall never again do anything that might endanger my class work. (At least I don't intend to – but a lot of that will depend on my Christ awareness, I know.)

This has all resulted in such a sense of being a professional at this – particularly the statement within that "This body is not your body it is My body" – that I see beyond question that I am nothing but the hand on the arm of God.

As a result of all this, I have been released from the silence which was imposed on me two and a half years ago about a statement I heard within – and I want to tell you about it.

It was either late in 1961 or early in 1962 – you were here, on your way home – and I was with you and Emma in your hotel room. It was the day you came out of your meditation with the statement, "I may now call you daughter."

On the way home from your hotel that day the Voice said to me, "You are one on whom the mantle will fall. Go and tell no man."

Well, my reaction was typically breezy. I thought, first, "Oh yes, who is that *really*? And if it *is* You, well, Dad, I don't know how You're going to pull *that* one off." It was absolutely inconceivable to me that my consciousness could ever expand into world work. Nonetheless, there was the statement. I said no more and thought no more about it. Simply realizing that if such were to eventuate it would certainly not be my doing – and again and again, the strong feeling that it was not anything that I wanted for me, anyway.

In fact, I would have wanted it so little – that I absolutely refused to do *anything* toward fulfilling this myself. I said back to God, "Well, if that's what *you* want you'll have to do it, because I won't even lift a finger to bring it about."

You may now remember in July of 1963, when I was in Honolulu for that wonderful summer class – that I wrote you that 6 months before the Voice had revealed something to me which I could not tell you – but that I would assume that if it were actually the Voice, and a valid experience, it would ultimately be revealed to you.

Now – here it is – and the question with it. Do you believe this to have been a valid experience? I am perfectly aware that you may have a hundred students who will claim to have heard the same, or similar thing. Perhaps, also, it could be *valid* to a hundred, or a thousand – in any event it came to me – and I believe it to have been the Voice.

Certainly, my road has been steady since then. It was, for instance, that summer that you told me, "Go home and teach or I will not teach you any more." And I have been at it ever since.

Now comes this experience with the heart-attack case – and I must look with new respect at my attained Consciousness. There is further evidence, too. Yesterday Edward asked me for help as a practitioner. He has never, never done this before. As you know all too well, a prophet is usually without honor in his own home – and Edward has always put forth the idea that we were on a perfect level as to our spiritual development. But he finally has been struggling with a problem which he has just not been meeting – and he has asked me for professional help. He will get it, too.

Also – a cousin of mine has come to two classes, and she has asked for help, and is getting it – and very, very grateful. I know it was hard for her pride to accept me in this new role, and obviously it was only that she finally recognized, somewhat, the state of my consciousness that enabled her to do it. Of course, now, having been helped by me, that is the proof of the pudding.

I realize that in writing you all this I am in grave danger of being misunderstood – but I have been strongly moved within to do it – and so I must just prepare for the consequences, whatever they may be.

And having gone this far – I may as well mention something else which seems to be coming clear to me. I had always thought that I was studying these European languages for singing. It now seems pretty clear that the Father has had me studying them for His own purposes and that it may very well be – when I am free from my private responsibilities to some extent – that I will be taking the message of the Infinite Way to Europeans in their own languages. Not that I am at all capable of doing that now – my foreign languages are only at a "travelling" level. But – if this is the design of the Father – then the time will be made available in the future for me to perfect myself in these languages.

Again – this is nothing I am going to decide to do of myself – if it is of the Father it must unfold. But I do seem to have a glimmer of what may happen.

I am most anxious that you shall give me your fatherly reaction to all of this. I say fatherly – because if you just think I'm off my rocker – say so – but do it gently, please.

I am enclosing a check in gratitude for your dedication of the Center.

As always,

Note: In 1962 when I heard the statement about "on whom the mantle will fall," I realized that, even if it were a true "Voice," it was referring only to my teaching work and not, in any sense, to the administrative activities of the Infinite Way. Joel had told us, privately and, in fact, it is also on one of his tapes, that after he was gone the world activities of the I.W. (publishing, tapes, etc.)

would be under the ownership, guidance, and control of Emma.

In 1977 Emma transferred all of that responsibility, and authority, to her daughter, Mrs. Geri McDonald; and so it still is.

I did not appropriate the name Infinite Way for my work. The Infinite Way is Joel's message. My work has been called Renaissance World, although it has always stated on my letterhead, "Based on the Principles of The Infinite Way." In that way I wanted to hold up Joel as my teacher and to express the gratitude I owed him for having brought me to illumination and re-birth (which is, of course, what Renaissance means) without, at the same time, riding on his coattails. I always felt that my work had to stand on its own.

Dear Barbara –   March 26, 1964

Please let me know if you have received answers to all of your letters and my thanks for your ever thoughtful and generous spirit of sharing. Have answered every letter received from you altho it is no longer possible to get my mail out on the same day of receipt. It looks as if those days are just gone. The mail is world wide and I now keep two students busy in Germany answering German mail and one in Switzerland answering French mail.

And now my heartfelt thanks for your letter of Mar. 21 and for your very generous spirit that enclosed the check.

Thank you for "seeing" that the spiritual life does not permit us to break the law knowingly or intentionally. This is the secret of Jesus' three temptations. Had he *fallen* from the mountain top he would have been protected –

but he dare not jump!! Had he been enhungered, stones might well have turned to bread – but *he* could not make it so!! The personal sense of *I* would defeat the demonstration. If you had need to live on candy for a year, it could not have harmed you – but when the personal sense of *I* tries to be God – it must fail.

Certainly this is a valid spiritual experience to teach you that *the personal sense of I is not God.*

Regarding the experience – since I do not know God's plan beyond to-day, I cannot answer. I know the "behind the scenes" work of the Infinite Way far into the future – but not the personalities of those who will carry it on. At one time I had an *inner* circle of twelve who Joel thought would be *the* ones! Three of them aren't even I.W. students any more! There is no more "12" or any number. What lies ahead is yet to be known. Only the functioning "behind the scenes" has been revealed to me and the ways of introduction into human consciousness.

It is well that those who turn to you are receiving help. Let this activity continue to unfold. In proportion as this healing consciousness deepens, it will widen the circumference of your work. This is how you can tell in what direction you are unfolding. It would be wonderful if an American student could teach in German and French. At present I have two German students to translate for me in Germany and one in French – so it would be wonderful to have an American teach in German & French. I do my own talking in German in interviews so I know how much better it would be to be able to teach in that language. We cannot live in the future so let us do what is given us each day and prepare ourselves by attaining deeper and richer healing Consciousness. Keep me posted as to your healing activities.

Am deeply thankful to you for your very generous spirit and for all your I.W. activity.

Our united love to all of you at home,

Joel & Emma

Dear Joel,   March 30, 1964

Well it finally happened. In my 5:30 meditation this morning the I AM announced Itself to me. I had thought that when this happened it would probably come with thunder, lightning and earthquake. Actually, it was almost startling in its quietness – only now I know that there is no God at all.[1]

I am in something of a quandry about my students – and I wish you would please answer me on this: From time to time – in fact almost every week – since I have been teaching I have had some inner development – some new light – which I have quickly shared with my students. (The students in my private class, that is). But somehow I feel that I cannot share *this* with them. Am I right on this?

Thank you for being my teacher.

As always,

Dear Joel,   April 1, 1964

Just a quick note to let you know that I will be in on Saturday morning for a week. Edward will join me Sunday.

---

[1] In April, when Edward and I arrived in Honolulu and were having luncheon with Joel and Emma, he turned to me with a sly, twinkling smile and said, "So you've discovered there is no God at all?" "Yes," I said. He responded, "Ah, but there's *something*" – and then I was blessed with that tiny giggle he used when he was especially pleased with something.

I would love to have a meditation with you if you feel so inclined. In any event I will check in when I arrive.

Love to you and Emma,

Dear Barbara: April 6, 1964

My own policy has been not to impart my revelations to my students until these revelations have worked in my consciousness for a sufficient time to prove by fruitage the full and complete meaning, application and fruitage.

The day after a revelation such as you have had, you cannot possibly know the full meaning of it. You cannot possibly know the fruitage of such a revelation, nor even the manner of imparting it. Such a revelation must work in consciousness until such time as the impulse comes from within to impart it.

It may be necessary to hold back until the fruitage has been so evident *in the experience of your students* that you can then tell them the why and the wherefore.

On my tape of Easter Sunday, which was completed last night, Friday night, and the enclosed paper, you will see that I am imparting a message given to me twelve years ago, and you will realize through this unfoldment why it has taken that long to be able to impart it. In these twelve years it has been proven beyond all doubt to me, and the fruitage of it has been so evident to students that now it is readily acceptable.

Aloha greetings,

Dear Joel,   April 14, 1964

This is just a quickie – not even to say "thank you" – because that can't be said in words. I now realize that the only real way I can say thank you is to get to work, and stay working, and try to take some of this awful load off your shoulders.

You know better than I that you gave me material for a lifetime last week – and I know that it will be unfolding for a long time.

On the healing activity – found that one person I had been working with on "supply" was given a Cadillac last week, with the insurance and license paid for a year. How about that for an "added thing?"

Also considerable fruitage in two situations of personal relationships in which the students are showing forth more maturity.

Dear Joel – please autograph your picture for me – I want to have it blown up to an 8 by 10 to hang in the center.

Love to you and Emma,

Dear Barbara: April 17, 1964

I guess I messed up the photograph in trying to autograph it, and I don't know that anything can be done about it, but anyhow, the face is going to shine out at you, because you are looking at it with a shining Spirit.

Since "beauty is in the eye of the beholder," I suppose I am going to be very beautiful to you.

Aloha greetings to all of you!

Joel

Dear Joel, April 22, 1964

Thank you so much for the picture – nothing was messed up at all – but I felt like adding to it myself "Joel called me a shining spirit." Wow! I have had so many swats with your Zen stick, that I get all giggly when you say something nice.

As you know from what I told you of my vision – you are not only beautiful to me – you are very, very big! How about that?

By the way – in line with keeping you posted on my activity – I forgot to tell you that L., at the time of the LA class, told me that she had never seen such a change in a person as in one of my students who had been to see L. at the time of the November 1963 class, and whom she had told about me, and who has been with me ever since. This, of course is not exactly a "healing" – but certainly represents a change of consciousness, which I value even more. In fact, there is a great, great deal of this change in consciousness going on in my students – more so than healings – because they don't seem to get sick.

For instance, I have two new students who were frank to tell me that they were coming to my class because they had been friends for 20 years with a student who has been with me since last December, and that they have seen her study everything for this past 20 years – but that in the last five months they have seen such a remarkable change in her that they just had to come and get whatever it was that she was getting.

Also, in the letter you gave me in Honolulu regarding the impartation of revelations – this is so true. And I did as you told me and said nothing to them for the first week. However, the second week I was given the flashcard, "Who made me a judge over thee?," to give to them to work on – and while there are some who are still floundering and don't even really know what it means (in spite of my explaining it) there are two so far who have seen far ahead of the simple words. For instance, one called me the other day, after working on it for only three days, and said, "Barbara, this seems to be the most important flashcard you have ever given us – this really would take us out of our humanhood, wouldn't it?"

Another came up to me last Monday night and said quietly, "This will give us our freedom, won't it?" So some of them are getting the point.

For some time I have been getting the flashcard given to me a week ahead and I work on it before I give it to them. I have, for instance, already been given, "Neither do I condemn thee, but go and sin no more." And this one is working wonders for me.

You see, I asked them to use that flashcard on person, place, condition and self – and that is where I, too, am using the one I got this week.

Well, I'm already over my allotted 1 page, so I had better close.

Love to all,

I am enclosing check for our private lessons. Many, many thanks.

Dear Barbara: April 25, 1964

It was nice talking to you, and I thank you for your letter of April 22 which has just arrived, and for your ever-generous spirit of sharing.

From your experience with me you will be better prepared for teaching others, because you will learn not to accept the surface appearance, but to go right through the appearance to the heart and Soul, *even if in doing it there seems to be a matter of Soul surgery involved.*

It is not only your student who has changed in this past year, but you yourself, and at least three-quarters of you is a newly-born person, *and the other quarter will yield to continued surgery.*[1]

Emma joins me in heartfelt greetings to you and Ed, and to all of the family,

Joel

Dear Joel,   May 6, 1964

Well, I anticipate the excitement that will be attending everyone next Tuesday (departure date I believe), especially since I have the disappointment of not being able to go.[2]

My work, however, is flowering nicely. I have been adding about 2 students each week since I got back. We are now up to about 20 on Monday nights and everyone is very, very appreciative of what they are getting.

In line with keeping you posted on this activity I have decided to enclose a couple of things which will speak for themselves, and which I prefer over having to recount my successes myself. The first enclosure is a letter from a Japanese boy, W.S. He has only been to 2 classes but has got something that he wants. His letter expresses this. I was really very touched when I received it and wanted to tell D. about it, too. You might show her the letter or tell her about it. Also tell her that now with her teaching "haoles"[3] and my teaching Japanese, the "twain has met."

I am enclosing also a poem which one of my "funny" students wrote me last week. I had asked them to write me something about the experiences they might be

---

[1]   Self-Surgery is the name of the game. The teacher can only point out the area that needs the surgery. The last "quarter" that he speaks of gets to the "heart" of the matter and, in my case, at least, is harder, and takes longer, than the first *three* quarters. When my students "squeak," I quote this passage about Soul Surgery to them.

[2]   Joel had asked me three times to go to Europe with him, but I just couldn't seem to work it out. I didn't have a crystal ball, but God did. It would have been wrong for me to go.

[3]   "Haole" is the Hawaiian word for Caucasians.

having in using the flashcard "Who made me a judge over thee" (this has really been productive with the entire class). I got quite a kick out of her and thought it might amuse you.

Also, I decided I would just send you my answer to Mrs. S. so you could see what kind of instruction they are getting. Naturally, I would welcome your comments or corrections to any of this.

Now as to the healing activity. Mrs. S. called me last week about her daughter who was going into the hospital with a blocked intestine for an operation. The pains subsided within a few hours and the doctor postponed the operation. The pains have never returned and so they are just letting the matter rest.

Edward had a catastrophic situation develop in his organization a couple of days ago which he asked for help on. The problem just dissolved.

Menstrual cramps relieved. One person, who has been very, very attached to her children – has become so unattached that she actually forgot to pick her child up at school the other day![1]

I must say for myself that I am so very grateful every day for having finally understood healing in the Infinite Way. I was never able to use affirmation nor denial and I used to think I was a big failure for not being able to do that type of healing. Also I was never able to do mental healing – I somehow just couldn't work it. But now I realize the Father was doing me a favor in preventing me from resting in that kind of demonstration. Please send me back the letters and poems, etc. – but not the check!

Love to you and Emma – and I shall certainly be with you in spirit on this exciting trip to Europe.

---

[1] I'm not sure that was a "demonstration!"

Dear Joel,   May 8, 1964

On the tape we heard last night you mentioned that a "worm was a worm, and then became a Butterfly." Now this metamorphosis certainly seems to be a part of natural law. And also, we certainly die and are reborn again and again, as we progress on the spiritual path. So it does seem to me that "evolution" at all levels is in accord with spiritual law.

Why, then, as I mentioned to you in Honolulu, couldn't a dog consciousness evolve gradually into consciousness at a human level – or a tree consciousness gradually evolve into an elephant consciousness, and so on?

Second question: you mentioned, "You've always lived and you've always lived *somewhere,*" ("though not here in America necessarily," you went on).

Does that "somewhere," however, mean on this planet and if so, how do we account for the continually expanding population? Or if not here, would it have been some other "where" than earth and possibly at a lower level of existence – less than man, for instance – so that one could assume that "men" live here (on earth) – "not quite men" evolve somewhere else – and "something more than men" live elsewhere?

Now I am keeping omnipresence in mind – and the fact that space and time are illusions of our eyes and minds – yet we do have scriptural work that says that God made *a* world – and I assume it to mean right here, right now, on this planet – but only that what He made we "see through a glass darkly."

Oh, this is very difficult even to frame a question about – but I have had the question come up in class when I have made the statement, "Creation is finished – God made the world and He is done with it – there is nothing that will ever be discovered by man that is not here right now" – and they then ask the question about the expanding population – and I told them I couldn't answer it very well and that I would write to you for an answer.

So here I am.[1]

Love to all,

Note: My understanding of this business of creation was limited in 1964. In 1975 further enlightenment came on this question. Robert Young (who has done a definitive Concordance to the Bible) in his book The Literal Translation of the Bible, points out that the book of Genesis has always been translated incorrectly, e.g. where it says, "...and God said let there be light and light was," etc., Young points out that the original is in the present tense, so that the correct translation would be, "...and God says let there be light and light is," or, "God separates the light from the darkness."

In 1989 I had the "Realization" that God is, not static, but living, and that God is constantly manifesting Itself as the "flow" that sustains and maintains the universe. Consequently, creation is not "finished," as I thought, except in the sense that the Laws of creation have been laid down and are immutable. But the act of creation, that is, manifesting the visible from the invisible, goes on all the time. So that, in that sense, God is always in the process of "making" the world.

---

[1] Apparently these are some questions I should have "asked again," since Joel did not answer them. I, too, have not yet been given a full revelation about it, so for me, it is still a mystery.

In other words, I saw that God did not make the world and then cut it loose but, like a good gardener, He continues to breathe life into all things and only our resistance and lack of understanding can keep it from being active in our lives, right here, and right now. That is why meditation is the "way" to freedom. Also, then, meditation – achieving "God contact" – is the way to be assured that God is, right now, making your world. You achieve this by learning the truth about how to "cast your bread on the waters."

Dear Barbara: May 11, 1964

This is Saturday, and probably the last mail before I take off for Portland.

I have never stopped to take thought about the matter of wealth. There was a Lord, and I've forgotten his name now, who owned practically all of the city of Liverpool, England, the great shipping center, and of course it was practically bombed out during the war, almost leveled to the ground, and on a trip to the States he told the reporters that he was ruined, that the entire city was gone, everything was bombed out, and he said, "I doubt that I have fifty million dollars left." And there was another man here in the Islands who has since passed on, but four times a year he needed two hundred thousand dollars to pay his income tax, Federal income tax, and believe it or not, a week before each of these was due, he would phone me and ask for help on supply, since he had to meet this great obligation and was finding it difficult. So you see how impossible it is to gauge such a thing as wealth. In thinking of any of our students, I never think of the human source of their supply or the human avenue of their supply, since I always associate them with the truth revealed in the message of the Infinite Way, namely, "I and the Father are one, and son, thou art ever with Me and all that I have is thine." It is my aim always that every student, whether wealthy or not wealthy, whether having means independent of their husband or not, should begin to realize that the relationship of Father and son, which includes the relationship of being heir, makes each one of us consciously dependent only on the realization of this relationship. Once we succeed in doing this, we have a passage out of an ancient wisdom which compels us to face the teaching that we are following, and see if we are measuring up to it, and that passage is this: "The way that does not provide for the wayfarer is no way to travel upon."[1]

The Infinite Way, then, which means, of course, the realization of our Christhood, is the Way that we are travelling, and if that Way does not provide for us, either there is something wrong with the Way or there is something wrong with our interpretation of the Way.

This does not mean that we are not to accept what the Grace of God gives us through our husband, or wife, or parents, or children; it merely means that our dependence must not be in that direction. Be assured that I rejoice in the fact that I can make the way of Emma's children a bit easier than it would be otherwise, but I in no wise permit myself or them to accept the belief that they are dependent on me, or that I am doing something very special for them, because I'm not. All I am doing is sharing a tiny measure of the wonderful Grace of God that has come to me.

Now, regarding your enclosures, first of all, please accept my sincere thanks for the check enclosed, and here, too, let me remind you that without a deep sense of gratitude, none of us has even touched the hem of the Robe.

I only wish every one of our students would know the measure of gratitude that I feel in my heart every single day for all Infinite Way students who are in any

---

[1]   Quote is from *The Book of Mirdad.*

wise engaged in this activity, and be assured I am knowing this truth also, that the Way upon which they have fared is the Way that meets their need.

Regarding your answer to Mrs. S., I would like to make one comment. Your final paragraph is excellent; oh, I mean the whole letter is good, but I am speaking now only of the final paragraph; is excellent in that you have cautioned her about the nature of protective work, but when you write a paragraph of this kind, always be sure to suggest the study of *Infinite Way Letters 1955*, chapter three. This gives them, not merely the brief sketch that you have given in this paragraph, but it gives them the entire principle of protective work so that they can read it, study it, incorporate it into their consciousness. In the same way, there are other paragraphs, and in some cases, whole chapters which should be referred to students for study when the occasion requires. I find that it is impossible to stress sufficiently the chapter, "New Horizon," in *The Infinite Way*, because without it one just does not have the major principles of The Infinite Way concretely established in consciousness, and with it one has a solid foundation for the entire message. There are chapters on human relationships – well, just refer to *The Contemplative Life*, end of chapter ten, and note all of those references, and see how much more valuable your work can be when, in giving your students specific principles, you likewise give them whole paragraphs or chapters that thoroughly and completely explain the principles.

Well, I must be off. Aloha greetings to all of the family and the students!

Joel

Note: Joel returned the following letter to me (in the interest of time, I am sure) with his comments on the margins. I have included them, as he wrote them, after the specific paragraph.

Dear Joel,   May 13, 1964

Well, I guess your show is on the road by now. Would mightily like to be there – but I will get a full report.   (Yes – Portland Special Class is special!).

Just to keep you posted on the healing activity. Had a call the other day from a student whose mother had cut her finger severely and it would not stop bleeding. It stopped.   (Nice).

Had a Mrs. D. who had "the spirits" and had been unable to sleep for a long time – a psychic disturbance. She had made reservations to go to Portland and Seattle hoping to get help from you. But she called me Friday night and said she was "free" and that they are "letting me alone." She has decided, therefore, not to go to Portland.   (Ditto).

Didn't mean to do you out of any business!
                              (I never mind competition!).

She told me she has been everywhere, to everyone, without receiving any help. She said, "You're the only one who didn't laugh at me."

Two deep humility experiences in two students this week. I was very glad to see it.

Added a new student Monday night.

But *I* don't seem to be worth much. Was given the flashcard "Neither do I condemn thee, but go and sin no more" – meaning, of course, don't fall back into mortality again – but I'm afraid I do. In fact I've been almost a total failure this week at using the flashcard. But it is, after all, just an exercise, and can be used in that way, even if I can't demonstrate it 100%. **(Have no interest in self).**

Love to you, Emma, D., and all,

Dear Barbara – May 13, 1964

Hundreds here – Every minute filled. God's universe is spiritual & Its son is spiritual – incorporeal.

What you are trying to account for is the illusion.[1]

Greetings,

Joel

Dear Barbara – June 10, 1964

You will have heard about Portland and Chicago so will not repeat.

But – Manchester Class, 1964, 3 tapes, Scriptural Meditation will be a text on this subject for years to come.

And London Studio, #1, was born of an Experience Sunday morning – probably only for serious students.

Love to all,

Joel

Dear Joel, June 17, 1964

How wonderful to hear your voice yesterday, and so clear. You sounded "right in the next room."

---

[1] Or, perhaps, this *is* his answer to my questions in my letter of May 8th.

I have already apologized to you over the phone for my long delay in writing, so won't go into it further except to say that my call for help Friday night was occasioned by one of the roughest weeks I have ever had. I finally ended up feeling entirely imposed upon, incompetent, and depressed – as I guess you gathered from my tone of voice.

However, as I told you yesterday, within 20 minutes after I talked to you I had my peace and by the next morning my lesson had come through. Actually, the way it came through was almost funny. I just woke up understanding that all the feelings of depression, loneliness, inadequacy, disturbance over my children fighting – everything – had been nothing more than *carnal mind suggestions,* and that they had been coming for the express purpose of damaging or frustrating my *work.* And then came the thought which was almost flattering – that the "devil" wouldn't have been working so hard on me unless my work was proving fruitful enough to disturb him; that the Christ was, evidently, being released, which posed a life and death threat to him – and for that reason I *was* important enough for him to work on. He entered through the only door of sufficient vulnerability that I am aware of, my "anxiety" about being a good mother, a good wife, and a good teacher.

Then followed the *Realization:* "He hasn't got the power!" And while the temptations have not ceased, not a single one of them has been able to penetrate my spiritual armor. And now, as I told you, I am living in a world with *one power.*

Then, this morning, another tremendous experience came to me, and I realized that it was just as well that I had been delayed in writing you because each day has brought something new to tell.

There is a classic story in literature that has always been a favorite of mine. The story of the strong man marrying a reluctant and rebellious young bride, and in his wisdom, being patient with her – educating her – and waiting until she grew up and returned his love before consummating the marriage. ("The Taming of the Shrew" is one example of this). It seems kind of corny, I realize – but it has appealed to me – and now I know why. It is the story of my spiritual life.

Many years ago, even before I came into the I.W. I had the experience of becoming the bride of Christ. I was fully aware of it – but not too much happened in my life. Then, after I came into the I.W. I became aware. Through reading one of your books one day, I realized that the Christ had given me Its "name."[1] Now I can see how patiently God has waited for me to grow up.

Some time ago, in talking to a couple of students of the I.W. they mentioned the "joy" of this pathway to me. Now, over the years I have noticed that there is one thing rather peculiar about me. I have always *known* what I did *not* know. Many years ago, for instance, while still a child I realized that I did not know how to pray. Then later, I realized that I was not yet grounded in I.W. principles – then also realized when I was. Later, I knew that I had not experienced Grace, and knew when I had; knew when I did not yet have the healing consciousness – and when I did.

So, I was frank to say to these people that I had never had any "joy" out of this path – that I had had, on occasion, peace, satisfaction, a sense of being cared for, of being taught, etc., but that I had never actually experienced the joy the mystics had written about. (Frankly, I doubted that they had, either – because I have seen in my students and others that it is possible to be fooled by ecstatic feelings, impartations, etc.).[2]

Well, after I had the realization that carnal mind is not power (and I mean "realization" – because of course, I have known this intellectually for years) I began to experience a sense of freedom that I had never known.

---

[1] As a "bridegroom" does.
[2] Joel labeled this, "Religious hysteria."

Then, this morning, in my car, I had an experience of joy. (It was like the pleasure of falling in love for the first time, only more so). And – like the girl in the story – my eyes were opened and I finally realized the *loving nature* of what I am "joined to." And now my work is a joy – washing dishes is a joy – serving my children is a joy. And, above all, the recognition, "If God be for me, who can be against me."

And so, the mystical marriage is consummated.[1]

Thank you for your letter.

I am enclosing check for May.

Love to you and Emma,

Note: I had just finished this letter when a telephone call came telling me that Joel had made his transition in London, just about the time I had my experience.

Wednesday afternoon
June 17, 1964

Dear Joel,

I have just talked with Emma and learned that you left this human picture this morning – and now I don't know what to do with this letter, since, in its way, it's kind of a love letter.

I guess I'll send it to Emma who, I am sure, knows all about this kind of love-affair.

---

[1] This experience happened to me that morning while I was on my way to my mother's office to write this letter. My entire car became flooded with light, and my body, too. This was to such an extent that I had to pull over and stop my car while this golden light, filled with love, showered down on me.

Thank you for being my teacher. It is good to know that you are "right in the next room."

Dear Emma,

Wednesday afternoon
June 17, 1964

About four years ago I wrote to Joel to this effect:

"My loyalty to you is unequivocal. Even if you now should make mistakes with me, I would never criticize you but continue to hold out my hand to you for what you have already done for me."

I knew at the time that I would one day be asked to prove that. I am sure you know that through two subsequent disturbances which we had, and right up until today, I have kept faith with that.

I have not sent flowers. My flowers to Joel are my word to you that I will never break faith with you, nor with him, nor with the Infinite Way.

I don't know why I am sending you the enclosed letter, except that I was inwardly moved to do so.

Love and gratitude,

EPILOGUE

And so my freedom to get Joel on the telephone was over, and not a day has ever passed that I haven't missed that. But the teaching was far from over. In 1975 he taught me, through words "heard," about malpractice (which I had not believed in), and how to break it. The method he gave me saved me from disaster and it has likewise saved many a student. The method was to stand fast, until the *conviction* came, "God is the *only* power and nothing but the Christ can enter mind or body."

Spiritual growth and deepening understanding have continued year after year. We have been given lesson after lesson, always rising higher. Many a night in class he has been at my shoulder, and the whole class was aware of his presence.

The spiritual integrity he asked me for has, to my knowledge, never been broken, and it has been a joy over the years to watch the changes, and the spiritual growth of my students.

In 28 years I have never found a reason to change my teaching method – a Socratic approach, a "workshop" format. The methods that we have uncovered have always worked.

I had, and still have, a *real* teacher. God Bless Joel, and the Master, Christ Jesus, and my great friends, from whom I have also learned: Lao Tzu, Gautama The Buddha, Hui Hai, St. Theresa, Molinos, A.A., and last, but far from least, my own indwelling Father, who, in many ways, has been the toughest teacher of all.

GLOSSARY

Added Things: Visible demonstrations, such as health, supply, companionship, etc., coming as a *result* of spiritual progress, but which, in themselves, are not spiritual demonstrations, since they can also be demonstrated mentally.

Affirmation and denial: Mental manipulation; (this is not a valid technique in *spiritual* healing).

Attachment: That which holds us to our humanhood; most importantly, *love* of anything in the human picture, *hatred* of anything in the human picture, *fear* of anything in the human picture, or *desire* for anything in the human picture.

Aware: One can only be "aware" of that which he has experienced.

Awareness: That amount of Infinite Consciousness of which the individual is aware. Awareness grows and changes with enlightenment.

Belief: Intellectual assent or agreement; an activity of the mind or intellect; the second of the "Four Milestones" of evolving awareness of Reality (the other three being hope, faith, and knowledge).

Attachment: That which holds us to our humanhood; most importantly, *hatred* of anything in the human picture, *fear* of anything in the human picture, or *desire* for anything in the human picture.

Body: The "instrument of physical awareness," comprising the five extroverted physical senses; a non-evaluating instrument of *sense* awareness. Body is Mind at a lower rate of vibration.

Carnal Mind (Human Mind): A state of hypnotism; the source of erroneous evaluation; the Misinterpreter.

Cause: A synonym for God. God is the *only* real Cause, which never has an effect. It is just cause "as."

Change of Awareness: A reconditioning process which involves a complete reversal of every former human standard of value; the yielding up of one's long-cherished concepts of Reality and one's habit patterns.

Christ: The *function* of God as Active Principle; the means through which the 'creative idea' (God *as* Father) is transformed into 'form' (God *as* Son); the Spirit indwelling every living being, which functions as the "evolver." *Synonyms:* Holy Spirit, Teacher, Savior, Guide, Rock, Comforter.

Christian: One who is living a God-governed life; *not* just a card-carrying member of the Party!

Communion: "Union with." That point beyond words and thoughts where the "human" self is completely out of the way and where the Father is praying in us; the highest stage of true Prayer (the other two being meditation and contemplation). This state of Prayer is Absolute Silence. Not even God speaks here.

Consciousness: A synonym for God; *Infinite* Awareness.

Contemplation: "To join with the temple;" the second stage of true Prayer. Contemplation consists of abandoning all intellectual effort and moving, to some degree, into conscious awareness of "the Presence." God sometimes speaks in this stage of Prayer.

Correct Letter of Truth: Valid statements *about* Reality and Spiritual Law; correct spiritual concepts. These concepts are not, in themselves, Truth, which is an absolute and which is a synonym for God.

Crucifixion: A series of "dark nights of the soul," experienced by every serious spiritual student. These crucifixions gradually wean the student from his attachment to his humanhood and from his erroneous concepts. The "Peeling off of the onionskins" spoken of in Oriental scripture. The final crucifixion moves the student — in the flesh — into the "Kingdom" (the Fourth Dimension) where he then operates under Grace.

Devil: The "hypnotizer." Universal human concepts accumulated down through the ages, which we have *accepted* and, therefore, turned into our "Belief System." The "collective *Un*conscious," which then acts hypnotically on every human mind. The "Universal Parent," the stumbling block to our being able to experience our own Real person and our own Real destiny. This Belief System, using the power *we have given it*, acts as a law of evil influence in our lives.

Discernment: The power to see what is not evident to the average mind; awareness of that which cannot be seen by the human eye.

Effect: Mind and Body; manifest form.

Enlightenment: Illumination, comprised of three experiences: the Nature of the Christ, the Nature of God, and the Nature of Reality.

Error (Sin): A mistake due to ignorance, e.g. lack of experience. *Synonyms:* sin, ignorance, mortal mind, carnal mind, devil, Satan, hypnotism, appearance, humanhood, human mind.

Error, Nature of: Illusion; a belief that we are separated from God, which is an impossibility, since God constitutes our very being.

Experience: To try out.

Faith: The *conviction* which moves one to action. That which makes one dare to act without certainty, without signs, without guarantees; the result of mental and physical activities which involve the whole man: his hopes, his emotions, his desires, and his beliefs: Fidelity; trust; the *third* of the "Four Milestones" of evolving awareness of Reality (the other three being hope, belief, and knowledge).

Flashcard: An intellectual (mental) exercise which involves the use of a statement from Scripture or from other spiritual writings, keeping it to the front of the mind so that, whenever any appearance of human discord crosses one's awareness, he can instantly remove his mind from that picture, bring up the Flashcard, and focus on that Flashcard; out loud if necessary, until he receives his release from that erroneous, hypnotic suggestion. This exercise works because the human mind cannot fasten on two things at the same time.

Four Cornerstones: The basis of spiritual understanding: 1) The nature of God, 2) the Nature of Man, 3) the Nature of Error, and 4) the Nature of True Prayer. Understanding of these constitutes the indispensable foundation for building a Spiritual Awareness.

Four Milestones: 1) Hope, 2) Belief, 3) Faith, 4) Knowledge; the four significant stages of man's evolving awareness of Reality.

Freedom, Spiritual: Freedom from the need to have anxiety or concern for any "human" problem; the ability to "see through," to "ignore what they say;" conscious awareness of Reality. Total freedom from "human emotions."

God: "That invisible 'something' that holds the universe in order, through the activity of Love. It functions according to *Its* divine Law." It is omnipresent, omnipotent, and omniscient; self-sustaining and maintaining, and it permeates and indwells all life — including yours.

God Experience: The *conscious* awareness of the Indwelling Presence. This results from the practice of mystical contemplation; an impartation from within which reveals the existence of a Presence greater than, and totally different from, the human mind; making interior contact with the real "I," the true Self; becoming *consciously aware* of the "knower" behind the "known." This contact is made through the Awareness Faculty, and *cannot* be made through the mind.

God, Nature of: That which is the "infinite Invisible;" Omnipresent, Omnipotent, Omniscient, eternally expressing itself in an infinite variety of forms for Its own purposes; the *real* "I" of each individual. *Synonyms:* Truth, Reality, Consciousness, Health, Supply, Love, Cause, Companionship, Life, Law, Principle, etc.

God, Tabernacling With: To "know" God; to experience God within, at will.

Grace: A "state of being." An actual state of awareness, in which all of the "pairs of opposites" are dissolved. That state which is "always sufficient."

Grace, Experience of: A momentary experience of Reality; a gift of God which brings with it the awareness that, in Reality, "there is nothing but love and it is all according to plan."

Healing, Mental: The "healing" of disease, lack, etc., all of which takes place in the realm of the mind.

Healing, Spiritual: Reality revealed; the change of awareness known as "the opening of the soul faculty;" "illumination" or "enlightenment," which takes place in the realm of the soul; release from an erroneous concept; "revealing" the perfection that already exists.

Humanhood: Our "mistake-making faculty;" ignorance; the "erroneous belief in the reality of good and evil."

Intuition: To be "inwardly taught." The interior spiritual faculty; the "seventh sense;" the Christ within functioning as teacher.

Karmic Bank: The sum of one's previous life experiences; conscious or unconscious memory of all previous life thoughts and behavior.

Karmic Law: (Old Testament) "...an eye for an eye, a tooth for a tooth." (New Testament) "...as you sow, so shall you reap." "Karmic Law is not *law* in the presence of the *realized* Christ." (Joel Goldsmith).

Meditation: Fastening the mind on something in order to understand it deeply; learning to focus the mind on a single idea; the first stage of Prayer; an exercise leading towards the God Experience.

Needle: Some person or thing which acts as the needle demanded by one's own Karmic Bank, for his own lessons; the "stumbling block" that is actually needed for one's spiritual growth. We usually are born to our 'needle,' give birth to it, or marry it.

Prayer: Communion; dynamic receptivity; "soul listening;" an activity of God, not of man, of which there are three stages: 1) meditation (learning to still the mind), 2) contemplation (abandoning all intellectual effort and moving into some conscious awareness of the Presence), and 3) communion (reaching the point beyond words and thoughts where the "human" self is completely out of the way and where the Father is praying in us). Never the prayer of.petition.

Reality: A synonym for God.

Realization: An *individual experience* of Reality; that moment when something becomes "real" to you; an experience which brings with it the ability to recognize the Truth that has *always* been there, and which was previously seen incorrectly. (A realization is always subjective. This is what distinguishes it from a Revelation, which can be either subjective or objective).

Revelation: That which is inwardly revealed or "shown;" an experience which elicits the reaction "whereas before I was blind, now I see." (A revelation nearly always makes one feel stupid, which is bad for the ego and good for the soul!). The validity of a *revelation* is tested by observing the spiritual fruitage which always follows a valid spiritual experience. (A revelation can come from within or without and, therefore, can be either subjective or objective).

Sin: To "miss the mark;" to "make a mistake;" a belief in a mortal mind, a carnal mind, or a devil. The only thing that we acknowledge as sin is a "belief in a life separate and apart from God;" the human "Belief System," in good and evil. *Synonyms:* error, ignorance, *acceptance* of an hypnotic suggestion or appearance.

Specific Healing: Remembering, or being given from "within" a specific truth which nullifies a specific "lie." For instance, if one needed to heal the error of *2x2=5*, one couldn't do it with the truth that 6x6=36. One would have to uncover the truth about *2x2*, which is "2x2=4." The *realization* of that specific truth nullifies the error.

"Twenty-Five Group": After Joel had developed some serious and dedicated students in New York, he began to bring them together when he was there and taught them to do World Work. The original number in New York was twenty-five, therefore the name "Twenty-Five Group." Subsequently, as students who were developing in other areas of the country became capable of World Work, he continued these private sessions and called them all "Twenty-Five Groups," no matter how many members there might be in each.

Voice, The (Inner): Any *valid* spiritual impartation or instruction from the indwelling Christ Consciousness. It can come as "words heard," but appears in this way very, very seldom. Most often the inner instruction is *sensed,* or *felt*. It brings with it a *conviction* of its validity, and this can only be *proved* by observing what changes take place in the life following such an impartation – no spiritual changes, no validity. It imparts only spiritual information, of interest to the soul faculty, *never* the things of interest to the human world. It may startle the student but it *never* brings fear nor anxiety and if the student feels either of these it is not a valid Voice, but is an impartation from "the whisperers" of the psychic world and is to be dismissed instantly. Such psychic impartations are dangerous and are to be avoided at all costs!

Whisperers, The: The inhabitants of the psychic world, still fully human.

World Work: Taking up, for the world, a specific problem that has come to one's awareness, and sitting as a transparency through which God can get "on the field." The most important function of world work is to awaken the soul faculty of every man, woman, and child on earth. But it can also involve specific healing for a specific problem.

Books by Barbara Mary Muhl

Published

THE ANATOMY OF SPIRITUALITY: *a Series*
Vol. I *The Royal Road to Reality*
Vol. II *Along the Royal Road*
These are step-by-step, self-taught textbooks of Infinite Way Principles and Practices.

This Pilgrim's Progress; A Correspondence with Joel Goldsmith
The story of the author's spiritual development, from beginner to Infinite Way teacher and practitioner. The book also affords a rare insight into how Joel Goldsmith dealt with a dedicated private student.

Forthcoming

Relationships That Work; A Guide for the Perplexed
The Ten "Non-Negotiables" for relationships.

Script, Kid, and Fantasyland; "The Truth that makes you free."
This book reveals the Nature of Error and how to deal with it.

What to Do Till the Psychiatrist Comes!
Tried and true methods discovered by Mrs. Muhl in bringing up six children and seven foster children. "Infinite Way principles work with children, too."